Pynchon and
Mason & Dixon

Pynchon and
Mason & Dixon

Edited by
Brooke Horvath and Irving Malin

DELAWARE

Newark: University of Delaware Press
London: Associated University Presses

Associated University Presses
440 Forsgate Drive
Cranbury, NJ 08512

Associated University Presses
16 Barter Street
London WC1A 2AH, England

Associated University Presses
P.O. Box 338, Port Credit
Mississuaga, Ontario
Canada L5G 4L8

The paper used in this publication meets the requirements of the American National Standard for Permanence of Paper for Printed Library Materials Z39.48-1984.

Library of Congress Cataloging-in-Publication Data

Pynchon and Mason & Dixon / edited by Brooke Horvath and Irving Malin.
    p.   cm.
    Includes bibliographical references and index.
    ISBN 0-87413-720-9 (alk. paper)
    1. Pynchon, Thomas. Mason & Dixon.   2. Biographical fiction, American—History and criticism.   3. Historical fiction, American—History and criticism. 4. Literature and history—United States.   5. Mason, Charles, 1728–1786—In literature.   6. Dixon, Jeremiah—In literature.   I. Title: Pynchon and Mason and Dixon.   II. Horvath, Brooke.   III. Malin, Irving.

PS3566.Y55 M37 2000
813'.54—dc21   00-029926

*This book
is dedicated
to the best-kept secret*

Contents

Acknowledgments

Acknowledgments begin with our thanks to publisher Henry Holt for approving this foray in Pynchon studies and, certainly, to Thomas Pynchon, whose novel has occasioned this book and whose work we have been following at least since the appearance of "Entropy" (the older and wiser of us having read this story first in the pages of the *Kenyon Review,* the younger but perhaps more polymathic of us in the pages of *Nelson Algren's Own Book of Lonesome Monsters*). We wish, of course, to thank the eleven contributors, each of whom made assembling this collection an experience as pleasurable as it was educational. Thanks, too, to Julien Yoseloff, Christine Retz, Melody Sadighi, Jean Harvie, and Brian Haskell of Associated University Presses and to Donald Mell of the University of Delaware Press for seeing this project through into book form with care, interest, and a most efficient expertise. Both presses entertained more stupid questions graciously than we suspect they are usually called upon to answer, and did so without making either of us feeling less competent than we had already adjudged each other to be. Thanks as well to Seema Kurup for helping with proofreading when one more misplaced comma or typo was simply beyond our abilities to ascertain and concerning which we were unable to rouse the necessary corrective energy.

The sample entries from Tim Ware's *Mason & Dixon* web guide are reproduced with the permission of Tim Ware; sample postings from the archives of the Pynchon List Server are used with the permission of their authors and site owner Andrew Dinn. We are grateful to be able to include these illustrations.

Finally, we wish to thank Melanie Jackson for permission to quote from Thomas Pynchon's *Mason & Dixon*.

Introduction

BROOKE HORVATH

MASON & DIXON IS AND DOUBTLESS WILL CONTINUE TO BE A book that matters. That much seems clear already even from a quick survey of the almost 150 reviews the novel received, most of them thoughtful, seriously receptive, even though (or because) many reviewers seemed to have felt as did Laura Miller of the *Village Voice:* that the task was "a bit like reviewing the Atlantic Ocean."[1] Righteously daunted but not put off, Miller found the novel Pynchon's "most grown-up and satisfying." Robert L. McLaughlin, writing in the *Review of Contemporary Fiction,* spoke for "old Pynchon hands" everywhere when he called *Mason & Dixon* "the novel we've been waiting for," as encyclopedic and esoteric as *Gravity's Rainbow,* as passionate in its opposition to "the forces of objectification and control," as filled with "outrageous jokes and passages so beautiful you want to cry." For McLaughlin, *Mason & Dixon* is "possibly the novel of our time." Similarly, Joel Stein of *Time Out New York,* if not ready to call Pynchon's longest-in-the-works effort *the* Great American Novel, was prepared to find it "the Most American Novel we could ask for," an assessment echoed by Malcolm Jones of *Newsweek*—"a huge, ambitious book that may not be *the* Great American Novel but, hey, it walks like a great novel, it talks like a great novel"—and one with which Louis Menard, writing in the *New York Review of Books,* concurred. Comparing *Mason & Dixon* to Claude Lévi-Strauss's great work of cultural anthropology, Menard wrote that Pynchon had produced "a *Tristes Tropiques* of North American civilization and an astonishing and wonderful book." With the publication of this novel twenty-four years in the making, Pynchon, in short, according to the *Chicago Tribune*'s Melvin Jules Bukiet, has shown that he remains "the most emblematic literary figure of our era."

Not everyone was on the bus, of course. Donna Rifkind, for instance, was not offering unqualified praise when she described *Mason & Dixon* as a "thrilling, sloppy monster of a novel." More

11

severely, James Gardner, the *National Review*'s "art critic," confessed he couldn't get past page 50 (*Slate*'s Walter Kirn did better, boasting of 400 pages read, 200 skimmed, and 100 "foregone," although I suppose he meant 173 left unread). Gardner's inability to make it very far into *Mason & Dixon* didn't, however, prevent him from dismissing the novel as yet another "heavy, boring, and unwieldy" book praised insincerely by mendacious critics who feign pleasure over obscurities they equate with profundity. Similarly, Kirn suggested the novel wasn't "intended for normal human beings" such as himself but for academics who earn their keep by untangling "linguistic complexity for its own sake." *People* magazine's Kyle Smith found himself unimpressed by a less-than-coherent fixation on slavery and genocide that was "no doubt cutting-edge when [Pynchon] began this project." Yet even these dissenting voices make a case for *Mason & Dixon*'s significance insofar as it is the business of a great book to trouble and discombobulate in important ways. A fair-sized crowd could doubtless be rallied of folks who find neither genocide nor slavery old hat, and it seems a fair question to ask why Smith wishes to find these concerns no longer relevant. Similarly, Gardner's comparison of *Mason & Dixon* to David Foster Wallace's *Infinite Jest,* Harold Brodkey's *The Runaway Soul,* and William Gass's *The Tunnel* suggests that something more than length and difficulty troubled the *National Review.* That something more, possibly the subject matter Smith dismisses, is likewise perhaps implicit in Kirn's hope that such fiction as Pynchon writes will soon fall entirely out of vogue and that we can return to writers we "get": less a criticism of *Mason & Dixon* than a wholesale rejection of serious fiction that refuses to pander, that insists on telling us the sometimes difficult, disturbing things we need to hear rather than the lies we long to be told, fiction that refuses to dumb down either what needs saying or how it needs to be said.[2]

But how many of those 148 or so reviews can or need to be cited to suggest why this book's appearance at century's end matters? Nor are those reviews the extent of the evidence suggesting that *Mason & Dixon* speaks strongly to our imaginations and concerns today. As I sit writing this introduction in mid-June 1998, the book—released in May 1997—has been the subject of several dozen published essays and news stories, a fair number of which, restless with anticipation, preceded the novel's publication and only a few of which originated in the offices of publisher Henry Holt.[3] Meanwhile, the "International Pynchon Week" conference sponsored by the Programme for International Pynchon Studies (Antwerp and London, June 1998) saw quick-working scholars already taking the lay of *Mason & Dixon:* beginning to measure its scope; to map the grounds for its aesthetic success; to chart its connections to Pynchon's earlier work, to postmodernism, and to American literary traditions; to cut interpretive vistos every which way through it without killing the thing off or coming off themselves as ghastly fops.[4]

It is likewise telling that the growing number of Pynchon sites on the Internet have already consumed hundreds of megabytes disseminating *Mason & Dixon* lore. Surfing the net, one can find historical documents, facsimile letters from Mason and Dixon, reviews, critical commentaries, author biography, suggested discussion-group questions, and more. For instance, there is Tim Ware's *Mason & Dixon* Web Guide, an annotated concordance that printed out only four months after the novel's appearance at seventy-five pages, with a standing invitation to users to submit additional entries, definitions, and the like. Or check out Andrew Dinn's "Pynchon Server List Archive," which houses thirty-six folders of one megabyte of mail each (again, as of June 1998), each containing the correspondence of several hundred subscribers "from prominent Pynchon academics to fanatical 'amateurs.'" At present, a mass *Mason & Dixon* discussion is underway.[5]

In short, forget *Mason & Dixon*'s too-brief appearance on the bestseller lists, forget the prizes that went elsewhere (where is Professor Corey when you need him?), forget the quick remaindering of the hardback. In a decade of big books—from Don De-Lillo, William Gass, Richard Powers, William T. Vollmann, David Foster Wallace—Pynchon has published another novel worthy of comparison to what Steve Moore once described as America's "huge, word-mad novels"[6]: from *U.S.A.* and *Absalom, Absalom!* to William Gaddis's *The Recognitions,* Jack Kerouac's *Visions of Cody,* Leslie Silko's *Almanac of the Dead,* George Garrett's *Death of the Fox,* and Pynchon's own *Gravity's Rainbow.* If we apply Italo Calvino's definition of a classic—"a book that has never finished saying what it has to say"—*Mason & Dixon* is sure to become one.[7] Or as Irving Malin puts it in his essay here, *Mason & Dixon* is a book that will never for any reader offer itself as "the same text twice."

The publication of this collection is, of course, another indication of *Mason & Dixon*'s importance. Brought together here are some critics new to Pynchon as well as some of those "old hands" to

Fabian
397; fiancé of Urania, in Williamsburg
Factors
251; "Warehouses of the" at Scanderoon
Fair Anchor, The
271
Falconer, Captain
258; of the Falmouth Packet; Dixon gives him Emerson's Watch for safekeeping, 318
Falmouth Packet
96; Falmouth is at the mouth of the River Fal, in Cornwall at the southwestern tip of England; a "packet" is a passenger boat carrying mail and cargo on a regular schedule; 317; 704
False Bay On the southern part of Cape Peninsula; the area is also known as Constantia; [MAP]
falsum in unum **Principle**
132;
Fang
24; aka Learnéd English Dog; 644
farinaceous
739; rich in starch, or having a mealy texture
Farlow, Robert
446; on M-D Line crew; 460; 492
Fatum in Denario vertit
674; Latin: "Misfortune turns into money" ("If you get a lemon, make lemonade")
Faust
558
Feather Row
185
Felípe
426; Voam's torpedo (electrick eel); 469
Fell
215; a barren field
Felucca
252; a narrow sailing ship usu. in the Mediterranean
Feng Shui
229; Feng Shui (pronounced "phong shway") is a Chinese philosophy, developed over 5,000 years ago, about the relationship between humans and their environment. It is about how everything in our external environment has a connection to our inner, spiritual world, and affects our well-being; 288; 487; "that undifferentiated condition before Light and Dark,—earth and Sky, man and Woman,—a return to that Holy Silence which the Word broke, and the multiplexity of matter has ever since kept hidden, Above from Below, the map from the mapped" (Tao De Jing, describing Feng Shui), 523; 542; [Great Feng Shui Website]
Fepp, Highwayman
111
Fermat's Last Theorem
336; Pierre de Fermat (1601-1665) was a lawyer and amateur mathematician. In about 1637, he annotated his copy (now lost) of Bachet's translation of Diophantus' Arithmetika with a theorem of which he never published the proof; [The Whole Story]

Sample entries from Tim Ware's *Mason & Dixon* Web Guide.

Subject: Re: MDMD(22) 648.21 Indian names

From: Doug Millison

Date: Sat, 2 May 1998 08:43:15 -0700

Reply-To: millison@online-journalist.com

Lines:

```
At 9:11 AM 4/29/98, S T Johnson wrote:
>648.21 Can anyone scry anything from the Indian's names? Was
>it common for them to take Chrisian names?
```

```
Yes if they converted to Christianity, or to be given European names by the
Europeans who had frequent contact with them. There was also a significant
population of mixed-race offspring of Europeans and Indians, likely to be
given European names.
```

```
D O U G   M I L L I S O N  |||||||||||||| http://www.online-journalist.com
```

Subject: MDMD(22) Charles Mason

From: "schwitterZ"

Date: Sat, 2 May 1998 08:21:02 -0700

Reply-To: mcmullenm@vcss.k12.ca.us

Lines:

```
Content-Transfer-Encoding: 7bit
X-Priority: 3
X-MSMail-Priority: Normal
X-Mailer: Microsoft Outlook Express 4.71.1712.3
X-MimeOLE: Produced By Microsoft MimeOLE V4.71.1712.3
Sender: owner-pynchon-l@waste.org
Precedence: bulk
Return-Path:
X-Orcpt: rfc822;pynchon-l-uunuu
```

```
648.5 'There may lie a Problem, for I am closely sworn not to.'
It's not at all clear to me why Mason is being so cryptick
here, help anyone?
```

```
Perhaps a pun on 'Mason'?
```

```
"The truth is much simpler and will perhaps disappoint those who are
attracted by far-fetched or diabolic adventures and suspected secretiveness.
The regular freemasonry has but one secret : an initiatic secret."
```

```
http://www.glrb.org/elivre.htm
```

Sample correspondence from Andrew Dinn's *Pynchon List Server Archive.*

whom McLaughlin referred. The collection opens with Irving Malin's "Foreshadowing the Text," an essay that gives the lie to reviewer Joel Stein's contention that the novel's "first, intricate, half-page sentence . . . simply tells you that some kids go to their room." Seeking to read *Mason & Dixon* closely—from dust jacket through opening paragraph—over the course of nine days, Malin casts his essay as a "journal" to escape the trap of "'final' form" even as he finds "the *transit* of explication" immediately entangled in puns and possible allusions to Pynchon's earlier work and hence in hallmark Pynchonesque concerns: the question of whether the reader finds or hallucinates the novel's "signs and symbols"; the difficulty of achieving certainty; the pursuit of pattern's chimera; the vagaries of readerly free will.

Like Malin, Brian McHale ("Mason & Dixon in the Zone, or, a Brief Poetics of Pynchon-Space") understands the novel's hallucinatory subjunctivity—its participation in the construction of what Malin terms "counterhistory"—as well as the conspiracy of author and reader in such free (postmodern) imagining. For McHale, America as "subjunctive space of wish and desire, of the hypothetical and the counterfactual, of speculation and possibility" is conjured in *Mason & Dixon* primarily via spatial means, including nested or stacked narratives, dreams, otherworldly dimensions, and "paradoxical interior spaces." Each world-packed narrative device leaks its alternative realities into the novel's "primary reality" to construct America as a swarm of microworlds. Yet unlike *Gravity's Rainbow,* the "paraspaces" of *Mason & Dixon* are horizontally oriented and posit "a resolutely earthbound this-worldliness" that proffers "the Other world" as shared hallucination lying "if anywhere, not above or below this one, but alongside or ahead of it . . . somewhere out there in subjunctive America."

If McHale is correct (compare Joseph Dewey's essay here), the worlds of Pynchon's latest novel represent not only those we have lost and prevented from coming into being but also, in embryo, that "landscape of nightmare" (the phrase is Jonathan Baumbach's)[8] through which we have been wandering for so long now. Not surprisingly, then, several essayists consider the causes and effects of *Mason & Dixon*'s this-worldy America to ask what values and events attended the nation's birth and with what consequences. For readers intent upon such matters, the novel's central symbol is the line Mason and Dixon charted through 244 miles of colonial frontier wilderness. Thus, Arthur Saltzman ("'Cranks

of Ev'ry Radius': Romancing the Line in *Mason & Dixon*") describes that eponymous line as "replete with suggestions of purposeful progress, reliable boundary, and stabilizing accuracy" that
reflect the Enlightenment belief in an orderly, divinely sanctioned
physical and moral universe. Under this reading, the line should
offer "the clearest sign of civilized human presence on the planet."
However, Saltzman continues, "Pynchon lays seige to [such] optimistic promise" and to the imperialistic "domestication by geometry" of both the natural and human worlds to reveal a "clockwork
universe" of infinite peril, indifference, impenetrability, chaos: a
universe "outlaw, dissolute, unfixed" and decidedly "contemptuous
of human petition" with the line itself a symbol of "the initial
menacing stroke from which 'bad history' originates."

Mason and Dixon's line lays down, then, what Pynchon describes
as "a conduit of Evil"[9] through which flows all that which, to
quote what is perhaps the novel's most cited passage, "chang[es]
subjunctive to declarative, reducing Possibilities to Simplicities
that serve the ends of Governments,—winning away from the
realm of the Sacred, its Borderlands one by one, and assuming
them unto the bare mortal World that is our home, and our Despair" (*Mason & Dixon* 345). Thus the line provides for Donald J.
Greiner ("Thomas Pynchon and the Fault Lines of America") an
explanation for the how and why of our present cultural malaise,
the answer to the question asked in *The Crying of Lot 49:* "how
had it happened here, with the chances once so good for diversity?"[10] As does Saltzman, Greiner finds Pynchon's answer beginning with a critique of the Enlightenment's attempts to impose
order on "pristine complexity," an effort that was bound to shat-
ter the ideals upon which the American experiment was founded
because it sought to erase mystery, Adamic innocence, freedom,
and "fresh beginnings" and to inscribe upon the continent con-
flictual "fault lines" determined by the wishes of wealth and power,
lines along which violence unavoidably erupted as "the sheer force
of colonialism obliterate[d] the otherness of resisting cultures."

Putting the mapping of America within the context of post-
colonial studies, David Seed ("Mapping the Course of Empire in
the New World") reads mapmaking and surveying as among the
means by which the "territorial imperatives" of imperialist politics
are realized, a politics blind to all casualties left in its wake: indigenous peoples, cultural pluralism, nature itself. Comparing
Mason & Dixon to earlier texts by William Bartram, William Byrd,
Thoreau, and others, Seed finds Pynchon destabilizing the ends

of "cartographic codification" through the proliferation of uninter-
pretable "secret lore" that inspires paranoia and calls into question the imperialist agenda, leaving America a "crypto-text" and
its surveryors the (possibly) surveilled.

In "Dimming the Enlightenment: Thomas Pynchon's *Mason &
Dixon,*" Victor Strandberg suggests that Pynchonesque rejections
of the Enlightenment's faith in order, reason, and progress such
as Greiner, Saltzman, and Seed sketch are to be expected from "a
hippie rebel against tradition, convention, and all forms of social
hierarchy." If the novel falters as an attack on the "moral turpitude" of Western oppression and as encomium to those who stand
outside the oppressors' values, this is only because eighteenth-
century writers already waged that war so successfully. Pynchon,
however, Strandberg concludes, achieves a victory "not ideological but metaphysical" by redeeming through art time's ceaseless
plunge into chaos and death.

The spiritual alternative to the secular nightmare sketched in
the preceding essays, an alternative touched on briefly by Strandberg, stands at the heart of Joseph Dewey's "The Sound of One
Man Mapping: Wicks Cherrycoke and the Eastern (Re)Solution."
Beginning with the question, why this story told to this audience
by this particular narrator, Dewey reveals how the narrative
choice of Wicks Cherrycoke alerts readers to Pynchon's religious
agenda: to explore and reject both "the damaged legacy of Christianity" and the secular Enlightenment that vied to replace it in
favor of Eastern wisdom, belief in the value of which is another
facet of Pynchon's beat/counterculture inheritance. Having experienced the failure of Western ideology and finding in his auditors a lost generation comparable to Americans of the Eisenhower
fifties, Cherrycoke makes of Charles Mason "a parable of gradual
enlightenment," Mason coming to recognize the earth "as an animated creature" and rejecting the hegemony of intellection and
"oppositional logic." Cherrycoke teaches his "Eastern solution,"
Dewey explains, through his story's "dozens of intrusive moments
of pure invention," which function as koans to punctuate the
narrative with "baldly supernatural phenomena."

If Dewey's reading hinges upon Cherrycoke's control over his
story, his honorable intentions, and ability to proffer viable solu-
tions to the problems posed, Bernard Duyfhuizen ("Reading at
the 'Crease of Credulity'") reminds us that questions of reliability and authority—Pynchon's, his narrators', his readers'—are
central to any understanding of his work. Drawing upon the work

of Gèrard Genette and focussing on the novel's narrative frames, intercalated texts, and sundry narrative voices, Duyfhuizen finds the combined effect of these narrative choices to be an instability that renders unreliable "the transmission of the narrative." Through such instability, Pynchon problematizes the possibility of historical certanty, coherence, and truth, thus the authority of and control exercised by those who give history its shape and meaning. Narrative instability, in short, implies instabilities of the sorts discussed by Malin and McHale, and the rejection of (narrative) linearity challenges both the rectitude of Mason and Dixon's line and our own confidence in anyone's ability to read anything "straight": a point that corroborates the essays by Saltzman, Greiner, Seed, and Strandberg even as it forces us to qualify our acceptance of those readings. "[R]eaders," Duyfhuizen concludes, "may be better off getting lost in [*Mason & Dixon*'s] wilderness of narrators and voices than trying to carve a clear and straight Visto through its thicket of words."

Another way of questioning narrative reliability is to ask how faithful to the historic record is Pynchon's novel. Does *Mason & Dixon* erect itself upon a firm historical base or stem from sheer imagining? Does it play fair with verifiable facts or misread, misuse, mislead? Such are the questions David Foreman asks in "Historical Documents Relating to *Mason & Dixon*." What Foreman finds is that Pynchon's borrowings from historical documents—Mason's *Journal* as well as the work of scholars Thomas D. Cope, H. G. Dwight, and H. W. Robinson—are largely accurate though not always so. Because discrepancies exist between sources and the novel, and because anachronisms and absurdities (what Dewey styled "intrusive moments of pure invention") widen the gap between history and fiction, "Pynchon forces us to see history as a construction" while remaining sufficiently "faithful to the historical record" to retain readerly faith in history's facticity and knowability.

Like Foreman, Jeff Baker ("Plucking the American Albatross") seeks to establish the factual accuracy of *Mason & Dixon*—specifically, Pynchon's portrayal of the Sons of Liberty and the Freemasons (the latter "speculated to have been at the heart of all the major revolutions of the eighteenth century")—as a means of assessing the legitimacy of Pynchon's conviction that revolutionary rhetoric was a "smokescreen" for the economic complaints of a colonial elite. Agreeing with other contributors to this volume that *Mason & Dixon* rehearses historical fact to lament America's "failure to live up to its promise as a new beginning," Baker, like McHale and Dewey, is particularly intrigued by Pynchon's introduction into his historical material of "cartoon-like irruptions and hippie-ish anachronisms." Agreeing with Dewey, Baker argues that Pynchon's rejection of realism is a reminder of the salvific magic and mystery modernity has largely had to do without; but this rejection of realism is also, Baker contends, the rejection of an aesthetic that has become a tool of the state, whose "horrible effects" reveal the betrayal of America's espoused beliefs—a reading that returns us to the concerns of Greiner, Saltzman, and Seed. And by connecting prerevolutionary America to the American 1960s, Baker continues, Pynchon highlights two moments in history when there were "generations who had a chance to really make a difference—to make America that 'gift from invisible powers'—but who sold out to the forces of trade and politics."

Whereas Baker concludes by emphasizing the implication of many of Pynchon's readers in the failures and betrayals *Mason & Dixon* anatomizes, Thomas H. Schaub ("Provisions for Survival: A New Compassion") is interested in how the novel revises Pynchon's own understanding of the politics informing his earlier work. As Schaub reminds us, Pynchon once located fiction-writing as a response to the world's politically engineered dangers somewhere on "a spectrum of impotence" between "not thinking" and "going crazy"[11] but nevertheless sought, Schaub notes, to sensitize and radicalize readers through texts whose uncertain plots required readers' active participation in the construction of order and meaning. Examining *Mason & Dixon*'s aesthetics in "relation to politics and the power to do something," Schaub wishes to know what happens when do-it-yourself plots are replaced by compassionate, sympathetic characterization as the work's focus and uncertainty is displaced to the level of overt content, becoming less a "condition of meaning than the fabulist's comment on his own art." By thematizing doubt, Schaub argues, the novel's meaning is "always in sight," no longer a result of the reader's efforts. The result, as in *Vineland,* is "a kind of forgiving pastoralism," a conciliatory attitude toward what "has gone before" as the strategy by which Pynchon now hopes to "[get] over the hump of apocalypse."

If Schaub's analysis of Pynchon's career reveals how one's reading of and response to history can change, McHale and Foreman suggest that this is so because, as *Mason & Dixon* illustrates, history is always a construction (and consequently, like its makers, always changing), albeit one that must be based on incontrovertable fact: an assumption that Foreman and Baker take pains to demonstrate and that underpins the readings by Dewey, Greiner, Saltzman, Seed, and Strandberg. That these constructions are always partial, subjective, and open to challenge returns us to Duyfhuizen while Baker, Dewey, and Schaub remind us that because *we* construct the historical moments we inhabit or imagine, we are therefore doubly obligated to analyze and assess those moments, those readings, to answer the questions (ethical, political, epistemological, aesthetic) to which such analyses give rise, and to act upon those answers—a recognition that returns us to Malin's understanding of this historical novel as a "meditation" whose function is to provoke meditation.

Collectively, these essays return us both to the concerns of reviewers, hyperspace surfers, and conference attendees as well as to a deeper understanding of the connections of *Mason & Dixon* to Pynchon's earlier work, to contemporary (postmodern) thought (indeterminacy and intertextuality, conspiracy and paranoia, pastiche and parody, iconoclastic historical revisionism and the breakdown of realism and other grand narratives), and to longstanding American concerns: Adamic innocence lost; the construction of otherness; the lighting out of what Greiner, following Leslie Fiedler, terms "bonded pairs" of civilization-escaping males; democratic ideals at odds with how we have lived our nation's life.

Writing in 1913 in an essay entitled "History as Literature," Theodore Roosevelt contended that "another writer of 'Canterbury Tales,' another singer of 'Paradise Lost,' could not add more to the sum of literary achievement than the man who may picture to us the phases of the age-long history of life on this globe, or make vivid before our eyes the tremendous march of the worlds through space."[12] Although not a novel Teddy would have been inclined admire, *Mason & Dixon* adds considerably to the "sum of literary achievement" in just the sense Roosevelt desired—down to his judicious use of "worlds" in the plural. To journey with Mason and Dixon is to engage in some hard travelling, but vistos are being cut even as we linger here gassing. It is time to turn to the essays themselves.

NOTES

1. All reviews cited are listed in Clifford S. Mead's bibliography, included in this volume. See also "Bibliography (1997—)" in *Pynchon Notes* 36–39 (1995–1996): 195–221.

2. For a full analysis of *Mason & Dixon*'s critical reception and speculation on what the negative assessments may mean, see Douglas Keesey, "*Mason & Dixon* on the Line: A Reception Study," *Pynchon Notes* 36–39 (1995–1996): 165–78.

3. For a listing of reviews, scholarly essays, and "features and news items," see Mead's bibliography. See also the *Pynchon Notes* bibliography and Robert Brown, ed., "Focus on Thomas Pynchon and the Law," a special issue of the *Oklahoma City University Law Review* 24, no. 3 (1999).

4. Twenty-two of the thirty-nine London presentations focused on *Mason & Dixon* with the Antwerp sessions of the previous week devoted to a celebration of the twenty-fifth anniversary of the publication of *Gravity's Rainbow.*

5. Tim Ware, "Thomas Pynchon's *Mason & Dixon,*" *Hyperarts Pynchon Pages,* (http://www.hyperarts.com/pynchon/mason-dixon/masondixon-nf.html [17 May 1999]); Andrew Dinn, *Pynchon Server List Archive* (http://waste.org/pynchon-l/ [17 May 1999]). Go to site for instructions on how to join this discussion group; archives can be accessed without subscribing. Other sites of interest, each including links to related sites and all offering material of various sorts on Pynchon generally and *Mason & Dixon* specifically, include:

—*Gen-X Susan's Pynchon Links:* very thorough set of links to Pynchonalia: 53 links at last count [http://www.city-net.com/~argus/pynchon.html (20 May 1999)].

—Tim Ware's *Hyperarts Pynchon Pages:* "Advice for Pynchon Newbies," web guides, concordances, forum, links to documents and related sites including "Pynchon News Service" and the very thorough "Gen-X Susan's Pynchon Links" [http://www.hyperarts.com/pynchon/ (20 May 1999)].

—*Letters of Wanda Tinasky:* links to many sites plus information about and samples of the letters reputedly written by Pynchon under the pseudonym "Wanda Tinasky" [http://members.aol.com/tinasky, n.d. (20 May 1999)].

—Publisher Henry Holt's *Mason & Dixon Main Page:* reviews and other material, including a guide to the novel for "reading groups" [http://hholt.com/pynchon/masonmain.htm 1997–1998 (20 May 1999)].

—*The Pynchon Files:* biographical information supported by documents, illustrations, citations, and more [http://www.pynchonfiles.com/ 1998–1999 (20 May 1999)].

—*Pynchon Notes:* home page for the biannual Pynchon journal [http://www.ham.muohio.edu/~krafftjm/pynchon.html 2 July 1998 (20 May 1999)].

—*San Narciso Community College Thomas Pynchon Home Page:* links to web conversations and essays, biographical and thematic information, introductions to Pynchon's other work as well as several general and *Mason & Dixon* specific sites and documents [http://www.pomona.edu/pynchon/ or http://department2.pomona.edu/pynchon 1995–1997 (20 May 1999)].

—*Spermatikos Logos:* links to "Main Pynchon Resources" available at other sites as well as documents and other attractions (songs inspired by Pynchon's work, "a collection of Pynchonesque images," criticism, "interesting quotations, remarks, paranoid soliloquies and other musings") [http://www.rpg.net/quail/libyrinth/pynchon/ n.d. (20 May 1999)].

—*The Subculture Pages:* links, biography, pictures, bibliography [http://fringeware.com/subcult/Thomas_Pynchon.html 1996–1999 (20 May 1999)].

6. Steven Moore, review of *The Tunnel,* by William Gass, *Review of Contemporary Fiction* 15, no. 1 (1995): 159.

7. Italo Calvino, "Why Read the Classics?," trans. Patrick Creagh, *New York Review of Books,* 9 Oct. 1986, 19.

8. Jonathan Baumbach, *The Landscape of Nightmare: Studies in the Contemporary American Novel* (New York: New York University Press, 1965).

9. Thomas Pynchon, *Mason & Dixon* (New York: Henry Holt, 1997), 701.

10. Thomas Pynchon, *The Crying of Lot 49* (New York: Perennial-Harper's, 1986), 181.

11. Thomas Pynchon, *Slow Learner: Early Stories* (Boston: Little, Brown, 1984), 18–19.

12. Theodore Roosevelt, *History as Literature and Other Essays* (New York: Scribner's, 1913), 11.

Pynchon and
Mason & Dixon

Foreshadowing the Text

IRVING MALIN

DAY ONE—

I am writing this critical "survey" in the form of a journal. I hope that this form emphasizes the *process,* the *transit* of explication. I am rebelling against the "final" form—often jargon-filled—of the academic paper.

I try to call attention to this ongoing, close reading of a text, but I may be accused of self-indulgence. I do not want to be impersonal and abstract—to suppress any autobiographical impulses—as if I could remove myself from the text.

I must admit that ever since last November (1996) when I first learned of a new Pynchon novel, I have wanted to write about it. He is one of the few contemporary American novelists I have not discussed. It is, of course, ironic that *Mason & Dixon* has received more critical praise than any of his other novels. My waiting has been, ironically, "rewarded."

Although I have tried to read critical books on Pynchon, I find that they have tended to point to "systems," to scientific traditions. I am trying here to confront his text—the book jacket and his opening paragraph—to read closely every word. I know that I cannot read "purely"; I have been "infected" by my reading of Pynchon criticism and his earlier novels and this text (months ago!). Is any explication ever innocent?

Perhaps the most interesting point about Pynchon's texts is their obsession with language, their insistence upon shape. His first novel is *V.;* the title is a letter. But the letter has a curious shape so that it has been read for possible references to "places" and "people." But *V.* is, first and last, a letter that consists of two lines that converge. And, if I want to continue madly, an inverted V coupled with the usual V becomes an X. Does this occult conjunction mean anything?

Then there is the odd title, *The Crying of Lot 49.* Again linguistic *duplicity*—is this the "right" word?—comes into play. "Crying"

27

is a pun; so is "lot." And even the number "49" hides religious meaning.

I do not even want to mention *Gravity's Rainbow,* but I must. Critics have wondered about the title. Is the juxtaposition of science and biblical reference meaningful? Does the shape of "rainbow" *as word* have anything to do with the scientific phenomenon?

Now I turn to the jacket of *Mason & Dixon.*[1] The book-jacket has "Mason" on top and "Dixon" on bottom. I find it curious that the names are not *completely* given. Pynchon, it seems, has decided to "shade" the first two letters of both and make "son" and "xon" *bold.* Why? Is he suggesting that even words are "split," that they contain "traces" or "shadows"? Is he pointing to obscure beginnings (of words)? Is he stressing "on" and, by shrewd implication, introducing his obsessive interest in on/off and other binaries? (Is a pun an example of the duality of things?) And does he see a duality (con)verging so that *one becomes two?* And does he recognize that his very name is another two-syllable one—like "Mason" and "Dixon"—which ends with "on"?

I should rest here, but I have "referential mania"—like the Nabokov madman in "Signs and Symbols." I notice that the word "and" is not used; rather there is an ampersand—and an unusual one at that! Why is Pynchon using a typographical symbol for a word? Is he musing again on the shape of text (of content)? I am going to consult my dictionary.[2] It seems that "ampersand" stands as the character for "and" in the dictionary definition. How strange! "Character" is, of course, a pun—part of a "typeface" and a person like Pynchon.

And to add to this manic flow, I seem to remember that in the center of the jacket I saw "Mason & Dixon" repeated beneath "Thomas Pynchon." What is going on? Is there some pattern pointing to twoness or reflection (a pun)? Is the jacket already hinting at clues to the huge text?

Then there is the color of the jacket. The book jacket is made to resemble parchment, an old document.

I must assume that there are reasons for the design, that it has been offered to us by Pynchon, that he is in control of the design.

On the other hand, I may be reading into a "simple" jacket signs and symbols. *My* signs and symbols! But isn't such madness always surrounding any Pynchon text? Don't the characters search for patterns or create ones that are *not* there? Are they ever *certain*—even about *uncertainty?*

I am going to stop here. On the second day (of "work") I plan to read the opening line of the text. I believe that Pynchon—who is, perhaps, one of our most careful (compulsive) writers—knows that these lines are significant. Indeed, he always worries about beginnings and ends—of texts, cultures, selves, actions.

DAY TWO—

I have been unable to sleep properly; I have had nightmares of huge letters, "ghostly demarcations"—is this phrase from Stevens?—because of performance anxiety. I am not sure that I have read the text "sanely."

I return to it. I see that there is a page with the words "*One*" and "Latitudes and Departures." The word "One" is underlined. I am slightly disturbed by the *word* used, instead of the *number,* but I'll accept it as merely a word introducing the first section. But what about "Latitudes and Departures"? I turn again to the dictionary—I'm convinced that Pynchon often uses this reference work, citing all etymologies. "Latitude," I see, comes from the Latin *Latus;* the Latin word means wide, "akin to lain." There are several meanings; some are archaic, such as "extent or distance from side to side" or "the range of exposures within which a *film* or *plate* will produce a *negative* or *positive* of *satisfactory* quality" (my italics). Another archaic meaning is *"freedom* of *choice* or *action"* (my italics). I am thrilled. The archaic repeats the notion of negative and positive (off/on?); it also alludes to "film" and "plate." Pynchon is probably amused by the reference to "film." (I think rapidly of the films in *Vineland* and *Gravity's Rainbow.*) I like the reference to "freedom of choice" because Pynchon is, as we all know, interested in the vagaries of "free will." How free is free? Will Mason and Dixon be free, or will they be servants of some higher, darker personage and/or deity?

The dictionary cites the usual meaning of "latitude," but it also mentions "angular distance of a *celestial* body from the ecliptic" (my italics). "Latitude" is an astronomical term. How interesting! And of course "latitudes" are thought of as parallel lines in the accompanying drawing. ("Lines" brings into play another reference to text.)

I am not going to refer to "departure" in the dictionary. But isn't it interesting that "departure" can mean a first step from "there" to "here." Is "departure" a beginning?

After all these beginnings—which, of course, *delay* the beginnings of the first paragraph—I now turn to the opening sentence, which is too long to quote in its entirety. The sentence is 117 words long, and the first thing I notice is the *archaic typeface.*

Nouns—but not all—are capitalized. Certain words such as "outbuildings" are oddly joined. The entire effect is quite puzzling. The typography and orthography seem to "defamiliarize"—to use Russian Formalism—the text and yet make me aware of the text as *shape.* Pynchon almost makes me aware of a "new wor(l)d."

I have to decide now on my approach. Should I read *every* word? If I do, I'll possibly say too much about too little. I'll be accused of "goofy" criticism. I'm almost tempted to consult "goofy" in the dictionary but this act would be, well, goofy.

The first sentence contains no reference to Mason and Dixon. This fact is mildly frustrating. Pynchon, instead, starts with a description beautifully phrased of *outside weather.* He uses as a first word "Snow-Balls." The word is shaped oddly (for us). It is a two-syllable word with two capital letters and a hyphen connecting nouns.

On with the madness. "Snow" is white (at first); then it becomes off-white as people step on it. It is, if you will, a "site" of change, transformation, "twoness." And, if I remember correctly, each snowflake is different! No snowflake is the same as any other, although the flake has six sides to it. It is a complex design hidden by the many snowflakes coming down, converging from above. Snow, at first, suggests whiteness—ah, Melville—and the whiteness is all or none of the spectrum of color. I should mention, at least in passing, that whiteness has been used by Aiken, Dickey, Melville, Ammons, and, of course, Coleridge. And it is subject to endless social interpretations in America. Race! When is someone "white"? Is a "white" person white or pink?

But wait. Is it too silly to relate whiteness to the word "witness"? Probably. But I am so afraid of Pynchon's "playfulness" that I feel I am his devoted servant. And "snow" is a word that reminds me of those other words like "snafu" which carry negative qualities. "Sn" seems to be associated with "bad" qualities.

And what about "snow" containing a "now," which could refer to time or, in its sound, could recall "know"?

I better turn to that hyphen. It links "Snow" and "Balls." Pynchon will continually play with the "mark" of connection. But is the mark merely a line? Again he makes me wonder, as I have never previously, about the meaning of punctuation. I guess that

in the back of my mind is that ancient notion that once words—
say *aleph* or *bet*—were pictures of objects, were shaped meaning-
fully. "Balls." A ball is a sphere, a circle; it is also a party. Twoness!
By capitalizing "ball" and joining it to capitalized "snow," Pynchon
makes me muse about the word and its "latitude." In the first
sentence "Snow-Balls" seem to fall from the sky. How perverse! I
usually think of manmade (child-made) snowballs. Who or what
is *shaping* the snowballs?

I better stop here. Again I am jittery. Another six pages—and
I have not even gotten to the verb—to the *action.* I'll never finish
at the rate I'm going. But I'm afraid that I'll miss something. If
Pynchon could spend twenty years on this text, then he could easily study all sides of a word.

To comfort myself I think of the Talmudists inquiring about the
Bible. Why is the first letter of the Old Testament—Genesis—a
bet rather than an *aleph?* Shouldn't the *first* word *begin* with the
first letter?

DAY THREE—

The "Snow-Balls," I am told, "have flown their Arcs." There are
several striking parts of the phrase. I turn again to the dictionary
to examine all the meanings listed under "flow." I take "flown" to
be a past participle of "flow," but I may find it to be related to
"fly." Under "fly" several interesting, unlooked-for meanings are
suggested: "Fly" is said to "move through outer space" and to "float,
wave, or soar in the air" and "to operate (as a balloon, aircraft,
rocket or spacecraft) in flight." Perhaps Pynchon is amused to
find the reference to "rocket" *(Gravity's Rainbow).* And the allusion delights his aesthetic gamesmanship.

The significance of flight—departure—is evident in many movements in Pynchon's previous novels. Flight or float is movement
from place to place as in Oedipus Maas's flight, but her flight is
crazy; it appears that *she does not control* it.

"Arcs" is, perhaps, the most subtle of the words. Several meanings are given for the word. They can suggest possible metaphors
for the future text. One is the "apparent path described above and
below the horizon by a celestial body (as the sun)." The "apparent" introduces the notion of seeming, of possible visionary sight-
ing. "Celestial" reinforces the astronomical references indicated in
a previous definition. "Arc" is also something "arched" or "curved"—

and perhaps arch suggests a *structure.* "Arc" can also mean an "angle." Arc also reminds me of "ark," a structure used to escape the terrifying overflow. Is Pynchon punning again? Is he informing us of "arc" as "rainbow"?

I return to the phrase "have flown their Arcs." Are the "Snow-Balls" (as structures) following a pattern, an "Arc"? Or do they, in a way, shape an "Arc," an angle of flow? Again the *pattern* enters the text, but the pattern is not clearly stated; it is fully ambiguous. But the pattern has been *reinforced* so that we are made aware that "Snow-Balls" are, if you will, *shapes shaped* or *shaping shapes*—there is a kind of circularity here.

Is Pynchon playing with sound? Snow and flow rhyme. The circularity here is broken by the "Arcs," which seem abrupt; the "c" closes the openness of "snow" and "flow."

In the next part of the sentence I read that the "Snow-Balls" "starr'd the Sides of Outbuildings." The noun "star" is turned into a verb as if an "object" can transit, can move, can begin a process. There is much beauty here, but what if objects can transform themselves (or be transformed) into *unexpected,* destructive forms—say, a dog who talks. "Sides" returns me to a word seen before—a *line,* not a *circle.* But perhaps the most curious word is "Outbuildings." What are they? Are they outhouses? Is there an "Inbuilding"? Does Pynchon suggest that buildings, structures, stand *out* because of certain aesthetic qualities? Even the "Outbuildings" stand out in the phrase because of the quirkiness of the word. I should look again at the dictionary. Eureka! An outbuilding is a "building (as a stable or woodshed) separate but accessory to the main house." I like the *separate but accessory* linkage. It reminds me of Mason and Dixon, who are "separate but accessories."

I should clarify some of the above. Pynchon has introduced earth (buildings) and air, combining the two elements; he has poetically transformed snowballs, stars, so that I see them freshly; and he has, in effect, forced me to regard "ordinary" words as poetic, special structures. He has made me stretch my imagination to the point that I see beauty—beauty that other writers would probably like to create or emulate.

DAY FOUR—

I must move more quickly; I am running against the clock, the *final lines.*

I look again at the first sentence. I see the simile of "Outbuild-ings" as of "Cousins." The family unit is suggested as a structure, a generational building. There is an occult association of outside and inside structures. (Pynchon makes much of the family.)

I am told that "Snow-Balls" "carried Hats away into the brisk Wind off Delaware. . . ." The forces of Nature are, of course, a re-curring concern. So are linguistic forces or fields of meaning (as indicated by Pynchon's apparent love of *interacting* definitions). The wind is important; it drives the "Snow-Balls" that, in turn, act upon hats, people, as well as "Outbuildings." I am fascinated by the use of the hat. Is the hat an ark of sorts, sheltering the head? Is it tied to the height—the height of stars and celestial bodies? I am probably reaching far for total unity. But the "Wind" is a kind of "divine" or spiritual force (as in Shelley's poem) driv-ing objects. Is there a pun on wind? Does "wind" suggest twists, curves, entanglements, coils? It does in the dictionary meanings. Once more I believe that Pynchon has used the dictionary as a significant text—in perhaps the same way he used scientific works for *Gravity's Rainbow*. Thus in a novel written in an old style, he has searched for archaic meanings and occasionally created words. By doing so, he again brings into play the text as a *field of energy*, not a still object. He has stressed linguistic magic or transforma-tion or transit. Thus the puns, the unexpected meanings.

"Delaware": the first state mentioned. But as I have tried to demonstrate, nouns are not always static in this text. "Star" be-comes "starr'd." The "state"—America itself—is a field of force, a process of forward (or backward) movement. Thus, we need sur-veyors like Mason and Dixon and Washington and Pynchon to determine where a state *begins and ends*. And, of course, I must survey the textual state, trying to read *between the lines*.

Is it mad to see "aware" in Delaware? Surely Pynchon would not break the noun into components? Or would he?

There is a comma and a dash as the sentence unfolds or flows. After the dash the "Sleds are brought in and their Runners care-fully dried and greased. . . ." In the winter scene we have moved from the flying snow to the return of sleds to the house. From *out*-doors to *in*doors! I like the drying and greasing of the runners (part of the sled) because "grease" seems to be needed to return the "sleds" to their original beauty and usefulness. "Greased" is not often used; the noun "grease" is the more common word. "Greased" and even "sled" *move, slide, run,* suggesting movement and action and—do I dare?—"transit."

"[S]hoes deposited in the back Hall, a stocking'd-foot Descent made upon the great Kitchen. . . ." Therefore the action in the sentence continues despite small stops of commas. Is "shoes" supposed to remind me of earth, "down" as opposed to air and height of hats? The body becomes a structure moving from high to low? I'm intrigued by the "back Hall." Should it be hyphenated? Back (and front by implication) hints obliquely at possible hidden movement or structure. We can't see what is in back of us. Nor can Mason and Dixon, who wonder later about whether they are moved by hidden forces and agents. Stocking becomes "stocking'd-foot"; again a noun becomes less static. Perhaps "Descent" is the significant word so far in the sentence. Things *have fallen*—"Snow-Balls," feet—and the notion of *fall* obsesses Pynchon because of religious, scientific, and sociological connections. He is hypnotized by the "lowlands," by Hell, by the downward movement of rockets.

The kitchen has been in a "purposeful dither." "Dither" suggests frenzied, hurried movements. Here it is described as "purposeful." There is, if you will, an oxymoron; I think of "dither"— how rarely the word is used—as meaningful; I must look up "dither" to amuse myself. It is in my dictionary. When its meaning of "shiver" is given, there is "the dithering of grass" (used by Stevens) as example. Stevens and Pynchon? I should file the comparison for future thought, but all I can think of now is that Stevens, like Pynchon, uses the arcane, unusual word. Stevens's English is almost *another* language. So is Pynchon's.

Day Five—

The sentence continues and the various words are linked obliquely. I recognize that my analysis interrupts the flow, thus changing or mutilating textual rhythms. At first I'm disturbed by this fact, but then I think that perhaps Pynchon wants me to recognize that my "logic" is insufficient or dangerous. I think of the surveyor who cannot really measure the field because he must stop and start as he notices markers (or marks). The text may reflect the hazards of charting fields.

The sentence continues: "punctuated by the ringing Lids of various Boilers and Stewing-Pots. . . ." I'm drawn to the word "punctuated" because it brings into play the notion of rhythmic haltings, pauses—there is an implied reference to text. What exactly are punctuations? Can we read a text without taking into account punctuation as well as diction? I have tried to show how the hyphen—and the dash—is an integral part of the sentence.

"Lids": the word, of course, suggests covering of space, a hiding of contents, an "out" closing an "in." And it brings into focus the idea of "seeing." Lids suggests eyelids. Doesn't it? Thus the reader-surveyor must see all the field, but he cannot see it *at once*. Total vision is impossible because the eyelid shuts—if only briefly. Blinks? Blanks?

"Stewing-Pots": The "stew" reminds me of mixed contents. Is a "stew" one or many? When we eat a stew, do we taste one thing, or do we taste many spices, etc.? Surely the text is a "stew" of sorts? I should refer to "stew" in the dictionary, but I'm afraid that there may be even more difficult, strange etymologies or usages.

The sentence informs me of the stew's contents—"Pie-Spices, peel'd Fruits, Suet, heated Sugar"—and the possible references of "peel'd" and "heated" to such earlier words as "lids"—isn't a lid a covering like a peel and isn't "Sugar" a kind of "Snow"?

Again Pynchon uses the rather odd (", —") punctuation, but the fact that I notice it reinforces my belief that he is calling attention to a text that consists not only of words but of "spaces" between words, and the punctuation subtly determines the flow, the transit of this sentence.

Now I learn more about the family. I see the "children" and am suddenly reminded of the generations in *Vineland* and the fact that these children are, ironically, my Fathers and Mothers. And young America has given birth to me. I cannot escape the heritage. Pynchon's historical text is a meditation on history—as "his story"? I must take the present "lid" off to see the Past. But doesn't the Past—the stew?—affect the lid in a perverse way?

"[H]aving all upon the Fly" is quite "ambiguous." Does Pynchon mean that they have "flown" at odd moments to the food? Are they flies, insects swooping *down* to the food? And isn't a "fly" an old kind of vehicle? That "upon" has, in effect, created the ambiguities and, of course, it makes me aware of "up" and "on," two "little" words which play a "big" part in later textual matters.

"[T]he Children, having all upon the fly, among rhythmic slaps of Batter and Spoon, coax'd and stolen what they might, proceed, as upon each afternoon all this snowy Advent. . . ." I have quoted this part of the sentence to demonstrate the rhythm Pynchon uses. Notice, first, that the significant verbs "coax'd" and "stolen" are used *after* two phrases. The real action seems to occur *after* description; I wait for the verbs—I am, in effect, "in the air," *suspended* by the Batter and Spoon.

The "rhythmic slaps" of the batter bring into play or reinforce the "rhythmic slaps" of the phrasing here. The entire sentence so far has rhythmically slapped me because it deliberately withholds knowledge of action. The verbs, for the most part, wait for the flight of descriptive phrases to end. There is the emphasis on flying or floating elements in the rhythm. I expect the verbs, but I am deliberately frustrated. There is a kind of *up* and *down* effect until I am slapped by the verbs.

Notice that the word "slap" introduces, if only somewhat briefly, the idea of *violence*. "Slaps" will eventually become more violent—there will be fights, wars, etc. Pynchon plants the seeds here, indicating perhaps that one minor act of violence leads to major acts of violence. Violence, indeed, cannot be *contained;* it can only be *continued* in an ever-increasing manner.

"[C]oax'd and stolen what they might": the verbs "coax'd and stolen" enter the text here and, like the noun "slaps," alert me to future coaxings and thefts in the text. History is, I may say, a matter of *persuasion and* (as?) *theft.* Mason and Dixon—and most of the others in the novel—recognize that adults use duplicitous language (coax) to achieve their ends, and if they can't use rhetoric, they will act as thieves (I am reminded of *The Confidence Man* here, another novel of coaxing and stealing).

Does Pynchon imply that childish acts, relatively harmless and "cute," undergird adult acts? If we follow the adventures of the surveyors and their "masters," the owners and their "slaves," we must admit that there is a linkage. The relatively harmless and simple actions here create a possible pattern—a kind of compulsion to follow through, to *increase* the possibilities of adult behavior.

I am not implying that the children are "evil"; I am suggesting that trifles, small acts, are meaningful for later life. The "past," after all, creates the "future."

Is "might" a duplicitous word? Does it carry the possibility of might as power? I simply raise the question. And "proceed"? The sentence proceeds "erratically"; so do the adult actions; the text is, in its entirety, a "process"—a secret one in which events seem to occur in a designed pattern, but the patterned process (or processive pattern) is never *fully* seen and comprehended. There are gaps, reversals, subtle changes. And thus the text reminds me of *Tristan Shandy,* another novel of *unexpected* movements and cessations in which there is no simple A-to-B-to-C structure.

The references to time in "afternoon" and to the religious day of Advent reintroduce the fact that *time,* although measured by clocks, which depend upon Greenwich Mean Time (measured by astronomical charts), is very rarely noticed by the characters until it is too late. And Time is seen in private ways, in personal anniversaries, celebrations, parties. It is ghostly, moving through the text so that Mason, although he wants to know exact time, also tries unconsciously to escape it. Time is "shadowy" and "spectral."

"Advent" is religious: "the period beginning four Sundays before Christmas and observed by some Christians as a season of prayer and fasting." But the word also brings to mind *adventure.* Perhaps the text, like *Gravity's Rainbow,* is an adventure—or series of adventures—timed to the Christian calendar.

There are, it seems, secular and religious times, calendars, so that Time is "relative"—Time is, curiously, a source of interpretation, and it, of course, can never be seen purely; it cannot be measured or charted. Thus if we apply the notion to History, I cannot understand the Past because I am not there; I am *here now.* Past and Present are strangely at war. Thus inferior History is merely a list of dates. But Pynchon's history forces me to see that the words are slippery, elusive, subject to personal charting. (And doesn't this remind me of Time in *The Tunnel* and *Pale Fire?* In these texts it is "spectral," open to personal interpretation.)

The "comfortable Room at the rear of the House" belongs to the children. It is a room of "Assaults." The house is divided; there is a back and front, twoness. Of course, back and front are perspectives. If the children are in the back room, then they will see the front as back. Any transit, any survey, any body, any text contains a back and front, but the to-and-fro movements transform spaces.

The last word of the first sentence is "Assaults." It seems to carry special weight because of its position. And certainly the sentence itself has assaulted our usual way of reading, our notion of (everyday) language. Is it curious that the *last* word begins with *A?*

Day Six—

The second sentence "rests." The emphasis is different from the "movements" of the first. There is a contrast, a "binary" opposition.

Pynchon makes much of the objects in the room. And the "objects" (nouns) are given interesting, useful adjectives. Consider, for example, the "scarr'd" table. The entire novel is *scarr'd*—there are references to wounds, tattoos, creases. And, of course, scars are *marks,* perhaps strange marks on a page. The "side-benches"— there is the use of side (edge) again—are "mis-match'd." Aren't Mason and Dixon mismatch'd? Aren't slaves and masters in South Africa and America mis-match'd?

The "Second-Street Chippendale"—I like the use of second, continuing the numerical and spatial references (two is "back" of one, depending on one's count). The Chippendale is an *"interpretation"* of the "fam'd Chinese Sofa." An interpretation? Isn't the entire text an interpretation of "America," an interpretation of interpretation?

The "Sofa" is likened with its high canopy to a "snug, dim tent": another structure! But "dim," which suggests soft light, is mysterious: why should Pynchon connect light and space (tent)? Dim, of course, returns me to the shadow-world as represented by the shaded names on the book-jacket.

There are "odd" chairs. Pynchon is punning once more. And the "odd," the "perverse," the "freakish" delight him. (See the Duck and Dog later.) But why is something odd? Perhaps it deviates from the norm. (The enlightenment surely had its oddities. I think of Swift.)

The Card Table is "sinister" (left?), and this word moves me to consider the sinister motives of the trading companies. The table "exhibits the cheaper wavelike Grain known in the Trade as *Wand'ring Heart,* causing an *illusion* of Depth into which for years children have gaz'd as into the *illustrated Pages of Books* ..." (my italics). I turn to the dictionary. "Wavelike" can mean "sinusoidal," and sinusoidal refers to the "sine curve," but it also can mean a "minute endothelium-lined space or passage for blood in the tissues of an organ." Thus Pynchon can use the word to repeat the *shape,* and he can use it to refer to passage of blood. And there is much blood in the text. But isn't the text somewhat curved? It refuses to move in a straight line; it contains digressions, off-center remarks, and journeys. No Pynchon text is ever straightforward in plot; each moves *erratically.*

The "Wand'ring Heart" is, no doubt, based on Pynchon's arcane investigations of historical furniture. I like the two-syllable "Wand'ring" not only because it brings into play "wandering" but because it "mismatches" "wand" (a magical *line*) and the circular ring. "The Heart" insists upon the body in the text, the structure that can be deformed by war and hallucination.

DAY SEVEN—

"An illusion of Depth" recreates the sense throughout the text that depth (associated with down under), like height, will always be imprecise; it changes because of perspective. Thus when we stand at a certain "line," we see things differently from the way we see things elsewhere on the line. The line itself, to put it another way, is not *stable*. Perspective influences perception. And if I apply this easy "cause" to the textual lines of the paragraph, I see the principle at work. A sentence can be lumpy, straight, jagged, depending on my pauses. I "rewrite" the sentence; so does Pynchon in his "revisions." We cannot be in the same place; our measures are mismatched. The uncertainty principle appears again. Text is illusive, elusive; so is the world.

I like the fact that Pynchon mentions the pages (illustrated) of a book. He seems always to return to textual matters as he "reads" the world. Is he, indeed, implying that the world—including planets, snowballs, furniture—is similar to a text (and vice versa). To quote Heraclitus: "No man steps into the same river twice." Perhaps no reader ever reads the same text twice.

The "*secret* compartments," "the *hidden* catches," the "sliding Mortises"—all these constructions reinforce the illusion of perception and the fact that we can never know all the shades of meaning. There is, perhaps, an interesting ambiguity here. If I know that there are "secret compartments," can I even think of them as secret? When does a secret *reveal* itself? How does it? Is this Pynchon sentence as full of "secret compartments" as I think it is? I ask these questions because I am "dithering," shaky, unsure of my perceptions (deceptions?). But I cannot really expect answers from others who may read the text differently, who may accuse me of finding things which are not there (wherever "there" is). Which "survey" is correct? And who can judge it?

The sentence continues with "the Twins" and their sister not being able to see ends. The Twins, of course, returns me to "twoness," duality, binaries. Although twins are supposedly equal, even they respond differently. There is the difference in behavior: one is usually more aggressive than the other. I want to leap here to Mason and Dixon. Obviously, they are quite different in their personalities, but they seem to be a single entity. Before reading this text, I always thought of them as a unit. That ampersand continues to bother me because it seems to join them.

I think suddenly of *Women and Men,* Joseph McElroy's mas-
terpiece, in which we are never sure whether or not to read the
phrase as one or to see division. Some readers maintain that despite the obvious differences, they are joined. There is a kind of
secret bond even when the male and female never really meet in
the text. Therefore, the concept of unity and difference is open to
question.

At the beginning of this journal I was fascinated by the idea of
beginnings. When does a text begin? And, of course, when does it
end? Does the last punctuation mark end the text? What about
the blank space under the lines? Does it not belong to the page?

Can "the Twins" ever be certain of the end? Surely, Mason and
Dixon cannot envision their ends. And are there not two ends to
the text? The last word of the text is "too." It ends with a pun! And
as I have been obsessively pointing out, puns mirror the twoness
in one word; they are profoundly significant because of their "secret," philosophical status.

Is the text about the "beginning" or "end" of America? Is the
end "foreshadowed" in the beginning?

DAY EIGHT—

The next sentence again "suspends" meaning. First we have a
lengthy description of the "Wall" before we are given other objects
in the room—we must wait for the end of the sentence. Presumably there is a "mirror" on the wall in which we will see other objects *exiled* to this back-room—these objects are "Remembrances
of a Time" passed.

I want to start with the first words: "Upon the Wall. . . ." The
wall is another reminder of a line, a border, an edge; it also fore-
shadows division (say the lines between "states" created by surveyors). "Upon" is an old "friend"—it has been used previously—
and it insists, by repetition, on the "up" and "on" syllables and
their suggestion of binary placements. "Up" implies "down"; "on"
implies "off."

This back room is a place of "banishment"; it is, if you will, a
hidden space for leftover, unnecessary objects. It is referred to
as a "Den of Parlor Apes for its Remembrance of a Time better
forgotten, reflecting most of the Room. . . ." The sentence is somewhat mysterious. I can see the linkage of "Den" and "Apes." ("Ape"
is a pun suggesting the animal and the notion of impersonation.)

What are *Parlor* Apes? Are these creatures human beings who act like animals? Although the reference is deliberately (?) mysterious, it does make me think that there is a thin line separating animals and men. And surely the Dog and the Duck we encounter later in the text remind us of metamorphosis, of easy slippage from one stage (or "state") of being to another.

The reference to a Time "better forgotten" implies that not all times are the same; some events must be forgotten, repressed in the back of the mind. Perhaps History itself is partially *hidden*— that history we would like to forget. And Pynchon apparently writes a "counter-history," including the repulsive, tormented, violent events not mentioned in our official versions of the past. Thus *Mason & Dixon* is a meditation on Memory—as are all of his novels. It is a many-sided reflection.

And the reflection ties itself to the mirror, the specters that later dominate the text (say Mason's "dead" wife). There is a gothic quality to the text because of all its references to "hidden," "ghostly," "shady"; and it may be argued that only the gothic can "reveal" the *cracks* in American culture. (Is Pynchon also playing with the fact that his ancestors have almost the same names as the inhabitants of *The House of the Seven Gables?* Is there intertexuality?)

We are offered "fray'd" carpets and drapes. Although they are uneven, both carpets and drapes *cover* things. They, like the lids, mentioned previously, serve as "obstacles" to the "underworld" of flour or wall or eye or batter.

The cat "Whiskers" hunts for food—it *stalks* objects. And the stalking prepares us for other stalking in the text. (Are not Mason and Dixon being followed by . . . who knows what company?) Whiskers's eyes are "finely reflexive to anything suggesting Food." Reflexivity has just been used in the reflection as in the novel itself—the wandering text reflects the odd transits of readers, writers, and, of course, surveyors. "Suggesting" may be Pynchon's suggestion that the text is filled with true/false suggestions, implications, readings, interpretations.

The mirror appears at this point. I now see it "upon the wall." It is an interesting object especially because it is in "an inscrib'd frame." The "inscrib'd frame" is inscribed by Pynchon's text. A double inscription! And the "frame" has been framed to appear just now in the sentence. The text demonstrates a reflexive quality.

The mirror commemorates a "memorable farewell Ball stag'd in '77 by the British who'd been Occupying the City, just before their Withdrawal from Philadelphia." I like the reference to "Ball" because it suggests the Ball of Snow. And I'm intrigued by the note of "Withdrawal" as the sentence finally ends. The paragraph ends with "Withdrawal," but it suggests that any departure implies an arrival somewhere else. Exits and entrances. Ends and Beginnings.

DAY NINE—

I have just reread my entries. Some are excessive or wild; some are wise. There is imperfection. I would change certain words, "erase" the evidence, but I prefer to allow the "original" remarks to remain. I don't want to cover them.

In a sense no text—including this journal—ever *ends*. It remains open; it avoids complete measurement.

NOTES

1. Thomas Pynchon, *Mason & Dixon* (New York: Henry Holt, 1997). On Pynchon's contribution to the dust-jacket design, see Ron Rosenbaum, "The Edgy Enthusiast," *The New York Observer,* 28 April 1997, 43.

2. All definitions come from *Webster's New Collegiate Dictionary* (1975).

Mason & Dixon in the Zone, or, A Brief Poetics of Pynchon-Space

BRIAN MCHALE

SUBJUNCTIVE AMERICA

With 773 pages of text to choose from, it seems extraordinary that two of the earliest North American reviews of *Mason & Dixon*—John Leonard's in *The Nation* and Anthony Lane's in *The New Yorker,* appearing on the same day, 12 May 1997—should quote exactly the same paragraph from Pynchon's novel. Is this collusion? Or even (heavily paranoid voices have whispered) conspiracy? The iconoclasts Alec McHoul and David Wills might see here, instead, the foundations being laid for a canon of quotations such as already circulates in the secondary literature on *The Crying of Lot 49* and *Gravity's Rainbow.*[1] And perhaps they would be right; nevertheless, something more than merely an instinct for consensus-building seems to have animated the reviewers' choice of this passage:

Does Britannia, when she sleeps, dream? Is America her dream?—in which all that cannot pass in the metropolitan Wakefulness is allow'd Expression away in the restless Slumber of these Provinces, and on West-ward, wherever 'tis not yet mapp'd, nor written down, nor ever, by the majority of Mankind, seen,—serving as a very Rubbish-Tip for subjunctive Hopes, for all that *may yet be true,*—Earthly Paradise, Fountain of Youth, Realms of Prester John, Christ's Kingdom, ever behind the sunset, safe till the next Territory to the West be seen and recorded, measur'd and tied in, back into the Net-Work of Points already known, that slowly triangulates its Way into the Continent, changing all from subjunctive to declarative, reducing Possibilities to Simplicities that serve the ends of Governments,—winning away from the realm of the Sacred, its Borderlands one by one, and assuming them unto the bare mortal World that is our home, and our Despair.[2]

43

Though neither says anything about it, I suppose that what at-
tracted Leonard's and Lane's attention to this passage is its foregrounding of the subjunctivity that is such a salient feature of
Mason & Dixon: the American West as subjunctive space, the
space of wish and desire, of the hypothetical and the counterfactual, of speculation and possibility.

Already in *Gravity's Rainbow,* certain key passages had been
cast in the subjunctive mode: if, for instance, Franz Pökler had
opted to commit incest with his putative daughter Ilse, then they
might have fled together to Denmark; but neither event actually
transpires in the world of the novel.[3] Relatively rare in *Gravity's
Rainbow,* such subjunctive events abound in *Mason & Dixon.*
Mason's appeal to his father for advice about marrying is paradigmatic in this respect: "All subjunctive, of course,—*had* young
Mason gone to his father, this *might have been* the conversation
likely to result" (208). Similarly, we are told what the English
captain of the *Seahorse* might have said to the French captain of
the *l'Grand* (39); the witty repartee that Mason would have liked
to have exchanged with Florinda at the Tyburn hanging (111);
the account Mason would have entered in his journal concerning
his first encounter with Susannah Peach if he had been keeping
a journal at that time (187); and even details of the exchange that
Mason might have had with Dr. Johnson and Boswell if they had
encountered one another in Scotland (744). All of these exchanges
and encounters, and many others like them,[4] belong to the cate-
gory that Gerald Prince has called the "disnarrated": though narrated, often at some length and in some detail, they are explicitly
identified as (probably) never having happened in the world of the
novel.[5] "Of course it happened. Of course it didn't happen."[6]

The subjunctive episodes mentioned above are supposed to have
occurred (if they had occurred at all) either before or (in one case)
after Mason's and Dixon's sojourn in North America. But subjunctivity (as the passage that caught Leonard's and Lane's attention attests) is especially associated here with the American
West, and instances of it multiply as Mason and Dixon approach
the western limit of their advance into the continent (e.g., 650–
51, 677, and 683). When they finally reach the Warrior Path of
the Native Americans, beyond which they are forbidden to go,
and must begin backtracking eastward across the Alleghenies
again, the narrative shifts into subjunctive and counterfactual
mode: "Suppose that Mason and Dixon and their Line cross Ohio
after all, and continue West" (706)—as, say, Lewis and Clark would

a generation later. This counterfactual hypothesis empowers the narrative to project a series of subjunctive spaces, the spaces that Mason and Dixon would have traversed if they had pushed on westward. Out there in subjunctive American they encounter (or they would have encountered) a succession of microworld enclaves: a simulacrum of the Bourbon Court; an underworld city; Spanish, Chinese, and Russian enclaves "with entirely different histories" from that of the Atlantic seaboard (708); a sky-worshipping sect; and so on. Out there they even identify (or would have identified) a new planet, the one that, in real history, Herschel would discover, and that would come to be called Uranus. By the time Mason and Dixon finally do turn back toward the East (still subjunctively), the settlements they first encountered on their outbound journey to the Warrior Path have undergone strange transformations. Subjunctivity, it appears, is contagious.

Moreover, within the subjunctive sequence of events, doubly subjunctive episodes occur. If Mason and Dixon had continued, extending their Line westward to the foothills of the Rockies, then eventually their chainmen would have outdistanced them and been lost; if, instead of turning back to claim their prize for discovering the new planet, they would have continued into the Rockies, then their chainmen would later have been found again (709). But, according to the primary hypothetical scenario, Mason and Dixon *do* return to claim their prize, so the chainmen remain lost—except in the world of the secondary hypothetical scenario. Similarly, if Mason and Dixon were to return to the East as triumphant discoverers of a new planet, then they would propose extending the Line eastward on buoys across the Atlantic. Along that seaborne line there would (hypothetically) develop a kind of floating city and theme park—a doubly subjunctive space, the space of Mason's and Dixon's hypothetical projection subordinated to the hypothetical narrative of their expedition beyond the Ohio and back again (709).[7]

Others have ventured into the subjunctive spaces of America before Pynchon's Mason and Dixon: Paul Muldoon, for instance, in his narrative poem set in an alternative America, *Madoc* (1991); or William Gibson and Bruce Sterling in their alternative history of the nineteenth century, *The Difference Engine* (also 1991). Though there are striking family resemblances among these texts, none is closer or more striking than the one between the subjunctive America of *Mason & Dixon* and the Zone of *Gravity's Rainbow*. "A great frontierless streaming,"[8] the Zone is a space of interregnum, an interval of freedom and unlimited potential between the collapse of one regime and the installation of new ones: "maybe for a little while all the fences are down, one road as good as another, the whole space of the Zone cleared, depolarized . . . without elect, without preterite, without even nationality to fuck it up."[9] Similarly, the American West of *Mason & Dixon* is poised at a moment when Native American and European social worlds coexist uneasily, when neither regime prevails and pluralism is de facto the order of the day. West of the Warrior Path, in subjunctive America, Mason and Dixon find (or would have found) a space honeycombed with microworlds and "entirely different histories,"[10] alternative scenarios and speculative projects, even a brand-new planet. Like the Zone, in short, the subjunctive America of *Mason & Dixon* is what Foucault would have called a *heterotopia,* an impossible space "in which fragments of a large number of possible orders glitter separately in the dimension, without law or geometry, of the *heteroclite.*"[11]

Already in *Gravity's Rainbow,* Pynchon had anticipated interpolating the Zone into North American space. There he proposed calling heterotopian America "the Zone of the Interior."[12] This is precisely the space of *Mason & Dixon:* the Zone of the Interior.

SPACE, TIME

The present epoch will perhaps be above all the epoch of space.
—Michel Foucault, "Of Other Spaces"

I have tended, in describing the pervasive subjunctivity of *Mason & Dixon,* to speak mainly in terms of the spaces projected by the narrative, when I might nearly as easily have spoken of its subjunctive sequences of events; I have tended, that is, to emphasize subjunctive space over subjunctive time. This is deliberate, for I will want to argue in what follows that *Mason & Dixon* is dominated more by spatial than temporal categories.

This argument has one enormous piece of counter-evidence to account for, namely the fact that *Mason & Dixon* is a work of historical fiction. Its subject is, in a sense, temporal difference, change over time: the differences, first of all, between the 1760s, when the narrated events occur, and the time of narration, 1786—between, in other words, before and after the Revolution;[13] and secondly, those between the late eighteenth century and our own late twentieth century. The differences between then and now are especially reflected at the level of style, in the novel's plausible pastiche of eighteenth-century diction, syntax, and typographical conventions. Or rather, the difference is reflected in the tension between the novel's eighteenth-century pastiche and its twentieth-century anachronisms. Here, for instance, is Mason's encounter with "a certain Amelia, a Milk-Maid of Brooklyn":

> Amy is dress'd from Boots to Bonnet all in different Articles of black, a curious choice of color for a milkmaid, it seems to Mason, tho', as he has been instructed ever to remind himself, this is New-York, where other Customs prevail. "Oh, aye, at home they're on at me about it without Mercy," she tells him, "I'm, as, 'But I *like* Black,'—yet my Uncle, he's, as, 'Strangers will take you for I don't know what,' hey,— I don't know what, either. Do you?" (400)

Substitute "like" for Amy's "as" ("I'm, like, 'But I *like* Black'") and you have a 1990s adolescent, thinly disguised as an eighteenth-century milkmaid—*Clueless* in the eighteenth century.[14] In other words, this is not historical fiction so much as "historiographic metafiction," in Linda Hutcheon's sense: fiction that, by flouting historical verisimilitude in various ways, including deliberate anachronism, invites critical scrutiny of the epistemological bases of historical reconstruction.[15]

Which is not to say that *Mason & Dixon* doesn't conform, in many respects, to the conventions of traditional historical fiction. For example, its protagonists, like those of traditional historical novels, are witnesses of history rather than central actors. Historical figures themselves, Mason and Dixon nevertheless observe rather than participate in the momentous historical events of their time: the Jacobite uprising of 1745 (311–14), the public upheavals and agitation preceding the Revolutionary crisis in America (40), and so on. So confirmed are they in their spectatorhood that when violent historical events do overtake them, such as when a French warship intercepts their vessel en route to Sumatra, Mason and Dixon suspect that they have mistakenly received "a piece of someone else's History, a fragment spall'd off of some Great Moment" (44)—a history not meant for them. Also as in traditional historical fiction, the protagonists interact with famous historical personages—Ben Franklin (chaps. 27 and 29), Col. Washington (chaps. 28 and 58, esp. 572–73), Jefferson (395–96), Dr. Johnson and Boswell (chap. 76), and so on.[16] Here, however, the *frisson* of glimpsing historical celebrities, which figures so centrally among the pleasures of traditional historical novels, is undercut by their being systematically "postmodernized"— reduced to comic walk-on roles, subjected to iconoclastic revision (Franklin is a womanizer; Washington smokes hemp), deprived of aura, contaminated by anachronism (Franklin wears shades; Washington's manservant does stand-up comedy).

Anachronisms abound, and not only in representations of famous figures; they threaten to explode historical verisimilitude at every point. Some are camouflaged (transparently) as predictions or anticipations: Ethelmer "predicts" rock 'n' roll (264), Cherry-coke "foresees" world wars fought to protect investments (422), Captain Zhang "anticipates" the American Civil War (615–16), and so on. Other anachronisms are interpolated without even a pretext of verisimilitude, especially in cases of contamination by late-twentieth-century popular culture. Amelia's "as" and her black outfit provide one such example; others include Vaucanson's automaton Duck, which exhibits Daffy's distinctive speech-impediment (375); the Kabbalists who frequent the Rabbi of Prague inn and salute each other with Mr. Spock's greeting, "Live long and prosper" (485; evidently Popeye is another habitué: see 486); the Baltimore slave-driver whose children bear the fashionable nineties names of Tiffany and Jason (699); and so on.

What is at stake here, clearly, is historicity itself—the pastness of the past and presentness of the present, the dependence of the latter on the former, the irreversibility of time, and so on. If there are any doubts that these really are the issues on Pynchon's agenda, he forestalls them by staging an explicit discussion on the relations between history and fiction (349–52). In this discussion, it is young Ethelmer who is made to speak for the "postmodern" position, defending fictitious history as the subversion of monopolistic "truth," while his Uncle Ives is given the traditionalist role of attacking fiction, with 'Brae slyly counterattacking by evoking the prestige of Shakespeare's history plays. So *Mason & Dixon* is not only a historical novel but also a novel *about* historicity, about the experience of being in history and how we grasp that experience—in other words, a historiographic metafiction, precisely.

Nevertheless, I want to argue that, while the temporal is certainly at issue here, it is space that dominates. Spatial dominance is perhaps discernible even at the level of style, where the difference between now and then, between the eighteenth century and the twentieth, is revealed by the discursive *proximity* of, say, Amelia's "as" to the text's studied archaisms ("dress'd from Boots to Bonnet," "instructed ever to remind himself," etc.). But it is at the level of the narrated world that the dominance of spatial over temporal categories is unmistakable. For it is here that time is *spatialized,* as Mason and Dixon, proceeding westward in space, recapitulate *in reverse temporal order* the history of the European presence in North America from the contemporary metropoles of the Atlantic seaboard (Philadelphia, Baltimore, New York) to the towns and farmlands of the Susquehanna country, to the frontier settlements of the Alleghenies, finally to the Trans-Allegheny wilderness into which, by the 1760s, Europeans had barely penetrated. Beyond this point, beyond the Warrior Path, lies America as it had been before the coming of the Whites, except that, in the subjunctive narrative of chapter 73, this space comes to be populated with alternative histories of America— French America, Spanish America, Chinese America, Russian America—other "temporalities," but localized in spatial enclaves, distinct microworlds.

So if *Mason & Dixon* is a work of historical fiction, or historiographic metafiction—as indeed it is—it is also, and predominantly, a "road novel"; its chronotope, Bakhtin might say, is that of the "open road."[17] Though its style mimics that of eighteenth-century fiction, and though its genre conventions, those of the historical novel, belong to the nineteenth, we have no difficulty in grasping the postmodernism of *Mason & Dixon*—not least because of its spatial dominant, which, as Jameson has argued, typifies the postmodern.[18]

A Brief Poetics of Pynchon-Space

The dominance of space in *Mason & Dixon* is secured through the quantitative proliferation, functional centrality, and perceptual salience (foregrounding) of spaces (in the plural). These spaces are of various kinds; they include, as we have already seen, the subjunctive spaces of nonrealized possibilities, but also the spaces of narrated inset worlds, subjective spaces of dream and hallucination, parallel worlds ("paraspaces"), paradoxical interiors, and so on.

Nested Spaces

Mason & Dixon is formally akin to the classic frame-tales: *The Arabian Nights, The Decameron, The Canterbury Tales*. Narratologically and ontologically, it is organized as a set of nested narrative frames and inset worlds. At each level of this structure, one or more narrators narrates a story, each of these stories implying a world. These story-worlds may approximate the "real worlds" of their respective narrators more or less closely—that is, the stories may aspire to be "realistic," or even "true"; alternatively, they may diverge more or less markedly from their narrators' real worlds. A character in any of these inset story-worlds may take it upon himself or herself to narrate a story, thereby becoming a narrator in his or her own right and projecting an inset story-world one level "down" (or, to vary the metaphor, one frame "in") from his or her own world. The structure, in short, is recursive: frame within frame, inset within inset, box within box, like a set of Chinese boxes or Russian *matrushka* dolls.[19]

Nested one level down, the world of Mason's and Dixon's adventures is subordinated to the framing narrative in which Rev. Wicks Cherrycoke tells their story to his family during an impossibly long winter night in 1786.[20] At the level of Mason's and Dixon's world, other narrators narrate—among them, Mason and Dixon themselves (167–71, 556–61, 587–94, 738–42), Luise Redzinger (356–60), Chef Allègre (chaps. 37 and 38), and Captain Zhang (chap. 64)—opening within the plane of their world windows onto other narrated worlds situated two levels down from the "top": doubly inset worlds, frames within the frame. Since this structure is recursive, nothing prevents characters located at this doubly inset level from becoming narrators in turn and projecting story-worlds inset three levels down from the top of the structure. Thus, the detective Hervé du T. narrates an account of the automaton Duck's powers (373–75), which is nested within Chef Allègre's narrative, which is nested in turn within Cherrycoke's. Only once does the system threaten to break down, namely in the case of the conflicting framings of the Jesuits' Captive's tale (chapters 53 and 54), which somehow belongs both to Cherrycoke's narrative and also to a pornographic novel being perused by Cherrycoke's niece 'Brae and nephew 'Thelmer.[21]

Most of these narrated worlds, at every level, appear to be compatible with the "real world" of *Mason & Dixon,* or at least so their narrators maintain—they are alleged to be "true" stories. Only a few—Dixon's tale of the slaying of the Worm of Lambton, Captain Zhang's tale of the Chinese astronomers Hsi and Ho—are more or less acknowledged to belong to an alternative, fictional reality. Nevertheless, any inset story-world, whether "truthful" or fictional, is by definition ontologically "weaker" than the world immediately "superior" to it (the world in which it is narrated), if only because its "reality" is dependent on its narrator's credibility, reliability, and authority. Questions of narratorial reliability and authority are highly germane to *Mason & Dixon* because the entire narrative of Mason's and Dixon's expedition derives from Cherrycoke, a self-confessed "untrustworthy Remembrancer" (8). No doubt his confession of unreliability belongs to the modesty *topos;* nevertheless, one is justified in wondering how, apart from those episodes when he physically accompanied Mason and Dixon (e.g., on board the *Seahorse* and during the actual surveying of the Line), Cherrycoke came to know what he claims to know about them. How does he know, for instance, what transpired during Mason's sojourn on St. Helena (105–6), or on the occasion of Mason's last visits to Dixon (750)? How does he know the contents of Mason's unsent letter to Dixon (146)? This is particularly mysterious in view of the fact that, in another context, he will scrupulously decline to speculate about the contents of Mason's lost correspondence with Maskelyne (720).

Examples could be multiplied. Ultimately, it is Cherrycoke who, in his role as narrator, is the source of the subjunctivity that colors (or taints?) the reality of *Mason & Dixon*. It is he who speculates, extrapolates, makes unfounded assumptions ("let us assume," 393), even on occasion outright fabricates (e.g., Mason's encounter with Johnson and Boswell, chapter 76, is acknowledged to be a fabrication). And it is Cherrycoke who, in narrating Mason's and Dixon's adventures, posits subjunctive America when he asks his audience to "Suppose that Mason and Dixon . . . cross Ohio after all" (706).

Dream-Spaces

All fictional narratives are honeycombed with subjective subworlds: states of affairs that characters wish or fear will happen, that they intend or project or fantasize or believe, along with the subjective worlds of their dreams and hallucinations.[22] *Mason & Dixon* hardly differs from other novels in this regard, though its protagonists' dreams, daydreams, and hallucinations are perhaps atypically ubiquitous. Mason's, Dixon's and, on at least one occasion Cherrycoke's dreams are reported at some length (e.g., 320–21, 538–39, 649–50, 718–19, 749–50); their daydreams (mainly Mason's), fantasies, and hallucinations also abound (e.g., 70–72, 163, 165, 169, 211, 722–23). Anomalies begin to appear, however, when "leakages" develop between dream-reality and primary reality. For instance, Mason confiscates a dagger from a figure who threatens him in dreams, and wakens with the dagger in his possession (70–72)![23]

More anomalous still are the shared fantasies, dreams, and hallucinations that recur throughout. Pynchon had already explored the disturbing potential of shared fantasy in *Gravity's Rainbow* where, for instance, Roger Mexico and Pig Bodine share the same vision (hallucination? anticipation?) of the cannibalistic "surprise roast," of which they are to be the main ingredients.[24] Similarly, Mason and Dixon share a fantasy of the life they never get a chance to lead in Sumatra—nothing anomalous here, except that the fantasized Sumatran women are said to develop "private lives" quite independent of the fantasists' scenarios (57). Later, on the North America frontier, Mason and Dixon will dream jointly about continuing their expedition westward into a land of wonders (677)—precisely the itinerary they will follow subjunctively in chapter 73. Later still, returned to England, they dream jointly of being spoken to by the Learnèd Dog (756).

Most unsettling of all is the hemp-induced hallucination they share of giant vegetables to be found growing somewhere "West of Cheat" (655–57). So detailed and circumstantial is this vision, that one might well wonder on what grounds it could be denied the status of full-fledged "reality," particularly since other, comparably fantastic episodes—the Octuple Gloucester, the automaton Duck—have presumably been admitted to this novel's world on equal footing with its historical references and verisimilar realities. And in fact, the evidence for the hallucinatory status of the giant vegetables is somewhat ambiguous. On the one hand, nothing about the episode indicates any deviation from chronological order (flashback or flashforward); nevertheless, two chapters later Mason's and Dixon's party is camped "yet east of Cheat" (665), suggesting that the discovery of "Gardens Titanick" west of the Cheat River can have occurred only in subjective reality. On the other hand, much later, in conversation, Mason seems to confirm the objective reality of Giant Vegetables—or does he?

Arguing with Dr. Johnson about evidences of the divine, he recalls wonders he had witnessed in North America:

> "Mounds, Caverns, things that went across the Sky?—had you seen one of these, 'twould've made y'think twice. . . . Even giant Vegetables,—if it had to be,—seeking Salvation in the Oversiz'd, how pitiable,—what of it, I've little Pride, some great Squash upon the Trailside? I'll take it, won't I." (747; Pynchon's ellipsis)

This is all rather tentative and hypothetical; all the more so, in view of the fact that only a few lines earlier Mason had said that he could testify personally "to little beyond the giant Mounds" (746). Do we infer, then, that he *can't* testify to the reality of giant vegetables after all?[25]

Whether or not we admit giant vegetables to the novel's world, the sharing of dreams and hallucinations thoroughly unsettles the distinction between dream and reality upon which novelistic world-building usually depends. If a hallucination shared by two already has a toehold in reality, then how many sharers would it take for a hallucination to attain full membership in consensual reality? That's the sort of question that shared hallucination provokes. The ubiquity of subjective realities here, and the unsettled relations between them and "primary" reality, lends weight to the hypothesis, entertained by Mason (610; see also 75), that his and Dixon's American experience belongs entirely to the dream realm. Many of Mason's and Dixon's early daydreams involve imagined landscapes (e.g., 163, 165, 169, 242); they will encounter the real-world versions of these landscapes when they finally reach America, as if they had been imagining America all along, without knowing it. When interrupted by the voice of the Learnèd Dog, Mason has been "dreaming of America" (756).[26] "Does Britannia, when she sleeps, dream? Is America her dream?" (345)

American Spaces

In the metaphorical geography of *Mason & Dixon,* the interiors of continents or islands, figure as other worlds. Cape Town seems "A town with a precarious Hold upon the Continent, planted as upon another World" (58). Similarly, James's Town, the settlement on St. Helena, "clings to the edge of an interior that must be reckoned part of the Other World" (107).[27] "Other world" here signifies *terra incognita.* Not until they reach North America, charged with surveying the unknown and tying it "back into the Net-Work of Points already known" (345), do Mason and Dixon get the chance to penetrate an otherworldly interior.

American space, as constructed by *Mason & Dixon,* is plural. As the surveyors proceed westward, each geographical boundary (river, ridge) marks the transition to a new region of space, a new microworld: "Over Susquehanna begins a different Province entirely, and beginning at the Mountains, another differing from that, and so on,—beyond Monongahela, beyond Ohio . . . " (467–68). The Susquehanna is *"not only* a River, being as well the Boundary to another Country" (474). South Mountain is a "last concentration of Apparitions" of the kind with which Mason's and Dixon's party have become familiar; "Beyond lies Wilderness, where quite another Presence reigns" (491). "Cheat is the Rubicon, Monongahela is the Styx" (663); but Yochio Geni (i.e., the Youghiogheny River) is also a version of Styx, across which Mason and Dixon are ferried by a sinister boatman (659–62). "Beyond Cheat they move in a time and space apt, one instant to the next, to stretch or shrink" (673). The most decisive boundary of all is the Warrior Path, marking a transition "Sort of like Death" (646); beyond it, "Distance is not the same . . . nor is Time" (647). Consequently Mason's and Dixon's journey beyond the Warrior Path transpires only in the subjunctive mode.

Paradoxically, as they map the unknown and score boundaries upon it, their surveying not only abolishes mystery but also creates it. This is especially the case with the uncanny enclave or pocket of space known as "The Wedge" or (with an anachronistic allusion to the Bermuda Triangle) the "Delaware Triangle" (323–24). Due to geometrical anomalies in closing the corner of the Maryland border, an ambiguous wedge remains, enclosing an "Unseen World" (469–70). This pocket-world is presumably similar in kind to those that will be discovered (or would have been discovered) during the subjunctive Trans-Ohio expedition of chapter 73.[28]

Otherworld Spaces

Parallel or adjacent to the spaces of this-worldly North America lie the spaces of some other world—or should that be worlds, in the plural? For it is never clear whether these fragmentary other worlds, glimpsed sporadically throughout, form a single integrated

Other World (as they apparently do in *Gravity's Rainbow*) or multiple worlds of potentially different kinds.[29] Some of these other worlds evidently hover "above" our own; extraterrestrial visitors "descend" from them to ours—perhaps in UFOs? (133–33, 142, 601, 648–49, 651, 769). Some apparently lie "below" our world's surface; one of these is the "ancient City . . . discover'd beneath the Earth" during the subjunctive expedition beyond the Warrior Path (707–8; see also 548, 602–3, 738–42).

However, most of these otherworld spaces seem to lie somewhere alongside or adjacent to our world, separated from it by a vertical barrier that is "something like a Wind" (172). There is precedent for this sort of wind-boundary in *Gravity's Rainbow*, where it separates the parallel worlds of Sundial, hero of an obscure comic book:

> Sundial, flashing in, flashing out again, came from "across the wind," by which readers understood "across some flow, more or less sheet and vertical: a wall in constant motion"—over there was a different world, where Sundial took care of business they would never understand.[30]

Wind is associated with boundaries between worlds throughout *Mason & Dixon*. The automaton Duck, for instance, can vibrate itself into invisibility, achieving a higher order of being, the duck equivalent of angelhood (378, 379); henceforth, only those sensitive to "shifts of Breeze between the Worlds" can catch sight of it (448). Similarly, "the old Gentleman"—Satan himself, presumably—appears only when "the Wind [is] changing, here in Pennsylvania, as between this World and the Next" (605).

This boundary is a porous one, evidently. One can push through it, as through "some Membrane," to "the other side of something" (188); or look through it, as Mason does when in the light of the Torpedo's electrical discharge he glimpses "an Aperture into another Dispensation of Space . . . and Time" (433). The many hauntings and apparitions of *Mason & Dixon* penetrate this porous world-boundary in one direction, while Mason and Dixon themselves venture across it in the other.

Even before coming to North America, both Mason and Dixon are already susceptible to otherworldly visitations. Dixon encounters a specter on his native moors (505–7), while Mason is haunted by his wife Rebekah's ghost on St. Helena (164–65, 171–72).[31] Rebekah will later visit Mason in America as well (408–9, 703–4), but here such hauntings are unexceptional. For

the American wilderness of *Mason & Dixon* is a haunted landscape, recalling nothing so much as the "ghoul-haunted woodland"
of nineteenth-century American romance—of Poe, or of Haw-
thorne's "Young Goodman Brown." Mason's and Dixon's surveying party are haunted by the Black Dog, the Glowing Indian, or
both (chap. 51); by a backwoods Golem (684–86); by the automaton Duck, which has become a supernatural being, capable of
"enter[ing] and leav[ing] the Stream of Time as she likes" (637);
by the "old Gentleman" who may or may not be Satan (604–7; see
also 408–9, 704–5); not to mention the supernatural Presence of
the Wilderness itself (634–36).[32] Nor are such encounters exclu-
sive to those accompanying Mason and Dixon. Others, too, experience apparitions and otherworldly encounters in America:
Peter Redzinger, for instance, experiences "rapture by beings
from somewhere else" (358), while even the house in Philadelphia
in which Cherrycoke spins out his narrative is visited by phan-
toms after all its living occupants have retired for the night (759–
60). And this is far from an exhaustive catalogue. Like the world
of *Gravity's Rainbow,* with its angels, its voices from beyond, its
revenants and cases of demonic possession, the world of *Mason
& Dixon* is all but overrun by interlopers from Elsewhere.

    Venturing "across the wind" in the opposite direction, Mason
claims to have sojourned in the otherworld space of the eleven
days "lost" in the Gregorian reform of the Julian calendar (556–61).
According to his account, Asiatic pygmies have been settled in the
eleven days as colonists; these time-colonists and the people of
our world mutually "haunt each other" (196–97). For his part,
Dixon seems to have encountered the land of the dead. Being
ferried out to a collier-brig in the fog, he hears the church bells of
an unknown town, and his keel-boat is surrounded by small craft
apparently manned by the dead of the locality (243–45). Unless,
that is, they are not dead but have only been deported to America, in which case what Dixon has encountered is a version of
America somehow displaced to the Northumbrian coast. Or is it
both at once? Is America the land of the dead?[33]

Zones of the Interior

    The dominant spatiality of *Mason & Dixon* is rendered espe-
cially palpable in a series of paradoxical interior spaces that
punctuate the novel: the Pearl of Sumatra public house in Ports-
mouth (24–25), the Jenkin's Ear Museum on St. Helena (chap. 17),

a coach of Jesuit design (354), Lepton Castle in the American wilderness (chap. 41). In each of these, the interior volume of space impossibly exceeds its exterior bounding surfaces. The coach, for instance, is "a Conveyance, wherein the inside is quite noticeably larger than the outside" (354); Lepton Castle's "ancient doorsill once traversed, the Surveyors find more room inside than could possibly be contained in the sorrowing ruin they believ'd they were entering" (412). Each "disquieting structure"[34] in this series encloses a space of labyrinthine complexity, as though containing an entire microworld.[35] Or perhaps more than one: the neglected garden in the Jenkin's Ear Museum, in particular, suggests a space of "Transition between Two Worlds" (180).

Spaces packed with worlds: what are these paradoxical interiors, if not a series of scale-models *en abyme* of the world of *Mason & Dixon* itself?

HORIZONTAL, VERTICAL

Subjunctive America, America as dream-world, America as land of the dead; inset worlds, subjective worlds, microworlds, the Other World, worlds *en abyme*: all of these categories of paraspace have precedents in *Gravity's Rainbow,* Pynchon's other novel of space. Nevertheless, the spaces of *Mason & Dixon* differ from those of *Gravity's Rainbow* in at least one striking respect: they tend to be oriented along a horizontal axis or to lie in the horizontal plane, by contrast with the vertical axis—the space of flight and fall—that dominates *Gravity's Rainbow.*

An orientation or aspiration toward verticality appears everywhere in *Gravity's Rainbow,* not only in its master-motif of rocket flight, but also in incidental motifs: for example, in the figure of Der Springer (the chess Knight, Gerhard von Göll's *nom de guerre*), the one able to leave the plane of the board (*"flight has been given only to the Springer!"*[36]); in the sentient pinball's temporary escape into the vertical dimension;[37] in the "long-haul" elevator ("the Vertical Solution") of some future high-rise Raketen-Stadt;[38] and so on. Answering symmetrically to these vertical ascents are the novel's descents: Slothrop's cloacal fantasy of descending the toilet bowl;[39] his hallucinated descent into the Mittelwerke;[40] Blobadjian's subterranean epiphany;[41] and so on. By contrast, in *Mason & Dixon,* though intimations abound of spaces lying above or below the horizontal plane—visits from UFOs, subterranean cities—these are, with rare exceptions, only rumored, not directly encountered. Motion, again with rare exceptions, is along the earth's surface, not above or below it.

Counter-examples spring to mind: Dixon's experiences of flight (218–20), or his tale of having penetrated the Hollow Earth (738–42).[42] These apparent counter-examples, however, only confirm the general pattern, for horizontality dominates even in what appear to be excursions into the vertical dimension. Dixon's flights over the moors with his teacher Emerson turn out to be essentially horizontal in orientation, parallel to the ley-lines inscribed on the earth's surface:

> In the Twilight they ascend, one by one . . . following southwesterly the Ley-Line [Emerson] shows them. . . . He is teaching them to sense rather than see this Line, to learn exactly what it feels like to yaw too much to its port or starboard. The Ley seems to generate, along its length, an Influence,—palpable as that of Earth's Magnetism upon a Needle. . . . (218; see also 440).

This accords with Emerson's general orientation toward the horizontal, including his theory "whereby Winds are imagin'd to be forms of Gravity acting not vertically but laterally, along the Globe's Surface" (220). What is this if not gravity's rainbow itself, horizontally reoriented![43]

Similarly, Dixon's descent into the Hollow Earth proves not really to be a vertical descent after all. Rather, Dixon and his mysterious guide follow a horizontal plane that wraps around to form the inner surface of a torus (compare Dixon's theory of the Hollow Earth, 602–3):

> "at the top of the World, somewhere between eighty and ninety degrees North, the Earth's Surface, all 'round the Parallel, began to curve sharply inward, leaving a great circum-polar Emptiness . . . directly toward which our path was taking us, at first gently, then with some insistence, down-hill, ever downward, and thus, gradually, around the great Curve of its Rim—And 'twas so that we enter'd, by its great northern Portal, upon the inner Surface of the Earth." (739)

Here, too, the seeming verticals of *Mason & Dixon* turn out to be horizontals.

This general reorientation from the vertical to the horizontal axis has thematic, ideological and ultimately metaphysical consequences. The opposition "horizontality vs. verticality" serves, here and elsewhere, as a kind of spatial code for encoding ideological positions and metaphysical commitments. Recall the affiliation of the verticality of rocket flight in *Gravity's Rainbow* with fascism, the Elect, the spurning of earth and the yearning for transcendence, and so on. Conversely, in *Mason & Dixon* the orientation toward the horizontal corresponds to democracy in political philosophy, and to a metaphysics of this-worldliness.

At least as late as the period in which *Mason & Dixon* is set, traditionally hierarchical social relations continued to be pictured in terms of a vertical "Chain of Being" from the highest to the lowest. Characters here—aristocrats mainly—invoke the vertical Chain several times (e.g., 194, 438); but on one of these occasions Dixon counters with his own alternative model of a horizontal, democratic chain, based on his experience of surveying: "Well, 'tis a horizontal Chain for me . . . such as Surveyors use. Which shall go before, I wonder, and which follow,—aye and which direction shall it point in?" (417–18). (Hearing this, Lord Lepton mutters, "You sound like one of these Leveler chaps.") Ironically, of course, the boundary that Mason and Dixon survey with chains will demarcate a space of undemocratic bondage: their surveyor's chains determine the Mason-Dixon Line dividing the chained (slave states) from the unchained (free states). As if in fantasy compensation for their historical role, in the subjunctive America of chapter 73 Mason and Dixon run their line through the middle of a town, freeing its slaves: "You survey'd the Chains right off 'em, with your own!" (708). Here, disguised as fantasy, one glimpses the spatial recoding of political philosophy in operation.

Related to the political meanings of the "horizontal vs. vertical" opposition are its metaphysical implications. Conventionally, Western deity is located overhead; transcendence is vertical ascent, a flight from earth to heaven. Not so in Iroquois theology, as Mason learns when he inquires of a party of Iroquois where their Spirit Village lies: "The Indians all gesture, straight out the Line, West. 'God dwells there? At the Horizon?' They nod" (651). (Asked in return where his own Spirit Village lies, "Mason rather uncertainly indicates Up.") The Iroquois' divinities dwell at the horizon, not overhead—a theology shared by the inhabitants of the Hollow Earth: "Their God, like that of the Iroquois, lives at their Horizon," Dixon reports (740).[44]

If a yearning for transcendence lingers in *Gravity's Rainbow*, it has been replaced in *Mason & Dixon* by a different metaphysics

entirely: something like a resolutely earthbound this-worldliness. Here the Other World lies, if anywhere, not above or below
this one, but alongside or ahead of it, "across the wind," somewhere out there in subjunctive America.

NOTES

1. Alec McHoul and David Wills, *Writing Pynchon: Strategies in Fictional
Analysis* (Urbana: University of Illinois Press, 1990), 108–9.
2. *Mason & Dixon* (New York: Henry Holt, 1997), 345. Henceforth all references to *Mason & Dixon* will appear parenthetically in the text.
3. Thomas Pynchon, *Gravity's Rainbow* (New York: Viking, 1973), 420–21.
See Brian McHale, *Constructing Postmodernism* (New York: Routledge, 1992),
67–68.
4. For other subjunctive encounters, see 336–37, 360–61, and 390.
5. Gerald Prince, "The Disnarrated," *Style* 22 (1988): 1–8.
6. *Gravity's Rainbow,* 667.
7. Compare Dixon's plan for a commercial promenade or Mall to be built along
the Mason-Dixon Line (701)—would that have been a "Mall of America"? Compare, too, John Shirley's floating city of commerce and entertainment, Freezone,
which appears in his science-fiction novel *Eclipse* (1985) but is more familiar
from his contribution to Bruce Sterling's influential cyberpunk anthology, *Mir-
rorshades* (1986).
8. *Gravity's Rainbow,* 549.
9. Ibid., 556; see also 265, 294, 333.
10. Compare the villages of the Zone, *Gravity's Rainbow,* 613–14.
11. Michel Foucault, *The Order of Things: An Archeology of the Human Sciences*
(New York: Pantheon, 1970), xviii.
12. *Gravity's Rainbow,* 711. See Brian McHale, *Postmodernist Fiction* (London:
Methuen, 1987), 49–56.
13. Compare the time-scheme of Pynchon's *Vineland* (1990), which flashes
back from the present-time events of 1984 to events of twenty years before, jux-
taposing, in effect, the before and after of the Revolution That Failed.
14. I am indebted to my colleague Cheryl Torsney for this phrase.
15. See Linda Hutcheon, *A Poetics of Postmodernism: History, Theory, Fiction*
(New York: Routledge, 1988).
16. Apart from the presence of these foregrounded historical figures, the historical texture of *Mason & Dixon* is "thickened" by allusions to a host of figures
who remain in the background, for example Christopher Smart (116–17); Mozart
and Mesmer (268); Peggy Shippen, Major Andre, and Benedict Arnold (308);
John Chapman/Johnny Appleseed (674); and so on.
17. Mikhail Bakhtin, "Forms of Time and of the Chronotope in the Novel," *The
Dialogic Imagination: Four Essays,* ed. Michael Holquist, trans. Caryl Emerson
and Michael Holquist (Austin: University of Texas Press, 1981), 98, 143–45. See
also Gabriel Zoran, "Towards a Theory of Space in Narrative," *Poetics Today* 5
(1984): 314.
18. Fredric Jameson, *Postmodernism, or, The Cultural Logic of Late Capitalism* (Durham, NC: Duke University Press, 1991), 154–80, 364–76.
19. See McHale, *Postmodernist Fiction,* 112–30. An alternative characteriza-

tion of this narrative structure uses the metaphor of the "stack" (derived from software design) rather than that of frame and inset; for details, see Marie-Laure Ryan, *Possible Worlds, Artificial Intelligence, and Narrative Theory* (Bloomington: Indiana University Press, 1991), 175–200.

20. This frame, visible at the beginning of the novel, reappears at intervals throughout, by contrast with *Gravity's Rainbow*, where the frame appears only at the very end, with disorienting effect.

21. Moreover, since the novel in question belongs to the *Ghastly Fop* series, which Mason also consumes, its characters appear to violate narrative levels, "ascending" from the fictional world of the *Fop* fictions into the "real" world of Mason and Dixon. See McHale, *Postmodernist Fiction,* 121–24.

22. See Thomas Pavel, "Narrative Domains," *Poetics Today* 1 (1980): 105–4; Umberto Eco, "*Lector in Fabula:* Pragmatic Strategy in a Metanarrative Text," *The Role of the Reader: Explorations in the Semiotics of Texts* (Bloomington: Indiana University Press, 1979), 200–260; Ryan, *Possible Worlds;* Ruth Ronen, *Possible Worlds in Literary Theory* (Cambridge: Cambridge University Press, 1994), 167–96.

23. Mason's confiscation of the dream-dagger accords with the Malay belief, about which he has learned, that the world of dreams is as real as the waking one. Later, Native Americans will claim to have entered Europeans' dreams (663)—a motif with more than a passing resemblance to that of the Dream-Hunters in Milorad Pavić's *Dictionary of the Khazars* (1984).

24. *Gravity's Rainbow,* 714. See McHale, *Constructing Postmodernism,* 68–69.

25. The situation is further complicated by the fact that the entire exchange with Dr. Johnson is acknowledged to be sheer speculation on Cherrycoke's part.

26. This phrase resonates with the title (and first line) of John Ashbery's lyric, "They dream only of America," *The Tennis Court Oath* (Middletown, CT: Wesleyan University Press, 1962).

27. Even homely Scotland figures as "the world across the new Line" (745).

28. Compare also Zhang's speculations about what might be concealed in the degrees of latitude "lost" from the Chinese circle of 365-and-a-quarter degrees when the Jesuits replaced it with the 360-degree circle of Western geometry (629–30).

29. Compare also the parallel worlds of *The Crying of Lot 49,* where Americans behave "as if they were in exile from somewhere else invisible yet congruent with the cheered land [they] lived in" (*The Crying of Lot 49* [New York: Bantam, 1967], 135; see also 72, 76).

30. *Gravity's Rainbow,* 472.

31. Both these locales—the open moors, the island of St. Helena—are said to be exceptionally ghost-ridden; see 108, 173–74, 504.

32. Mason's supernatural encounters continue after his return to Europe: he will sight fairy lights in Ireland (724) and will spend a night with his son at a haunted inn (766–77).

33. Compare the Turok land of the dead in *Vineland.*

34. *Gravity's Rainbow,* 537.

35. Other related labyrinthine spaces include James's Town on St. Helena, whose interior complexity is belied by its small exterior dimensions (126); the inner rooms of the Company Seraglio at Cape Town (151); the coach-travellers' inn, its complex topography recalling that of a Middle Eastern bazaar or souk (362); and the Jesuit College at Quebec (514).

36. *Gravity's Rainbow,* 494; see also 376.

37. Ibid., 584.

38. Ibid., 735–76.

39. Ibid., 60–71.

40. Ibid., 295–314.

41. Ibid., 354–55.

42. The motif of the hollow earth has many precedents, in fiction and in popular culture; think of Jules Verne's *Journey to the Center of the Earth,* Edgar Rice Burroughs's "Pellucidar" novels, Rudy Rucker's *The Hollow Earth* (1990)—and of course Vheissu in *V.*

43. Cherrycoke's dream of flying westward along the Line, and his vision (if that's what it is) of airborne conveyances somewhere in the West conform to this pattern of flight parallel to the horizontal (649–51).

44. In his declining years, Mason is beset by fears of evil Spirits "from beyond the Horizon . . . who dwell a little over the Line between the Day and its annihilation" (769), a troubled and dysphoric version of horizontal theology. But this evidence is ambiguous: Mason also fears "Beings from the new Planet," "Souls falling to Earth, becoming incarnate" (769, 760).

"Cranks of Ev'ry Radius":
Romancing the Line in *Mason & Dixon*

ARTHUR SALTZMAN

I

Most writers go unremarkably along, safe from assault in restaurants or *The New York Times;* they need only take their phones off their hooks to ensure all the authorial distance they require to be productive. The legendary anonymity of Thomas Pynchon is quite another matter, of course, to which the mythic difficulty of his fictions certainly contributes. While the author seems at once everywhere and nowhere, a celebrated absence eluding the baited breadth of editorial pages, MLA conventions, and Internet sites, his labyrinthine novels render each reader a Theseus making his allusive, competitive way and tethered by his own slim thread—particle physics, onomastics, economic theory, or any of a hundred other kabbalistic guides—to thicken the "grand Gothic pile of inferences."[1] Who among his contemporaries is more inherently hypertextual than Pynchon, who seems born to be endlessly reapportioned and squabbled over by squatters online. (Such is the justice of the piecemeal.) If *Gravity's Rainbow* is the *Ulysses* of a later generation, it is in part because it is likewise available to so many equivalences, divisible—intriguingly, edifyingly so—by so many factors and resonant terms. This way to the ingress, ladies and gentlemen!

The long-rumored *Mason & Dixon* has arrived with the promise of numberless new accesses to try and plots to plow. One interesting tendency among the reviews of the book, however, is the contention that it is surprisingly—for most, gratifyingly—straightforward in design. Here we have the generous framework of Reverend Wicks Cherrycoke's reminiscence/invention/elaboration upon events that are offered by means of (for Pynchon) a forthright chronological development. As Rick Moody put it in his review for *Atlantic Monthly,* "The action of *Mason & Dixon* is refreshingly

63

linear, compared with the complexity of Pynchon's earlier work."[2] Moody does not underestimate the wealth of research and learning in the novel; nevertheless, given the premise that Cherrycoke is offering his family an after-dinner entertainment, it is strategic not only to pack his tale with harrowing action and exotic incident but also to attempt to render the narrative feast digestible. So what we face in *Mason & Dixon* is a basic set of dissonances. Most apparent are those between the eighteenth-century language and contemporary references and intellectual vantages, whereby we are suddenly, metafictionally wrested out of the novel's context to view its characters as specimens; no less significant are those tensions between our expectation of multilayered research and intimations of conspiracy on the one hand, and the clear commitment to telling a whacking good yarn on the other.

In fact, the linear seductions of the story of Charles Mason and Jeremiah Dixon prove to be as vulnerable to chance, negotiation, ambiguity, expediency, and error as the Line that immortalizes them. Whereas the primary shape of *Gravity's Rainbow* is the arch, whose manifestation as the trajectory of a lethal rocket is the template for dozens of other arches emerging throughout the novel, in *Mason & Dixon* it is the line. The line validates the surveyor's unconflicted vision for the landscape; it allows the astronomer to lay out constellations and the navigator to set his course; it is replete with suggestions of purposeful progress, reliable boundary, and stabilizing accuracy; it indicates a moral vector, the sign of efficiency and rectitude; it is, in the estimation of William Emerson, another of the novel's stargazers, the clearest sign of civilized human presence on the planet.[3] And in *Mason & Dixon,* Pynchon lays siege to its optimistic promise and inexorably wears down the migratory dedication of this picaresque duo. The Bible may foretell that "the crooked shall be made straight, and the rough places plain," but Pynchon's novel chronicles a world more recalcitrant. The findings in *Mason & Dixon* instead attest to the argument of Immanuel Kant: "Out of the crooked timber of humanity no straight thing was ever made."[4]

Mason and Dixon are appointed by the British Royal Society to their historically significant task because of their expertise in surveying and astronomy. These mutually fortifying pursuits— think of astronomy as landscaping at a higher altitude—mark the two men as master empiricists, devotees of computation, and true children of the Age of Enlightenment. Surveying and astronomy are disciplines inspired by discipline, whereby countryside and cosmos alike may be realized as English gardens. By this reasoning, lines on maps are like dendrites expanding the empire of Mind. Drawing out the Mason-Dixon Line is intended as an extension of the reign of civility, public programming, and good sense; like Wallace Stevens's jar in Tennessee, it serves a policy of aesthetic coercion, of domestication by geometry. Thus mapmaking is another imperialistic transgression. Our heroes are commissioned to guarantee stateliness among the colonies, as presided over (so the astronomers would maintain) by a governable republic of stars. Accordingly, when Dixon tries to allay suspicions at a Pennsylvania tavern, he introduces himself and his companion in a way that equates right thinking and right angles, scrupulous measurement and moral scruples:

> "[W]e're out here to ruffle up some business with any who may be in need of Surveying, London-Style,—Astronomickally precise, optickally up-to-the-Minute, surprisingly cheap. The Behavior of the Stars is the most perfect Motion there is, and we know how to read it all, just as you'd read a Clock-Face. We have Lenses that never lie, and Micrometers fine enough to subtend the Width of a hair upon a Martian's Eye-ball." (342)

This is the optimistic logic that fortifies Mason and Dixon during their intercontinental drift from England to the Southern Hemisphere (to observe the Transit of Venus, an event visible once every eight years) and ultimately to America (to establish the famous border between Pennsylvania and Maryland). And this faith in the friendly coalescence of first principles is a prime target for abuse in Pynchon's novel. Through parody, revisionist history, mandarin playfulness, and the introduction of numerous corruptive influences both literary and political, Pynchon undermines the motives, the findings, and the societal efficacy of such efforts. *Mason & Dixon* continually impeaches the dream of precision, reviving the wilderness against our most elevated, exacting presumptions.

II

Depending on one's perspective, we inhabit an orderly universe whose instances of randomness are occasional and, in the broader view, negligible; or, we inhabit a random universe whose evidences of order are infrequent and, in the broader view, unconvincing. To borrow the language of Joyce's Ithaca chapter of *Ulysses,* there is a related contest depicted in "the reiterated examples of poets in the delirium of the frenzy of attachment or in the abasement of rejection invoking ardent sympathetic constellations or the frigidity of the satellite of their planet," which is to say that heavenly commentary denotes "verifiable intuition" or "fallacious analogy."[5] The persistent encroachment of the latter position is a regular feature of *Mason & Dixon,* and it is the melancholy Mason who is especially susceptible to its effects. Pynchon casts the dour widower as Hardy to Dixon's Laurel, Guildenstern to his Rosencrantz, Vladimir to his Estragon; he explains that what lies between him and Dixon is not so much distrust as "a Lapse of Attention" (120), thereby recalling Vladimir's having to urge his fellow loiterer to "return the ball" and maintain the interplay between them.[6] As the more diligent stargazer of the two, Mason has placed greater trust in the capacity of the stars to sanction and elaborate us. It is he who typically refers to his faith in the universe as some sort of glossary of all Being, at once elegantly devised and disclosable. Hence his reminder to his companion that their honor consists of their standing as "Astronomers under the commission of our King. . . . Surely, at the end of the day, we serve no master but Him that regulates the movements of the Heav'ns, which taken together form a cryptick Message . . . we are intended one day to solve, and read" (59). The rewards of steady observation presumably await them like a guaranteed salary.

By this reckoning, Mason and Dixon's initial mission, to observe the Transit of Venus, is designed to *verify* the Lord's exacting handiwork, "His artisanship how pure" (93); contemplation of God's purest divisions beneath His perfect firmament move mortal boundary-makers to pious emulation (361). Our narrator quotes poet Timothy Tox to attest to Man's adoration of "The Line":

> Yet soon or late, the Line will find its Way,
> For Skies grow thick with aviating Swine,
> Ere men pass up the chance to draw a Line.
>
> .   .   .   .
>
> Sharing a Fate, directed by the Stars,
> To mark the Earth with Geometric Scars.
>
> (257)

Confidence and obsession similarly combine in the defense of astrology offered by Mason's "Lens-brother," Maskelyne: "For if each Star is little more a mathematickal Point, located upon the Hemisphere of Heaven by Right Ascension and Declination, that all the Stars, taken together, tho' innumerable, must like any other set of points, in turn represent some single gigantic Equation of a Sphere,—to us unreadable, incalculable" (134).

Maskelyne's closing disclaimer regarding the illegibility of the skies does not disqualify the capitalized enthusiasm for a clockwork universe studiously, unperturbably going about its business. Still, the frustrations of this "lonely, uncompensated, perhaps even impossible Task" must become corrosive over time, and even the heartiest astrologers suspect that the cast of the zodiac have deserted their readers. Indifferent, impenetrable forces, contemptuous of human petition, occasion "Questions whose Awkwardness has only increas'd as the Astronomers have come to understand there may be no way of ever finding the Answers" (44). We may remember Walt Whitman's "When I Heard the Learn'd Astronomer," in which columns of figures and careful diagrams make the speaker "tired and sick"; he opts for "mystical moist night-air" and the company of stars, which he does not accost with mathematics but simply admires "in perfect silence."[7] (At one point, Mason ruefully recalls that "'Star-Gazing' in those parts was a young man's term for masturbating" [171]—a pleasant enough pastime, perhaps, but one that hardly warrants such meticulous analysis.) Indeed, the vigil around the world for the Transit of Venus is rewarded by what we might call, in deference to another Pynchon novel, the Transit of V-ness. In *Mason & Dixon,* too, delineation (or "stenciling," again in keeping with the language of *V.*), by tracing glimpses of light, actually deepens the darkness:

> Observers lie, they sit, they kneel,—and witness something in the Sky. Among those attending Snouts Earth-wide, the moment of first contact produces a collective brain-pang, as if for something lost and already unclaimable,—after the Years of preparation, the long and at best queasy voyaging, the Station arriv'd at, the Latitude and Longitude well secur'd,—the Week of the Transit,—the Day,—the Hour,—the Minute,—and at last 'tis, "Eh? where am I?" (97)

Talk about ghostlier demarcations! "'And Men of Science,' cries Dixon, 'may be but the simple Tools of others, with no more idea of what they are about, than a Hammer knows of a House" (669).[8]

Mincing themselves with incessant calculation, watchers of the sky seem to discover as much chaos as coherence. William Emerson, Dixon's teacher and another dedicated astrologer, contends that the "Telescope, the Fluxions, the invention of Logarithms and the frenzy of multiplication" have "all been steps of an unarguable approach to God, a growing clarity"; yet he goes on to admit to being "repeatedly appall'd at the lapses in Attention, the Flaws in Design, the squand'rings of life and energy, the failures to be reasonable, or to exercise common sense," which taken together cause him to doubt the character of God (220). Indeed, by all indications in this novel—sea battles and warpaths, sentient animals and vengeful vegetables, robot ducks and nagging ghosts, lecturing dogs and rogue wheels of cheese, drunken carousing and caffeine overdoses, conflicting cryptics and secret societies, deceptive clocks and distorted calendars, political skullduggery and flagging sanity, as well as several competing emplotments of history—the Great Chain of Being does not stretch plumb but is badly, irremediably snarled (417–18). If we are to countenance what Cherrycoke calls the "Vocational Habit . . . of seeking God there, among the Notation of these resonating Chains" by which surveyors measure their intentions, it is evidently the energy of celestial transgression, even unto the "shambles of Eternity" and unmindful of "all Metes and Bounds," and not some placid geometric heaven, which charges them (483–85). The Mohawk term for stargazing—"sky fishing" (651)—suggests a humbler approach, well short of dreams of conquest. Mason and Dixon may make their intrepid petitions across strange landscapes or into the night sky, but the difference between their efforts and the superstitious whispers of sailors into the void of a pickled ear is disconcertingly small (179). A "savage Vacancy [lies] ever before them" (709).

The possibility that the luster above is merely beautiful, not otherwise edifying, triggers a crisis that future centuries might call existential. It threatens to relegate Mason and Dixon to the status of "Bystanders. Background. Stage-Managers of that perilous Flux,—little more" (545). Nor is the situation more favorable on the ground. ("As above, so below" is a favorite refrain in the text.) A captive bewilderment—"a kind of stunn'd Attendance," as Cherrycoke reports it (188)—defines the horizontal plane as well as the vertical. While telescopes reveal a vexed heaven, theodolites expose the lie of "settlement" altogether, as bearings, boundaries, and trespasses in *Mason & Dixon* are as shifting as impulses, as relative as mental health. Flouting their essential pieties, the Mason-Dixon Line does not represent a Platonic unspooling through a divinely sanctioned course but a frail suture, continually thwarted, compromised, or otherwise askew. The ragged seam between infant states results from desire, not insight. The Reverend Cherrycoke makes it plain that

> there exists no "Maryland" beyond an Abstraction, a Frame of right lines drawn to enclose and square off the great Bay in its unimagin'd Fecundity, its shoreline tending to Infinite Length, ultimately unmappable,—no more, to be fair, than there exists any "Pennsylvania" but a chronicle of Frauds committed serially against the Indians dwelling there, check'd only by the Ambitions of other Colonies to north and east. (354)

A map is a veiny abstraction, whose lines are woven like a spell against confusion. The frontier exists in the permanent subjunctive (345), and everywhere the travels of Mason and Dixon take them turns out to be another frontier—outlaw, dissolute, unfixed.[9] The condition of their lives, like that of the terrain, is of "no fix'd place, rather a fix'd Motion" (707), a fluxional reality that refutes their protracted ceremony of ordinance. There is no paraphrasing of the wilderness that will suffice. Although they may begin as heirs of Pointsman, empiricism's loyal lieutenant from *Gravity's Rainbow,* Mason and Dixon continually confront a world like the one described by Geli Tripping, a witch who tells Slothrop, "Forget frontiers now. Forget subdivisions. There aren't any. . . . You'll learn. It's all been suspended. . . . You only have to flow along with it."[10]

America may appear to be ripe for the creative "polygony" of surveyors under royal contract (586), but Nature abhors straight-edge rule. Certainly the difficult environment that the surveying team drags its slow chain-lengths along balks at their labor, leaving them with precious little confidence in the bearings they battle for each day (339). So warns a Chinese mystic:

> "Ev'rywhere else on earth, Boundaries follow Nature,—coast-lines, ridge-tops, river-banks,—so honoring the Dragon or *Shan* within, from which Land-Scape ever takes its form. To mark a right Line upon the Earth is to inflict upon the Dragon's very Flesh, a sword-slash, a long, perfect scar, impossible for any who live out here the year 'round to see as other than hateful Assault." (542)

The general resistance to shapely culmination is an inescapable theme in this novel. Certainly the political impetus behind the assertion of the Delaware-Maryland boundary-line is either mocked as futile flirtation (337) or condemned as "the very Shape of Contempt, through the midst of a People," and thus, as the initial menacing stroke from which "bad history" originates (615, 692–93).[11] Systematic deforestation, Indian massacres, and orderly slave-trade, all of which the Line encourages, show it to be "a conduit for Evil" (701)—not a ray fired by the Age of Reason across the globe to illuminate the wilderness but an agent of darkness.[12] And the darkness deepens the deeper Mason and Dixon drive "into a world of less restraint in ev'rything," until, Mason suspects, they will "reach at last an Anti-City,—some concentration of Fate,—some final condition of Abandonment . . . " (608–9). When they do leave America in the end, they imagine that the continent casts off its lines as if it were a departing ship, so frail a mooring do lines provide (704). Not an annotated Eden, elegantly graphed, but an unmarked Elysium—an unlined innocence or "Paradise of Chance" (421)—will be the explorers' reward.

A fantastic rainstorm sends a river of "Blood, Semen, Excrement, Saliva, Urine, Sweat, Road-Mud, dead Skin, and other such *Data* of Biography . . . lixiviated 'neath Heaven" rushing down the gutters (88–89); Benjamin Franklin makes an organic battery out of a hand-holding Line of Fops by firing electrical current through them (294); a gigantic Surinam Eel, a living Line of Fire, remains mysterious and unpredictable in defiance of "the keenest minds of the Philosophickal World, including a Task-Force of Italian Jesuits dedicated to Torpedic Study" (431–32). These are but a few symbolic examples of the mockery, distrust, or desecration of linearity in *Mason and Dixon*.[13] After years of transecting, Mason admits, he has not "*trans*-cended a blessed thing" (746). The Mason-Dixon Line is a joint mirage.

III

"In the Forest," Mason and Dixon are told, "ev'ryone comes 'round in a Circle sooner or later. One day, your foot comes down in your own shit. There, as the Indians say, is the first Step upon the Trail to Wisdom" (677). In the long view, sequences are revealed as cycles after all in this novel. Acquaintances return, as do storms, skirmishes, ghosts, heavenly transits, and a malevolent mechanical duck. The Trail of Wisdom spirals inward, and part of the lesson has to do with appreciating the way that even one's most intrepid progress is rounded with a sleep. When the surveyors close the boundary at the northeast corner of Maryland, "at this purest of intersections mark'd so far upon America," we are asked to contemplate the achievement as a crisis for "the Geometrickal Pilgrim":

> Yet, Geomancer, beware,—if thy Gaze but turn Eastward by an Eyelash's Diameter, thou must view the notorious Wedge,—resulting from the failure of the Tangent Point to be exactly at this corner of Maryland, but rather some five miles south, creating a semi-cusp or Thorn of that Length, and doubtful ownership,—not so much claim'd by any one Province, as priz'd for its Ambiguity,—occupied by all whose Wish, hardly uncommon in this Era of fluid Identity, is not to reside anywhere. (469)

The American utopia is pocketed by null sets, simultaneously uninhabitable and open to "all who Wish."

Marooned in so perilous a landscape, taking aim "amid a profligacy of stars" (492), Pynchon's men of science resemble May Swenson's cross spider, who, transported to the orbiting Skylab to spin an experimental web in outer space,

> tossed a strand straight as light,
> hoping to snag on perihelion and invent
> the Edge, the Corner and the Knot.[14]

On the first night, she consumes both the web and the thought behind it. On the second night, further infected by chaos and the betrayal of geometry, she somehow concocts another web of sorts:

> A half-made, half-mad
> asymmetric unnameable jumble, the New
> became the Wen. On Witch it sit wirligiggly.[15]

It likewise nets nothing. She is soon crushed by the "Black Whole." Although their Line leaves them less anonymous, Mason and Dixon similarly pioneer in restless spaces to "wirligiggly" effect. They may intend to leave their prints with the firmness of edict, but, at least in Pynchon's rendition, they map fancy and document loss.

NOTES

1. Thomas Pynchon, *V.* (Philadelphia: Lippincott, 1963), 226.

2. Rick Moody, "Surveyors of the Enlightenment," review of *Mason & Dixon,* by Thomas Pynchon, *Atlantic Monthly,* July 1997, 108.

3. Thomas Pynchon, *Mason & Dixon* (New York: Henry Holt, 1997), 219. Further page references to this novel are noted parenthetically in the text.

4. Immanuel Kant, quoted in Gertrude Himmelfarb, review of *Isaiah Berlin,* by John Gray, *Wilson Quarterly* 20, no. 2 (1996), 74.

5. James Joyce, *Ulysses* (New York: Modern Library, 1946), 576.

6. Samuel Beckett, *Waiting for Godot* (New York: Grove, 1954), 9. Regarding the comparison of Pynchon's duo to Beckett's, see the discussion between Mason and Dixon about their having signed a fatal agreement that leaves them no choice but to go on despite their confusion and skepticism about things (478–79), an episode that closely echoes Vladimir and Estragon's interchange about their ambiguous appointment with Godot. Dixon's continual suspicion that the two of them are "being us'd, by Forces invisible" (73) also echoes the fear pronounced by Beckett's tramps. Finally, it bears noting that as they age, Mason suffers from a troubled head and Dixon from bad feet (gout), maladies that mirror Vladimir's and Estragon's, respectively.

7. Walt Whitman, "When I Heard the Learn'd Astronomer," in *Poems, Poets, Poetry,* ed. Helen Vendler (Boston: St. Martin's-Bedford Books, 1997), 300.

8. Intimations of government conspiracy pervade the novel and intensify the possibility that Mason and Dixon are "the simple Tools of others" in more than a philosophical sense. Mason and Dixon cannot help but see a parallel between themselves and Hsi and Ho, the legendary Chinese astronomers who are compelled to predict eclipses for their emperor in order to help him win bets. Here, too, cosmology defers to politics, with Mason and Dixon "ever at the mercy of Place-jobbery, as much as any Nincompoop at Court" (209). See also Dava Sobel's book *Longitude* (New York: Walker, 1995), which details how the placement of the prime meridian was but one of the "purely political" decisions governing scientific pursuits relevant to Pynchon's novel (7).

9. The term "subjunctive" significantly reappears in one of the Reverend Cherrycoke's *Undeliver'd Sermons* when he contends, "The final pure Christ is pure uncertainty. He is become the central subjunctive fact of a Faith, that risks ev'rything upon one bodily Resurrection . . . " (511). In other words, "doubt is of the essence" in spiritual as well as the American territories.

10. Thomas Pynchon, *Gravity's Rainbow* (New York: Viking, 1973), 294.

11. For more on the "great disorderly Tangle of Lines" that is human history, see 349–51. Like Hamlet himself, every fact may defy domestication as "a figure with an interesting Life of its own" (351). Later in the novel, we are advised to rely upon fictions as much as we might upon "poor cold Chronologies" to deliver a coherent sense of reality (695–96).

12. At one portentous juncture, a somber Mason wonders, "Shall wise Doctors one day write History's assessment of the Good resulting from this Line, *vis-à-vis* the not-so-good? I wonder which List will be Longer" (666).

13. The Line often descends to the ridiculous, too, as seen in the legal confusions over marital status in a house heedlessly halved by the recent division of Pennsylvania and Maryland (446–47).

14. May Swenson, "The Cross Spider," *In Other Words* (New York: Knopf, 1992), 39.

15. Ibid., 40.

Thomas Pynchon and the Fault Lines of America

DONALD J. GREINER

NEAR THE END OF *THE CRYING OF LOT 49,* JUST BEFORE A MEET-ing with what may or may not be the mysterious Tristero, Oedipa Maas reaches a conclusion that lifts her out of individual paranoia and into cultural malaise. Commenting on America, Oedipa asks:

> how had it ever happened here, with the chances once so good for di-versity? . . . Behind the hieroglyphic streets there would either be a transcendent meaning, or only the earth. . . . For there either was some Tristero beyond the appearance of the legacy America, or there was just America and if there was just America then it seemed the only way she could continue, and manage to be at all relevant to it, was as an alien. . . .[1]

Published in 1966, in the midst of the complicated decade known today as the Sixties, *The Crying of Lot 49* was a clear-eyed de-piction of shattered faith in the American experiment and its founding ideals. The novel appeared, for example, just after the botched invasion at the Bay of Pigs, the assassination of Presi-dent Kennedy, and the military commitment to the Vietnam War in 1965; and just prior to the murder of Martin Luther King, the assassination of Robert Kennedy, and the riots at the 1968 De-mocratic National Convention. The culturally sanctioned wave of good feeling following victory in World War II was destroyed.

I

In *Mason & Dixon* Pynchon looks back two centuries, from the 1960s to the 1760s, to investigate the formation of the very ideals that would be negated in *Lot 49*. The timing of the publication of *Mason & Dixon* is both appropriate and dramatic. Appearing at

the end of the twentieth century, the span of one hundred years
that historians have already identified as "the American century,"
Mason & Dixon is an appointment with the millennium, a continuing echo of Pynchon's poignant question, "how had it ever
happened here, with the chances once so good for diversity?"

Pynchon is not alone, of course, in publishing a *summa* of the
American century at the end of the era. *Mason & Dixon* joins John
Updike's *In the Beauty of the Lilies* (1996) and William Vollmann's
The Ice-Shirt (1990), *Fathers and Crows* (1992), and *The Rifles*
(1994) as long, sweeping meditations on the mystery of the "New
World" and on the inevitable sullying of the American ideal. Sum-
maries at a millennium are not new in American literature. In
1894, for example, Samuel Clemens published *Pudd'nhead Wilson,* one of his darkest novels, about the disappointment of America. He expressed the spirit of cultural despair in the following
excerpt from Pudd'nhead Wilson's calendar: "October 12, the Discovery. It was wonderful to find America, but it would have been
more wonderful to miss it."[2] Pynchon does not share Clemens's
cynicism, but in *Mason & Dixon* he suggests that the New World
had already "missed it" even before officially becoming the United
States when, in the 1760s, two surveyors were employed to create
geographical order out of continental complexity.

The early notices of *Mason & Dixon* point to what Michiko
Kakutani calls another variation on Pynchon's "favorite theme"
of conspiracy versus chaos: "This time, the overarching tension
is between Enlightenment rationalism and absurdist despair;
between the orderly processes of science and the inexplicable
marvels of nature."[3] Yet *Mason & Dixon* is more a treatise on the
meaning of America than a reprise of Pynchon's familiar theme.
The novel is, in the words of Paul Gray and Laura Miller, "an epic
of loss" and "a sad book, an old man's book"[4] rather than a paradigm of paranoia. As Anthony Lane notes, Charles Mason and Jeremiah Dixon "*were* heroic, in a quietly dogged way, and you feel
by the close that they deserve a medal for surviving not just the
rigors of their professional task but the incalculable travails of
Pynchon's fiction."[5] I would add that their exploration through
the American wilderness becomes the reader's journey through
the fictional tale. Lured by the promise of America, by an unsul-
lied domain of fresh beginnings and tomorrow, both Mason and
Dixon on the one hand and the reader on the other must recon-
noiter the slips and slides of history, the twists and turns of the
unexpected, the dark remains of the day.

In the eyes of the European settlers, America *should* have been innocent, but the two surveyors and the reader learn that no one is ever free. If between 1763 and 1767 Mason and Dixon discover that not themselves but forces as various as the Royal Society, the British Navy, the East India Company, the Jesuits, and even extraterrestrials pull the strings, so the reader realizes that the author manipulates the reader through the text. *Mason & Dixon* turns the eighteenth-century explorers and the exploring reader toward the west of the setting sun. John Leonard writes that "if *V.* was Henry Adams and Ludwig Wittgenstein shooting alligators in New York sewers, and *Gravity* a conjoining of Spengler, Freud, Rilke, Celine and S. J. Perelman, and *Vineland* a lysergic-acid Icelandic saga, *Mason & Dixon* is a 'Westward Ho!' to the Culture of Death."[6] Death, defeat, and the New World: not exactly what Columbus, the Pilgrims, Mason and Dixon, and the Founding Fathers had in mind.

II

I suggest that we read Charles Mason and Jeremiah Dixon as American Adams, as Pynchon's end-of-the-century, ironic take on a venerable American literary paradigm: that of bonded males leaving the safe but restricted hearth to follow the exciting but dangerous lure of freedom beyond the border. Illustrations of the paradigm are as various as Ishmael and Queequeg on the ocean, Huck and Jim on the river, and Sal Paradise and Dean Moriarty on the road; but the constant feature remains two or more men turning their backs on home in order to plunge into the adventure on the other side of the clearing. Yet of all their American literary forebearers, Mason and Dixon most closely follow the footsteps of Natty Bumppo and Chingachgook. The first mythic hero in American literature, Leatherstocking joins the great Mohican chief to form the first inviolable friendship in American fiction. Pynchon's late twentieth-century irony, however, becomes clear as soon as Mason and Dixon set foot on the American continent. Whereas Natty turns west to escape the sound of the axes, Pynchon's bonded males bring the axes with them. Their contract, after all, calls for them to hack an east-west line to mark the separation of Maryland and Pennsylvania. They are New World Adams who push westward yet who find not an Edenic paradise or a soiled hell but both—a potential garden trampled by the very humans who seek to cultivate it. Pynchon significantly points to another irony after Mason and Dixon complete their arduous trek on the far side of the border: rather than follow Leatherstocking and Chingachgook and light out for the setting sun, they turn back to England. Pynchon's end-of-the-millennium vision inhibits eighteenth-century space. There is no place to run. The novel undercuts Frederick Jackson Turner's famous thesis and shows that "the frontier" closed not in the 1890s but the moment the first settlers stepped ashore. In both the 1760s and the 1990s, America has become "our home, and our Despair."[7]

The classic account of this literary paradigm was articulated in 1955 by R. W. B. Lewis. Titling his seminal work *The American Adam,* Lewis probed the turn toward tragedy when Adamic heroes clash with culture and "pay the price of their own innocence."[8] One does not know for certain, of course, but Pynchon may have been exposed to Lewis's thesis when he was a student. Matriculating at Cornell in 1953 at the age of sixteen, Pynchon had switched majors from engineering physics to English by the time Lewis published *The American Adam* in 1955.[9] Pynchon then served in the United States Navy from 1955 to 1957 before returning to Cornell to graduate in 1959 with a degree in English.

Lewis's description of the archetypal American literary hero applies to traditional canonical novels of both the nineteenth and twentieth centuries, the very fiction featured in university literature classes in the 1950s. His definition of the American Adam is relevant:

> The matter of Adam: the ritualistic trials of the young innocent, liberated from family and social history or bereft of them; advancing hopefully into a complex world he knows not of; radically affecting that world and radically affected by it; defeated, perhaps even destroyed—in various versions of the recurring anecdote hanged, beaten, shot, betrayed, abandoned—but leaving his mark upon the world, and a sign in which conquest may later become possible for the survivors.[10]

Lewis goes on to point out that "the evolution of the hero as Adam in the fiction of the New World . . . begins rightly with Natty Bumppo."[11] Taking his start outside time, and thus "liberated" from social history, Leatherstocking locates himself in what Lewis calls "space as spaciousness, as the unbounded, the area of total possibility."[12] Time, in other words, is the enemy of the

American Adam, who thrives on apparently limitless potentiality in what at first appears to be unbounded territory.

The boundless spaciousness of an entire unsettled continent seems to welcome Mason and Dixon when they land in the New World in 1763, but they soon learn that the potential for hostile encounters lurks behind every tree. Although filling the tale with talking dogs, giant cheeses, mechanical ducks, and other assorted highjinks, Pynchon nevertheless takes care to situate *Mason & Dixon* in the context of a violent American history that challenges the ideal of American innocence. The reader is aware that the Revolutionary War is less than a decade away by the time the two surveyors complete the Mason-Dixon Line in 1767, but Pynchon also reminds the reader of a military disaster that took place eight years before Mason and Dixon cut down their first tree: Braddock's defeat. The French victory over Braddock's English forces in 1755 sent shock waves of uncertainty and fear through the settlements east of the Allegheny Mountains. General Edward Braddock was commander-in-chief of British Armies in America. Leading an expedition against Fort Duquesne on 9 July 1755, he was surprised by an attack of French and Indians. Braddock lost over half his command, was routed, and died of wounds four days later. Pynchon repeats references to Braddock's defeat throughout the novel to remind the reader of the tenuousness of the colonialists' hold on the new Eden of supposedly boundless possibility.

The overt reference to Braddock's defeat frames Pynchon's covert allusion to Natty Bumppo, for *The Last of the Mohicans* is subtitled *A Narrative of 1757*. The point is that General Braddock and the Leatherstocking of *Mohicans* were fighting in the same conflict, what today is known as the French and Indian War. Braddock's death at Fort Duquesne in 1755 presages the massacre at Fort William Henry that Natty and Chingachgook witness in 1757. When *The Last of the Mohicans* was published in 1826, Cooper's readers would have been aware of these two catastrophic losses by the British and colonialists at the hands of the French and Indians a mere twenty years before the colonialists finally revolted against the English. Pynchon, of course, cannot assume that his readers have historical acuity similar to Cooper's, so he calls attention to Fort Duquesne and then leaves it to the reader to ferret out the allusion to Fort William Henry. Natty Bumppo and Chingachgook are American Adams present at the Fall. Even Cooper, the consummate American romantic, concedes the realist's challenge to the Adamic myth and thus acknowledges the romantic-realistic tension in American culture. Mason and Dixon follow the trail of Leatherstocking and Chingachgook into the unforeseen darkness of the new-found forest.

III

Men of the Enlightenment, personifications of the Age of Reason, Mason and Dixon confidently set out in the belief that their mandate is to bring order to chaos. Whether attempting to define longitude on the high seas at night, or to mark a transit of Venus, or merely to establish property lines between adjacent estates north of London, they exemplify the eighteenth-century's faith in the precision of scientific measurement. Surveyors, astronomers, mathematicians, and explorers, they accept the perils of personal discomfort to advance what they consider to be the precise progression of humanity. Acutely defined lines of demarcation, in other words, are visible signs of human progress away from the gloom of superstition and toward the glare of rationalism.

The immediate reason Mason and Dixon are employed first to chart and then to hack a boundary line hundreds of miles long in the New World is to adjudicate a property dispute between the Penns of Pennsylvania and the Calverts of Maryland, a rational assignment that would seem to be an end in itself. Yet Pynchon the postmodernist knows that the rational gives way to the unexpected. The pristine path first walked in American fiction by Natty Bumppo and Chingachgook and now followed by Mason and Dixon turns out to be a plunge into the unknown and thus into the unmeasurable. Like Leatherstocking, Mason and Dixon consistently appeal to human reason, but they discover that either Magua or mechanical ducks crouch around the next bend. The border the two surveyors identify, measure, and build at the cost of four years of their lives turns out to be the line that history names in their honor, thereby unexpectedly linking them forever to the tension between North-South, urban-agrarian, and freedom-slavery that explodes a century later in the Civil War. As Natty mutters disapprovingly when he comes across a desecration of trees indiscriminately felled by settlers in *The Prairie*, "I might have know'd it! I might have know'd it."[13]

My point is that the boundary of order and precision Mason and Dixon establish between quarreling Pennsylvania and Maryland is a fault line. Equally significant is that the east-west Mason-Dixon Line inadvertently runs into a second fault line that signals a border Americans should not have crossed: the north-south Warrior Path originally surveyed by the Indians. Whether Yankee-Rebel or Indian-White, alien cultures collide and clash at markers intended to establish reason. Pynchon exposes the precariousness of the rational in one of the most resonant passages in his entire canon:

> Does Britannia, when she sleeps, dream? Is America her dream?—in which all that cannot pass in the metropolitan Wakefulness is allow'd Expression away in the restless Slumber of these Provinces, and on West-ward, wherever 'tis not yet mapp'd, nor written down, nor even, by the majority of Mankind, seen,—serving as a very Rubbish-Tip for subjunctive Hopes, for all that *may yet be true* . . . safe till the next Territory to the West be seen and recorded, measur'd and tied in, back into the Net-Work of Points already known . . . changing all from subjunctive to declarative, reducing Possibilities to Simplicities that serve the ends of Governments,—winning away from the Realm of the Sacred, its Borderlands one by one, and assuming them unto the bare mortal World that is our home, and our Despair. (345)

The compulsion to map and measure, order and own, generates not reason but the forfeiture of dreams. The lie of Manifest Destiny is the result. What, Pynchon asks, is left for humanity in this Age of Enlightenment when all the vistas of possibility have been surveyed?

Pynchon's Adamic heroes confront the specter of time and its threat to boundlessness that R. W. B. Lewis identified as a defining characteristic of the American literary innocent. Benjamin Franklin, an architect of Enlightenment know-how, instructs the newly arrived Mason and Dixon with a warning: "I see our greatest problem as Time,—never anything, but Time" (287). Although called by the populace "a Magician," a "Figure of Power," and "the Ancestor of Miracle" (488), Franklin understands that humanity's limitation in time eventually curtails its joyous possibilities in space. Mason and Dixon may follow Natty and Chingachgook on the trek west, but with every step they are a minute older. As Cooper points out in *The Prairie,* at the moment Leatherstocking reaches the western edge of the American plains, he is an old, old man. The next frontier is death.

Time even affects the legal and thus the culturally blessed

stature of the border Mason and Dixon labor to mark. The longer
the judicial process takes to clarify the official authority of the
Line, the more Colonialists lay claim to the real estate and thereby
confuse the issue. The two surveyors are hired to separate Pennsylvania and Maryland, but the delays of time inadvertently
permit the encroachment of other territories: "Waiting until the
legal status of the Wedge becomes clear. Is it part of Pennsylvania? Maryland? or the new entity 'Delaware'?—which on paper at
least belongs to Pennsylvania" (470). Pynchon's American Adams
are unaware that a culturally sanctioned entity eventually to be
known as the United States is taking shape in the wake of the
newly defined borders. The birth of a nation signals the fall from
spaciousness into time and presages the deaths of Mason, Dixon,
Natty, Chingachgook, and the Indians.

Arbitrary geographical borders become culture's fault lines
when the boundaries are mere playthings of the powerful and rich.
The Calverts of Maryland, for instance, fail to connect Mason and
Dixon's Enlightenment precision with the larger issue of the slow
but inexorable creation of America:

> Indeed, a spirit of whimsy pervades the entire history of these
> Delaware Boundaries, as if in playful refusal to admit that America,
> in any way, may be serious. The Calvert agents keep coming up with
> one fanciful demand after another, either trying to delay or obstruct
> as long as possible the placing of the Markers, or else ... giddy with
> what they imagine Escape, into a Geometry more permissive than
> Euclid, here in this new World. (337)

To refuse the "seriousness" of America is to ignore the complex
nature of the social experiment being authenticated by Mason
and Dixon's markings. Natty, Chingachgook, and the Indians flee
the echo of the axes that Mason and Dixon wield to mark the line,
but the two trail blazers are also caught up in the progress of
diminishing space. As a member of their party remarks, "There
is a love of complexity, here in America ... pure Space waits the
Surveyor,—no previous Lines, no fences, no streets" (586). Yet the
speaker is partly mistaken, as most newcomers to America were
in the 1760s. The landscape offers complexity and space, but the
speaker is ignorant of what Mason and Dixon learn, and what
Natty and Chingachgook already know: that "previous Lines" run
through the supposedly boundless forest. The sheer force of colonialism obliterates the otherness of resisting cultures.

The Warrior Path existed long before Mason and Dixon set out to walk the Line that bears their names. Indeed, the humanity of Pynchon's great novel is fully articulated in his acknowledgment of prior boundaries established by the Indians. There is a difference, of course, and the distinction is crucial: whereas the Calverts and the Penns desire a line to sanctify the permanence of property, the Indians design the Warrior Path to be a locale of fluid motion. To them the Path is a river of unimpeded flow. To cut across the Path with the Mason-Dixon Line is to dam a freeway. The intersection of the east-west Mason-Dixon Line and the north-south Warrior Path previews the inevitable collision of cultures in a newly settled land that should have been innocent. Innocence, in other words, is always in dialogue with corruption.

The implied agreement with the Mohawk fighters is that the Warrior Path designates the westernmost extension of the Mason-Dixon Line:

"We'll be crossing Indian trails with some regularity,—these don't trouble the Mohawks in particular. But ahead of us now, there's a Track, running athwart the Visto, north and south, known as the Great Warrior Path. This is not merely an important road for them,— but indeed one of the major High-ways of all inland America. So it must also stand as a boundary line,—for when we come to it, we shall not be allow'd to cross it, and go on." (646)

The advancing Americans define the Warrior Path in concrete terms as a geographical entity that may be quickly crossed without littering or disturbing the trail. As Mason remarks, "It'll take us a quarter of an hour. We'll clean up ev'ry trace of our Passage" (646). The Mohawks, however, define the Path in abstract terms as a spiritual line of demarcation not to be violated by European intersection. Like the east-west boundary that will arbitrarily identify Yankee and Rebel a century later, so the north-south Warrior Path is a fault line that when disturbed explodes into the cataclysm of extermination. Pynchon's sad irony is that both sides claim the authority of nature. A Mohawk warrior explains to Mason: "As the Stars tell you where it is you must cut your Path, so do the Land and its Rivers tell us where our Tracks must go" (675).

In one of the novel's most poignant moments, Pynchon describes the American future to be born from the intersection of the two fault lines: "Were the Visto to've cross'd the Warrior Path and simply proceeded West, then upon that Cross cut and beaten into the Wilderness, would have sprung into being not only the metaphysickal Encounter of Ancient Savagery with Modern Science, but withal a civic Entity, four Corners, each with its own distinguishable Aims. Sure as Polaris, the first structure to go up would be a Tavern" (650). Businesses would soon proliferate for miles in each direction along both trails, and just behind the tavern owners, the merchants, and the prostitutes would be "Fleets of Conestoga Waggons, ceaseless as the fab'ld Herds of Buffalo, further west,—sunlit canopies a-billow like choir-sung promises of Flight, their unspar'd Wheels rumbling into the soft dairy nightfalls of shadows without edges, tho' black as city soot" (650–51). With a splendid stroke of historical connection, Pynchon links the accelerating tension at the crossing of the fault lines in the 1760s to the defeat of General Braddock and the massacre at Fort William Henry in the 1750s. Armies of Indians were the deciding factor in both disasters; and now, as Mason and Dixon approach the Warrior Path, their ax men begin to desert in fear, fully aware that the ghosts of 1755 are "growing": "as the latent Blades of Warriors press more closely upon the Membrane that divides their Subjunctive World from our number'd and dreamless Indicative, Apprehension rising" (677).

The Indians fear a future that the Europeans cannot see. Picturing the Mason-Dixon Line as "a great invisible Thing that comes crawling Straight on over their Lands, devouring all in its Path" (678), the Mohawks discern no purpose in the boundary except to create a corridor for its own sake. Enlightenment notions of precision, measurement, and property mean nothing to them. Dixon fails to persuade Mason to stop at the intersection, and his warning becomes Pynchon's lament for the sullying of the promise of America: "and what of its intentions, beyond killing ev'rything due west of it? do you know? I don't either" (678). But Pynchon knows, and what he knows is that the Mason-Dixon Line became "an Avenue of Ruin" (679)

Mason & Dixon is Pynchon's elegy for the American dream. Both the last, best hope for humanity and the continent of despair, America at one time was, in the famous words of F. Scott Fitzgerald, "a fresh, green breast of the new world. Its vanished trees, the trees that had made way for Gatsby's house, had once pandered in whispers to the last and greatest of all human dreams; for a transitory enchanted moment man must have held his breath in the presence of this continent."[14] Like Fitzgerald,

Pynchon knows that man *did* hold his breath—and then cut down the trees. How had it ever happened here, Pynchon asks in *The Crying of Lot 49*. *Mason & Dixon* is his answer. It happened way back in the past because, in the rush to establish Enlightenment order on pristine complexity, the new American Adams hacked out the fault lines of the future.

NOTES

1. Thomas Pynchon, *The Crying of Lot 49* (Philadelphia: Lippincott, 1966), 181–82.

2. Samuel Langhorne Clemens, *Pudd'nhead Wilson and Those Extraordinary Twins,* ed. Sidney E. Berger (New York: Norton, 1980), 113.

3. Michiko Kakutani, "Pynchon Hits the Road with Mason and Dixon," review of *Mason & Dixon, New York Times,* 29 April 1997, B1.

4. Paul Gray, "Drawing the Line," review of *Mason & Dixon, Time,* 5 May 1997, 98, and Laura Miller, "Pynchon's Line: The Great American Recluse's Postparanoid Epic," review of *Mason & Dixon, Village Voice,* 6 May 1997, 43.

5. Anthony Lane, "Then, Voyager," review of *Mason & Dixon, New Yorker,* 12 May 1997, 98.

6. John Leonard, "Crazy Age of Reason," review of *Mason & Dixon, The Nation,* 12 May 1997, 67.

7. Thomas Pynchon, *Mason & Dixon* (New York: Henry Holt, 1997), 345. Further references will be noted parenthetically within the text.

8. R. W. B. Lewis, *The American Adam: Innocence, Tragedy, and Tradition in the Nineteenth Century* (Chicago: University of Chicago Press, 1958), 91.

9. See Nancy Jo Sales, "Meet Your Neighbor, Thomas Pynchon," *New York,* 11 November 1996, 60–64.

10. Lewis, *The American Adam,* 127–28.

11. Ibid., 91.

12. Ibid.

13. James Fenimore Cooper, *The Prairie: A Tale,* ed. James P. Elliott (1827; Albany: State University of New York Press, 1985), 83.

14. F. Scott Fitzgerald, *The Great Gatsby,* ed. Matthew J. Bruccoli (1925; New York: Cambridge University Press, 1991), 140.

Mapping the Course of Empire
in the New World

DAVID SEED

IN HIS STUDY *CULTURE AND IMPERIALISM* EDWARD W. SAID AR-
gues for the primacy of territory in the expansion of empire:

> Underlying social space are territories, lands, geographical domains,
> the actual geographical underpinnings of the imperial, and also the
> cultural contest. . . . The actual geographical possession of land is what
> empire in the final analysis is all about. . . . Imperialism and the cul-
> ture associated with it affirm both the primacy of geography and an
> ideology about control of territory.[1]

Geography then forms part of the process of territorial appropriation, which is the very basis of empire. Pynchon's *Mason & Dixon*
takes as its central narrative the survey carried out by the eponymous protagonists of the border between Maryland and Pennsylvania from December 1763 to December 1767. His subject is
therefore mapmaking on the eve of the American Revolution,
placed within the context of British and French imperial rivalry.
Pynchon dramatizes the mounting tensions between the latter
empires as well as the conflict between the British American
colonies and the imperial center. But the novel also demonstrates
the incompatibility of interests between the European settlers
and the native Americans who are being slowly but steadily displaced as the colonies extend westward and codify that process
through mapmaking. Graham Huggan has proposed that in the
context of empire the map should be seen as a "manifestation of
the desire for control rather than as an authenticating seal of coherence." For him a map exists to "empower its makers," not to
provide a supposedly objective codification of terrain.[2] Throughout his novel Pynchon similarly demonstrates how surveying and
mapmaking are implicated in vested commercial and political interests as well as in the processes of colonization.

84

From the very beginning of his career Pynchon has demonstrated an awareness of the cultural implications in topographical representation. This was first made explicit in his famous description of Baedeker-land in *V.:*

> Its landscape is one of inanimate monuments and buildings; near-inanimate barmen, taxi-drivers, bellhops, guides. . . . [I]t is two-dimensional, as is the Street, as are the pages and maps in those little red handbooks. . . . [T]he tourist may wander anywhere in this coordinate system without fear.[3]

Pynchon captures the sheer abstraction of this descriptive system that filters out from their cultural contexts historical buildings and means of communication. As Geoff King writes, "the Western colonial map is an abstraction that tends to extinguish other dimensions of reality in an act of violent appropriation," a process that can be seen at work here in the minimalizing of the humanity of the inhabitants of Baedeker-land.[4] The barmen and other functionaries are "near-inanimate" because they are defined by performing functions, supposedly easing the movements of tourists from place to place. Pynchon's use of Baedekers to describe Florence and Egypt then mimics this representational process, but his focalization of chapter 3 of *V.* through a train conductor, waiter, and similar figures reverses the conventional perspective of tourism by foregrounding the viewpoints of those either marginalized or blanked out completely by Baedeker. This instance would thus confirm Brian Jarvis's argument that Pynchon dramatizes the suppressions of his culture through narratives where spatial suppressions are discovered.[5]

William M. Plater has argued that in Baedeker's handbooks the tour "has been routinised and economised" and that for Pynchon "the tour is the basis of plot."[6] *Mason & Dixon* is not really an exception to this generalization as the protagonists are constantly making excursion from their main journeys. These divergences from the main historical sequence of their survey as often as not result in discoveries and encounters that generate much of the novel's meaning. *Mason & Dixon* is a polyphonic work where surveying is deconstructed by contrasting speakers into a process that is viewed from radically differing perspectives. The survey and the map that will be its end result are therefore destabilized as concepts subjected to endless reinterpretation as the narrative progresses.

The novel's preamble, which describes Mason and Dixon's experiences in the Cape of Good Hope and St. Helena, establishes the connections between imperialism, narration, and mapping; in short, the preamble establishes that mapping is cultural. The Cape is perched precariously on the edge of an enormous spatial expanse referred to simply as the "Hinterland." This term, however, also suggests the paradoxical suppressions within a settlement based on the business of slavery and Eastern trade. Partly this is a sexual geography. On the one hand there is the Company world with its own brothels; on the other, there is the abiding fear of a "Lust that crosses racial boundaries."[7] Pynchon focuses this attempted system of separations on the Cape Dutch, who segregate diet but who cannot exclude Eastern household goods, for instance. These cultural processes are played out in miniature within the household of Cornelius Vroom, a local "patriarch" whose authoritarian Protestantism rationalizes apartheid along moral or religious lines. Through Vroom come stories of the interior:

> Vroom is a bottomless archive of epic adventures out in the unmapped wilds of Hottentot Land, some of which may even hold a gleam of truth, in among the narrative rubbish-tip of this Arm-chair Commando, wherein the mad Rhino forever roles his eye, the killer Trunk stands erect and a-bellow, and the cowardly Kaffirs turn and flee, whilst the Dutchman lights his Pipe, and stands his Ground. (60)

The term "epic" carries a pointed irony here because the brief narrative fragments endlessly recycle an opposition between colonizer and wilderness that arises from the frontier. Geoff King explains: "that which lies across the frontier line is in some cases experienced as an unreal 'other' that guarantees the reality of civilization."[8] Hottentot Land is first described in this novel as the source of fabulous stories (just as in the American chapters "wonders" precede the journey of Mason and Dixon westwards) and then functions as a metaphor of the suppressions within the culture of colonization. The latter simultaneously desires and demonizes the East as a source of riches that might compromise perceptions of cultural homogeneity. The African interior can thus be read as a displaced spatialization of cultural threat whereas Mason and Dixon discover countless signs of ethnic and commercial permeation *within* the household and the Cape settlement generally.

The Cape episode establishes a mode of cultural reading that contrasts with Mason and Dixon's initial response to the African continent as an "unreadable Map-scape," largely unexplored and therefore unknown. The first locations in the novel are situated not within a territorial expanse but within an imperial maritime network of trade routes where India becomes a major point of reference with respect to colonial rule, the treatment of indigenous populations, and the plenty of burgeoning consumerism. The lists of foodstuffs and trade items that recur throughout the novel identify its historical moment as the beginnings of modern consumerism and the emergence of a new kind of European "less respectful of the forms that have previously held Society together" (330). In describing this period of transition Pynchon foregrounds all attempts at cartography as already encoded culturally and therefore complicating representation as a continuous struggle between political and commercial vested interests.

During the eighteenth century, "survey" and related terms became assimilated into the discourse of landscape description. The narrator of Goldsmith's *The Traveller* (subtitled *A Prospect of Society*) shifts his attention onto the Swiss with the words "turn we to survey / where rougher climes a nobler race display" (ll. 165–66), and in *The Seasons* Thomson uses the equivalent to Mason and Dixon's "Visto" (a line of vision) to describe the emergence into view of a garden that implicitly represents the culmination of a whole process of landscape composition: "At length the finished garden to the view / its vistas opens and its alleys green" ("Spring," ll. 516–17).[9] Mason himself in his journal, one of Pynchon's source-texts, uses the same kind of language when describing striking views like that from the Allegheny Mountains (the "Boundary between the Natives and strangers"): "From the solitary tops of these mountains, the Eye gazes round with pleasure; filling the mind with adoration to that pervading [sic] spirit that made them."[10]

Before we see how Pynchon recontextualizes such responses, we should note similar rhapsodic moments in William Bartram's *Travels* (1791). Bartram started his travels around the Southeast with a surveying party commissioned by the Georgia merchants who were demanding millions of acres from the Creek Indians in payment for "debts." At one point a dispute occurs between the surveyor and an Indian chief who argues that the compass (that "wicked instrument") "would wrong the Indians out of their land"; and sure enough a later instance actually demonstrates that the Indians have been displaced from Lake George. It is a consolation to Bartram, however, that the proprietor has preserved an Indian mound intact. Soon after describing this place he gets overcome by the beauties of nature and rhapsodizes to the deity: "it has pleased thee to endue man with *power* and *preeminence* here on earth, and establish his *dominion* over all creatures ... " (emphasis added).[11] The quotation from Mason's journal describes an essentially empty landscape where no native inhabitants came awkwardly between the contemplative British viewpoint and his God. Bartram by contrast demonstrates a fleeting recognition of displacement but smothers any inferences by shifting the reader's attention to flora and fauna. The gambit does not quite succeed in hiding the issue, however, and it is ironic indeed that Bartram's triumphalist description of humanity's supremacy of species comes straight after an image demonstrating the Indians' attenuation to mere traces in the landscape.

Pynchon ensures that such implications are brought out by a sustained interaction between the surveyors and the places they visit. The editors of the *Post-Colonial Studies Reader* have argued that postcolonial space is "characterised firstly by a sense of displacement in those who have moved to the colonies," and this is exactly what Mason and Dixon experience.[12] Whether in the Cape, St. Helena, or Maryland, they are innocents abroad, struggling to understand each new set of cultural circumstances that confronts them. Pynchon distinguishes between the two men's characters: Mason the rather earnest, rather puritanical observer; Dixon the opportunist preoccupied with hidden powers. Surveying for them becomes a means of trying to understand and encode the New World. A dialectic takes place between self and location in both cases because by the end of the novel each scientist has lost his grip on rationality—Dixon becoming manically obsessed with going ever further west and Mason sinking into a depression. At one point a surveyor named Shelby verbalizes an ideology of open space, describing America as expanse: "pure Space waits for Surveyor,—no previous Lines, no fences, no streets to constrain polygony however extravagant" (586). But the novel gives the lie to this geometric fantasy of America as *tabula rasa,* which resulted historically in the commodification of the landscape into commercially disposable lots. Instead it is described as an ancient land where evil lies waiting. There are very rarely panoramic descriptions. Instead we get local scenes crowded as often as not with characters from diverse ethnic and religious origins. Even before Mason and Dixon go to America, a character comically exclaims at its dangers: "Snakes! Bears! Indians!" (201).

More seriously, news of massacres in America and South Africa suggests that "whites in both places are become the very Savages of their own worst Dreams, far out of Measure to any Provocation" (301). Once the survey gets under way, Mason makes a detour to the town of Lancaster to see the site of a recent massacre, which is already being converted into spectacle through sketches and mementoes. At this stage in the novel he still works on the naive presumption of place being there just to be seen. It is only as the novel progresses that the darker side to the American landscape emerges. Mason, for instance, comes to feel threatened by trees. There is just "too much going on" in the forest for comfort. Like Conrad's Marlow in the Congo and the European travellers in Cooper's Leatherstocking Tales, he imagines the trees concealing malign and threatening presences. The trees literally cannot be surveyed. Then at their farthest point westward Mason registers a pleasing view across the landscape only to have that pleasure rudely shaken when an Indian brandishes a freshly taken scalp under his nose.

The surveyors' progress westward brings their hold on the real under greater and greater pressure. Dixon finds himself forced to confront the ubiquitous fact of slavery ("this public Secret, this shameful Core" [7]) while Mason's perception of hidden forces reaches crisis point. The latter experiences a hallucinatory vision in a mirror of all the forces running counter to his scientific rationalism:

> a procession of luminous Phantoms, carrying bowls, bones, incense, drums, their Attention directed to nothing he may imagine, belonging to unknown purposes. . . . There may be found, within the malodorous Grotto of the Selves, a conscious Denial of all that Reason holds true. (769)

The vast majority of references in the novel to optical instruments are ones directed outward to the landscape or the stars, whereas here Mason appears to be looking inward to a psychological landscape peopled by figures carrying out mysterious rites. The two surveyors attempt to apply experience while actually experiencing counter-processes that ultimately bring about their mental collapse.

The surveying method used by Mason and Dixon (the "secant

method") consisted of "running arcs of great circle which inter-
sect the desired parallel of latitude at predetermined intercepts."[13]
Mason himself had established a reputation as an astronomer
and Dixon for expertise in eclipse and transit expeditions. In other
words, their survey represented an attempt to project astronomical measurements onto the earth's surface. At the beginning of
chapter 47 Pynchon gives us an example of the kind of calculation they had to carry out, but he has earlier explored the notion
of surveying as a symbolic transformation of America from dream
to settlement. Thus the fabulous imagining of America as Earthly
Paradise is only "safe till the next Territory to the west be seen
and recorded, measur'd and tied in, back into the Net-Work of
Points already known, that slowly triangulates its Way into the
Continent, changing all from subjunctive to declarative, reducing Possibilities to Simplicities that serve the ends of Governments . . . " (345). Like the introduction by Stalin of a non-Islamic
alphabet among the Central Asian peoples described in *Gravity's
Rainbow,* this process of measurement westernizes America by
bringing it at one and the same time under mathematical and political control. The imposition of geometrical measurement can be
seen graphically in the map of the Delaware peninsula that accompanied Mason's article on latitude calculation in the *Transactions of the Royal Society* for 1768, where the north-south line
ignores natural boundaries like watersheds.[14]

Although Mason and Dixon are obviously engaged in paid employment, one of the first casualties in the novel is their lingering conviction that they are contributing to the advancement of
science. Chapter 35 presents a dialogue on the nature of historical truth. The subversive modern point of view is put as a submis-
sion of history to vested interest: "History is hir'd or coerc'd, only
in Interests that must ever prove base" (350). And the Mason-
Dixon survey is no exception since Pynchon shows that it involves
disputes over mineral rights (coal, lead, etc.) and of course the appropriation of land. This is entirely consistent with the history of
surveying, which from the fifteenth century onwards was used to
examine the state and boundaries of estates; and it confirms J. B.
Harley's assertion that "the surveyor, whether consciously or otherwise, replicates not just the 'environment' in some abstract
sense but equally the territorial imperatives of a particular political system."[15] The most famous eighteenth-century narrative
of surveying was undoubtedly William Byrd's *History of the Dividing Line,* which describes the commission established in 1728
to settle border disputes between Virginia and North Carolina.

Map accompanying Charles Mason's 1768 article for the Royal society on latitude calculation.

Byrd's line constituted a border separating two quite distinct regimes: Carolina, where the climate makes cultivation so easy that the menfolk have become personifications of slothfulness, putting all the labor on their women, and where taxation is minimal; and, on the other hand, an efficient colonial administration in Virginia. The dividing line Byrd's party traces cuts through plantations, whereas in Pynchon's novel the Mason-Dixon western line at one point actually bisects a house.

The line therefore can be taken as the symbolic sign of cartographic codification as the map of America gradually comes into being. This process is not without its casualties. Byrd records how the Tuscaroras waged war against the settlers from 1711 to 1713 because of "some injustice" about their lands and seized the hapless John Lawson, surveyor general of North Carolina, slitting his throat for his pains.[16] Byrd glosses urbanely over the decimation and dispossession of the Tuscaroras that followed, whereas Pynchon dramatizes the consequences of the line by introducing an authoritarian Jesuit, a kind of anti-Mason, who tries to actualize the line as a wall: "Walls are to be the Future. Unlike those of the Antichrist Chinese, these will follow right Lines." Then playing on the moral and geometrical meanings to "right," he predicts an enforced orthodoxy: "if we may not obtain Consent, we will build Walls. As a Wall, projected upon the Earth's Surface, becomes a right Line, so shall we find that we may shape, with arrangements of such Lines, all we may need" (522). True to the spirit of the novel, which is based extensively on dialogue, the priest can scarcely utter this purpose before his audience starts raising objections, for instance to his "orthodoxy" (a "deprav'd worship of right Lines" [522]), which already enacts a heterodoxy of opinion even before the plan can be formulated.

The line proposed in the above quotation is not a means of measurement so much as of control. Line or wall here represents an attempt to impose an official ideology that the newly pluralistic cultural landscape of America resists. Dixon unconsciously helps this meaning to emerge when his Tangent Line reminds him of the Roman road running north through Yorkshire. The imperial analogy is clear since the network of straight Roman roads guaranteed ease of military movement. Although its origin is different, the image of the line anticipates the electric fence that bounds the Reservation in *Brave New World:* "Uphill and down, across the deserts of salt and sand, through forests, into the violet depth of canyons, over crag and peak and table-topped mesa, the fence marched on and on, irresistibly the straight line, the geometrical symbol of triumphant human purpose."[17] Huxley represents a quasi-military process taking place here, where the contours of the landscape have become obstacles to overcome. What he depicts ironically (the implicit human and animal cost of this line), Pynchon renders as a dramatic clash between rival viewpoints. Thus Father Zarpazo's exposition above of the line/wall trope, which is juxtaposed appropriately to an inset Gothic narrative of a captive novice, cues in Pynchon's introduction of the former's antagonist, the Chinese Captain Zhang, who proposes the counter-argument: that boundaries should "follow Nature," "so honoring the Dragon or *Shan* within, from which Land-Scape ever takes its form" (542). This argument is based on the analogy of landscape-as-body, whereby a right line becomes a wound or "sword-slash" inflicted on the living terrain. It further suppresses the factor of colonial appropriation by drawing attention to features like coast-lines, which exist independently of ownership. The ongoing duel between Zarpazo and Zhay thus dramatizes a conflict between starkly antithetical perceptions of place as a site on the one hand, and living, contoured environment on the other.

The boundary between Maryland and Pennsylvania, like that between Virginia and North Carolina charted by William Byrd's party in 1728, followed a line of latitude westward that triggers a dream by Pynchon's clergyman-narrator of the "long unscrolling of the land" (649), as if the surveying party were following the line, not codifying it. The line thus comes to signify the course of empire, to signify the direction of historical time, and if it crossed an Indian warpath the intersection would form a settlement, "a civil Entity, four Corners, each with its own distinguishable Aims" (650).

In his first two novels Pynchon had drawn attention to the rectangular grids in American cityscapes and Baedeker street-plans. *Gravity's Rainbow* pursues the symbolism of differential calculus by breaking entities down into similar segments. In *Mason & Dixon* the right line and rectangles signify the systematic colonization of the American "wilderness." Pynchon's 1993 article for a series about the deadly sins takes mid-eighteenth-century Philadelphia as symptomatic of a commercialization of the New World:

Philadelphia, by Franklin's time, answered less and less to the religious vision that William Penn had started off with. The city was becoming a kind of high-output machine, materials and labor going in, goods and services coming out, traffic inside flowing briskly about a grid of regular city blocks. The urban maze-work of London, leading into ambiguities and indeed evils, was here all rectified, orthogonal.[18]

Here the rectangular grid images a new process of commercial activity, which is revealed in *Mason & Dixon* through the transfer of goods and the technology of the very instruments used in the survey that would facilitate commercial expansion.

If the line denotes a scientifically rationalized appropriation of the terrain that had already become actuality in the layout of Philadelphia, that which cannot be coerced into the rectangular grid takes on a sinister dimension. Surveying self-evidently privileges sight and conversely that which cannot be surveyed becomes the unseen. The Delaware Wedge, a small anomalous area left out of a survey, becomes another of Pynchon's symbolic areas of anarchy, a place hospitable to the unofficial transactions that the culture attempts to suppress:

> Yet there remains to the Wedge an Unseen World, beyond Resolution, of transactions never recorded,—upon Creeksides and beneath Hedges . . . where one may be lost within minutes of entering the vast unforgiving Thickets of Stalks,—indeed, all manner of secret paths and clearings and alcoves are defin'd . . . . Anybody may be in there, from clandestine lovers to smugglers of weapons, some hawking contraband. . . . (470)

Omitted from the survey, the place belongs to no one but those who use it. In that respect the Wedge is the most recent instance of locations like the dump in Pynchon's short story "Low-Lands," which escape the ordering of legal and cartographic systems.

In *Gravity's Rainbow* Pynchon shows paranoia as an extreme skepticism toward appearance that produces inferences of conspiracy. Now the imperial rivalry between Britain and France is used to justify a paranoid vision of a worldwide network of Jesuit observatories that for one character in the novel makes it plain that "the inner purpose . . . can only be,—*to penetrate China*. The rest being but Diversion" (224). This lodges in Dixon's memory since he anyway demonstrates a predisposition to see hidden forces at work. He names one of his optical instruments a "cryptoscope" because it identifies "Powers hidden and waiting the Needles of Intruders" (301). When he visits Annapolis he again

suspects that he is surrounded by men in disguise and even comes
to distrust his own enterprise. Speculating about why they have
to run their line, he reflects, "something invisible's going on" (478).
Such reactions, shared to a lesser extent by Mason, reflect the two
surveyors' ignorance of American politics and reach their paranoid peak in their fear that a covert rival survey is going on: that
a "secret force of Jesuits" (479) is stealing astronomical observations from Greenwich, transforming them into a secret code, and
storing them until an ultimate message will be revealed.

Such a fantasy reflects the two surveyors' thirst for signs. The
heavens for Mason form a "cryptick Message" (59), but early in
the novel even his natal signs are examined as predictors of his
destiny. Mason emerges in other words as the bearer as well as the
decipherer of signs, and during his visit to Annapolis Dixon experiences a similar wavering between subject and object that he
rationalizes through wordplay: "yet I suppose my own *Surveillor*
might be secreted anywhere in our Party" (394). Dixon imagines
himself becoming the object of survey, or rather of surveillance
before the fact, since the term did not enter the language until
the 1790s.

The interlocking fear of conspiracy and preoccupation with cryptic signs that stay in the foreground of chapters 48 through 50
raise questions about the Mason-Dixon survey by destabilizing
it as a codifying process. Graham Huggan has questioned the
coherence "implied by the map's systematic inscription on a supposedly 'uninscribed' earth,"[19] and Pynchon too has questioned the
notion of the American landscape as a blank page from early in
the novel, describing the Delaware Triangle, for instance, as "inscriptions made upon the body of the Earth, primitive as Designs
prick'd by an Iroquois, with a Thorn and a supply of Soot, upon
his human body" (324). The landscape-as-body trope strategically
reveals that territory is being seized, not just mapped out, and
thereby makes absolutely explicit a process that eighteenth-
century writers scarcely note. William Byrd, for example, explains
Indian names for natural features like rivers, appropriating them
through translation into English and assimilating them into territorial designations through British superimpositions like "Sur-
rey," "Isle of Wight," and "Prince George." Both Byrd's party and
Mason and Dixon's include Indian guides as they head further
westward, which makes an irony in itself since, as J. B. Harley has
argued, "in the 'wilderness' of former Indian lands in North America, boundary lines on the map were a medium of appropriation

which those unlearned in geometrical surveys found impossible to challenge."[20] The last quotation above from Pynchon's novel draws an analogy between landscape and the human body that implies the integrated nature of Indian culture before the settlers came and also suggests a signifying system quite independent of print.

As Mason and Dixon travel onwards, they encounter characters who radically question the nature of their undertaking. A German mystic delivers the equivalent to Father Mapple's sermon in *Moby-Dick,* an exercise in nominalism, when he declares: "in Reality, we live upon a Map" (482). Here the real is displaced either toward Heaven or toward Hell with only the representation being apprehensible. A different possibility is spelt out by a community of Kabbalists who argue that "America, withal, for centuries had been *kept hidden,* as are certain Bodies of Knowledge. Only now and then were selected persons allow'd Glimpses of the New World" (487). The body metaphor has now become a means of desubstantializing the American landscape into a secret lore only interpretable by a chosen elite. Their preoccupation with secrecy, with the hidden dimension to meaning, leads them to distrust the immediate so much that the Mason-Dixon Line itself becomes a cryptic text to be read in its own right.[21]

Pynchon draws on the captivity narrative genre in chapter 50 to describe how a frontier wife is taken out of her familiar household space—kitchen and kitchen garden—and progressively estranged from familiar settlements geographically as well as in diet and dress. Her story is not one of suffering at the hands of the "unimagin'd dark Men," however, but rather dramatizes her discovery, when taken to Quebec, of an enormously elaborate communications network figured as follows: "Kite-wires and Balloon-cables rise into clouds, recede into aerial distances, as, somewhere invisible, the Jesuit Telegraphy goes ahead, unabated" (515–16). The surveyors' presumption of lateral measurement and communication is refuted by this image of their rivals, who circulate the new currency of information through three-dimensional space. The concept of surveying as a discrete act now becomes transformed into a *system* of surveillance where power is exercised through the transmission of information.

If surveying is conceived as a process of codifying the landscape, Pynchon's novel subverts its apparently straightforward representational purpose by proliferating signs and signifying systems. Mason and Dixon's cherished mathematical system is

woven into cultural symbolism by one group representing Heaven
and Hell as expanding and contracting spheres; a hollow-earth
theory is used by others to internalize dimension; and when Mason and Dixon visit a cave near Antietam Creek, each projects
a different symbolism. The former records in his journal his response to the place as a reminder of mortality. The cave reminds
him of a Gothic temple that evokes the "abodes of the Dead."
Dixon on the other hand reads on the cave walls "ancient Inscriptions, Glyphs unreadable" (497). The earliest recorded instance of
the term "glyph"—meaning a "sculptured mark or symbol"[22]—is
1825, and indeed Dixon's response has much more in common
with the American Renaissance, when Champollion's decipherment of the Rosetta Stone fired the imagination of American
writers and heightening their sense of the world as text.[23] In
Pynchon's novel the visit to the cave triggers a moment of similar insight from Mason, who exclaims that experiential data have
become text, "and we are its readers, and its Pages are the Days
turning. Unscrolling, as a Pilgrim's Itinerary map in ancient
Days" (497–98). The analogy is a misleadingly clear one, however,
because it does not recognize how far America has become a
crypto-text for the surveyors, scarcely accessible to decipherment.
An itinerary would be predictable, whereas Mason and Dixon are
constantly being confronted with the unexpected.

In this novel, then, Pynchon foregrounds the act of interpreting territory through the interplay between different voices,
contextualizing the Mason-Dixon survey within the political
ferment of the 1760s. His most famous precedent in American
literature of imaginatively exploiting the concept of surveying
was Thoreau, who was a surveyor by profession. In his journal he
records the tedious frequency with which clients would give him
a tattered deed and expect him to identify their land. Surveying
became for him a kind of "dry knowledge" that cramped his perception of the landscape. Thus he records: "I have lately been surveying the Walden woods so extensively and minutely that I now
see it mapped in my mind's eye ... as so many men's wood-lots."[24]
He could no longer see this terrain (unlike the Maine woods) as
wilderness, and his withdrawal to Walden Pond reflected a desire
to escape from issues of property and ownership. Throughout
Walden he accordingly exploits wordplay and metaphor to enact
the imaginative appropriation of the landscape. Surveying, specifically plumbing the depths of Walden Pond, becomes a metaphor
of intellectual enquiry. Pynchon similarly explores metaphorical

dimensions to surveying in *Mason & Dixon,* to locate the survey not just within a play of mind but also within a set of territorial and political imperatives. The novel demonstrates a postcolonial alertness to mapping as a culturally inflected exercise, an exercise in territorial appropriation where the first casualties to be displaced are the native Americans.

NOTES

1. Edward W. Said, *Culture and Imperialism* (London: Chatto & Windus, 1993), 93.

2. Graham Huggan, "Decolonizing the Map: Post-Colonialism, Post-Structuralism and the Cartographic Connection," *Ariel* 20, no. 4 (1989): 117, 118.

3. Thomas Pynchon, *V.* (Philadelphia: Lippincott, 1963), 408–9.

4. Geoff King, *Mapping Reality: An Exploration of Cultural Cartographies* (London: Macmillan, 1996), 145.

5. Brian Jarvis, *Postmodern Cartographies: The Geographical Imagination in Contemporary American Culture* (London: Pluto Press, 1998), 67.

6. William M. Plater, *The Grim Phoenix: Reconstructing Thomas Pynchon* (Bloomington: Indiana University Press, 1978), 71, 81. The 1909 Baedeker handbook to the United States reduces the Indians to inanimate status by devoting the majority of its section on "Aborigines and Aboriginal Remains" to mounds, shell heaps, etc., as if these peoples were extinct.

7. Thomas Pynchon, *Mason & Dixon* (New York: Henry Holt, 1997), 62–63. Subsequent references to this novel are given in text.

8. King, *Mapping Reality,* 106.

9. The most famous line in English poetry containing the term "survey" ("I am monarch of all I survey") opens William Cowper's 1782 "Verses Supposed to be Written by Alexander Selkirk" and links visibility with territorial rule. Robinson Crusoe similarly converts his island from a wilderness to a personal domain by carrying out a "particular survey" of its landscape.

10. *The Journal of Charles Mason and Jeremiah Dixon,* ed. and transcribed by A. Hughlett Mason (Philadelphia: American Philosophical Association, 1969), 129. Virtually all of this journal was written by Mason.

11. William Bartram, *Travels through North and South Carolina, Georgia, East and West Florida* (New York: Penguin, 1988), 58, 103.

12. *The Post-Colonial Studies Reader,* ed. Bill Ashcroft, Gareth Griffiths, and Helen Tiffin (New York: Routledge, 1995), 391.

13. *The Journal,* 21.

14. Mason's article was "Observations for Determining the Length of a Degree of Latitude in the Provinces of Maryland and Pennsylvania in North America," *Philosophical Transactions of the Royal Society* 58 (1768): 274–328.

15. J. B. Harley, "Maps, Knowledge, and Power," in *The Iconography of Landscape,* ed. Denis Cosgrove and Stephen Daniels (Cambridge: Cambridge University Press, 1988), 279.

16. *The Prose Works of William Byrd of Westover,* ed. Louis B. Wright (Cambridge: Harvard University Press, 1966), 303.

17. Aldous Huxley, *Brave New World* (London: HarperCollins, 1994), 94.

18. Thomas Pynchon, "Nearer, My Couch, to Thee," *New York Times Book Review,* 6 June 1993, 3.

19. Huggan, "Decolonizing the Map," 120.

20. Harley, "Maps, Knowledge, and Power," 285.

21. The signs in the novel of conspiracy—coded messages, references to the Illuminati and Kabbalism, etc.—have more in common with the 1790s than the 1760s. In the former decade were published two classic accounts, John Robison's *Proofs of a Conspiracy* (1798) and Abbé Barruel's *Memoirs, Illustrating the History of Jacobinism* (1797–98). The relevance of Robison to the American context is discussed in Neal Wilgus, *The Illuminoids: Secret Societies and Political Paranoia* (London: New English Library, 1980), 20–33.

22. *Oxford English Dictionary,* 2nd ed., s.v. "glyph."

23. This subject is discussed in John T. Irwin's *American Hieroglyphics: The Symbol of the Egyptian Hieroglyphics in the American Renaissance* (New Haven: Yale University Press, 1980).

24. Henry David Thoreau, *Journal,* ed. Bradford Torrey (1906; rpt., ed. Torrey and Francis H. Allen, New York: Dover, 1962), 10:233.

Dimming the Enlightenment:
Thomas Pynchon's *Mason & Dixon*

VICTOR STRANDBERG

"Mason, pray you,—'tis the Age of Reason," Dixon reminds him,
"we're men of Science."
> —Thomas Pynchon, *Mason & Dixon*

In April 1984, when Thomas Pynchon published his *Slow Learner,* the times looked bad for the American Left. At home, President Reagan was soon to crush the last of the old-time liberals, Walter Mondale. Abroad, the Cold War opened its jaws wider than ever to consume even more trillions in American debt, with no Gorbachev—to say nothing of 1989—comprising even a remote possibility on anyone's radar screen. Given these circumstances, Pynchon's rare act of self-disclosure in the introduction to *Slow Learner* assumes increased importance as a source of insight concerning his whole career.

By 1984 Pynchon's decades of disenchantment with the Eisenhower-Nixon-Reagan political culture had critically intensified his long search for an alternative ethos. That search— which produced the Whole Sick Crew in *V.,* the hippie community in *Vineland,* and the motif of rebellion in *Mason & Dixon* (the Weavers' Rebellion, Bonnie Prince Charlie's Scots uprising of 1745, the Black Hole of Calcutta, the Levelers, resistance to the Stamp Act)—finds its rationale in a set of cultural attitudes that Pynchon usefully clarifies in the *Slow Learner* introduction, attitudes that change very little over the thirty-four years from *V.* through *Mason & Dixon.* Here we find a set of precepts that governs Pynchon's whole career.

The most fundamental of these precepts is Pynchon's intense discontent with the military deadlock of the 1950s—that formative decade when Pynchon graduated from Cornell and began his two-year stint in the U.S. Navy. His harshest judgment applies to the political leaders he held responsible for the Bomb-dreading postwar standoff, creating what Faulkner called (in his Nobel address) "a general and universal physical fear" of such proportions that "there are no longer problems of the spirit. There is only the question: When will I be blown up?"[1] But where Faulkner called upon artists to resist this attitude, Pynchon, as late as 1984, wallowed in it:

> Our common nightmare The Bomb . . . was bad enough in '59 and is much worse now, as the level of danger has continued to grow. . . . Except for that succession of the criminally insane who have enjoyed power since 1945, including the power to do something about it, most of the rest of us poor sheep have always been stuck with simple, standard fear.[2]

It is notable that Pynchon makes no distinction between the clearly "criminally insane" Soviet leaders such as Stalin and Beria and their surely less culpable Western adversaries such as Churchill and Truman. Instead, his view of history was importantly shaped, he says, by the "mighty influences" of Edmund Wilson's Marxist-Leninist history *To the Finland Station* and Machiavelli's *The Prince* (*Slow Learner* 18). These are classic works, to be sure, but by the 1950s Wilson had long since renounced his infatuation with the Soviet regime, and *The Prince* seems an oddly cynical book for a Bomb-fearing peacenik to be influenced by. It would seem that for Pynchon the finer distinctions of historical judgment were to be subordinated to the larger purpose of social criticism.

In pursuit of that purpose, Pynchon recalls three specific epiphanies of cultural enlightenment in *Slow Learner.* First, he learned from his military experience the perversity of class hierarchy (one thinks perhaps of the coprophiliac general in *Gravity's Rainbow*):

> Whatever else the peacetime service is good for, it can provide an excellent introduction to the structure of society at large . . . . One makes the amazing discovery that grown adults walking around with college educations, wearing khaki and brass . . . can in fact be idiots. And that working-class white hats . . . are much more apt to display competence, courage, humanity, wisdom, and other virtues associated, by the educated classes, with themselves. (*Slow Learner* 6)

Second, he learned that his own attitudes were not above reproach either, in that the "racist, sexist, and proto-Fascist" talk in an early story, "Low-lands," represented not only "Pig Bodine's voice, but, sad to say . . . my own at the time" (11). But at least he had some pretty elegant company, in so far as "John Kennedy's role model James Bond was about to make his name by kicking third-world people around" (11). In the end, however, these transgressions too fall under Pynchon's quasi-Marxist view of class:

> It may yet turn out that racial differences are not as basic as ques-
> tions of money and power, but have served a useful purpose, often in
> the interest of those who deplore them most, in keeping us divided
> and so relatively poor and powerless. (12)

Most significantly for his work, Pynchon's discontent with his times shaped his aesthetic sensibility. Apart from a dismissive mention of *The Waste Land* and *A Farewell to Arms,* the only artists Pynchon cites in his introduction to *Slow Learner* are the cultural outcasts, rebels, and innovators of his lost youth. In music, he makes no mention of the great classical-romantic composers; instead, he venerates "jazz clubs," Bird, Elvis, Spike Jones, bop, rock 'n' roll, and swing. In painting, none of the Old Masters rates a mention, but he says he took "one of those elective courses in Modern Art, and it was the Surrealists who'd really caught my attention" (20). Likewise, in literature his favor falls exclusively on contemporary voices of social protest and emotional liberation: *Howl, Lolita, Tropic of Cancer, Playboy* magazine, Norman Mailer's "The White Negro," and above all the Beat writers, who promoted "a sane and decent affirmation of all we want to believe about American values" (9)—these were the models Pynchon claimed to follow. Most importantly, he cites his exceedingly dubious but fervently held belief in "a book I still believe is one of the great American novels, *On the Road,* by Jack Kerouac" (7). It is fair to say that none of these aesthetic fashions would find much resonance with the aristocratic elegance of the Age of Reason.

Finally, perhaps influenced by the existentialist zeitgeist propagated by European thinkers like Heidegger and Sartre, Pynchon declares that "when we speak of 'seriousness' in fiction ultimately we are talking about an attitude toward death" (5). In Pynchon that attitude evoked the notion of the absurd, a fundamental precept of the greatly popular black humor movement. "A pose I found congenial in those days," he remarks, "was that of somber glee at any idea of mass destruction"—a view that soon came to encompass the idea of entropy, the "spectacle of universal heat-death and mathematical stillness" (13). But though this idea comes up pervasively in his big novels (as well as in his early story "Entropy"), the real focus of the theme of death is not the physics of entropy but the individual's subjection to the moving arrow of time:

> that human one-way time we're all stuck with locally here, and which terminates, it is said, in death. Certain processes, not only thermo-dynamic ones but also those of a medical nature, can often not be re-versed. Sooner or later we all find this out, from the inside. (15)

Clearly, this is not a man who will be much impressed by the Enlightenment-driven precepts of an Alexander Pope: that "Or-der is Heav'n's first law"; that "God said, *Let Newton be!* and all was Light."[3]

In sum, we find at the base of all Pynchon's work the tem-perament of a hippie rebel against tradition, convention, and all forms of social hierarchy. To pass judgment on our age in *V.* and *Gravity's Rainbow,* Pynchon accordingly amplified the violence and madness of two World Wars with a choice selection of war-ravaged sites: Berlin, London, Peenemunde, Malta, and South-West Africa, where the German overlords' killing of sixty thousand Hereros became the precursor of one hundred times that many Holocaust victims. Ignoring the great advances accomplished by Western Civilization in the twentieth century—in science, civil rights, women's equality, expanding middle-class prosperity and health care, the defeat of worldwide fascist-communist tyranny—he launched his career in *V.,* his prize-winning first novel of 1963 (the year after the Cuban Missile Crisis), by using the Fashoda Crisis of 1898 as his portal to the twentieth century. That episode was a matter of drawing amoral lines of force across the map, with the British painting Africa red from north to south while the French preferred purple going west to east. Barely averting war, those empires in collision near the Sudanese town of Fashoda proved a reliable harbinger of a cataclysmic age.

Given this worldview, it is not surprising that Thomas Pynchon's journey to the eighteenth century in *Mason & Dixon* is calculated to display the underside of the Enlightenment. Those same two empires that collided at Fashoda were going at each other a century and a half earlier on another continent, with a third em-pire—our America—about to emerge out of that confrontation. It is especially useful to Pynchon's purpose that the Line that would divide the new nation from 1776 to the present was created before the nation itself, a feature not of physical but moral geography. ("An emerging moral Geometry," Pynchon calls the map of the Wedge region in Delaware—a wedge that did in fact split the country by the 1860s.[4]) In the name of that geography, Pynchon casts a cold eye on the century of order, reason, and progress that gave birth to the modern age.

Pynchon's vehicle for rendering judgment is that quintessential plaything of eighteenth-century literature, the mock-epic— a Fieldingesque mock-epic in prose, in this instance. A quick checklist shows a dozen or more mock-epic conventions at work in *Mason & Dixon*, apart from its inordinate length and imitation of eighteenth-century style. First, we have at stake the destiny of whole races of people: European settlers, Indians, and slaves. The setting ranges, epic-wise, across whole continents, from South Africa to the Appalachians. There is the on-the-road plot, which descended to Pynchon in a line running from *The Odyssey* to Arthurian legend to *Don Quixote* to *Tom Jones* to *Huckleberry Finn* to Jack Kerouac. There is the obligatory visit of the epic hero (Dixon) to the Underworld, in the North Pole "hollow earth" episode. There is much recourse to magic and the supernatural, with Rebekah's ghost taking a somewhat similar role to that of Odysseus's Athena appearing to the hero (Mason) at critical junctures (*The Odyssey* is cited on page 690). There are, in the epic mode, long-winded digressions such as the Captive's Tale of Eliza Fields and the outer framework of storyteller and listeners (the Reverend Wicks Cherrycoke and his family members). There is the epic theme connecting gods and men, which Pynchon magnifies into a catalogue of world religions in *Mason & Dixon*, evoking the whole range of Christian denominations (Anglican, Quaker, Methodist, Jesuit) along with Deism, Judaism, Confucianism, Buddhism, and Hinduism. There is the concluding reunion of father and son, with Mason in the Odysseus role and Doctor Isaac as Telemachus. (Another father-son motif, the Mason-Masklyne rivalry over Bradley's legacy, suggests a biblical analogy to Isaac, Jacob, and Esau.)

There are, finally, the profusion of allusions, not to classical-biblical figures as in Milton or Pope, but to the neoclassic tropes and names that characterize the world of Mason and Dixon. Collectively, Pynchon's deployment of these motifs appears to represent a kind of moral geometry that does to Augustan England what the Mason-Dixon Line does to America. The better part of that geometry, in Pynchon's view, resides in the figures who stand outside the Augustan vanities of the time: religious revivalists like Whitefield and Wesley (9, 100, 260, 405); the melancholiac Dr. Johnson (35, 745–47); the pre-romantic mad poet Christopher Smart (116); and fictional characters like Laurence Sterne's Uncle Toby in *Tristram Shandy* (364), along with Pynchon's reverend narrator, Wicks Cherrycoke. The latter's fierce social criticism, as when he decries the practice of giving Indians hospital blankets infected with smallpox as a "Wicked Policy of extermination" (308), prefigures the gradual departure of Mason and Dixon from Enlightenment rationalism. Concerning race, they come to see the vaunted Enlightenment as little more than a Heart of Darkness:

> Mason did note as peculiar, that the first mortal acts of Savagery in America after their Arrival should have been committed by Whites against Indians. . . . They saw white Brutality enough, at the Cape of Good Hope. They can no better understand it now, than then. Something is eluding them. Whites in both places are become the very Savages of their own worst Dreams, far out of Measure to any Provocation. (306-7)

On the wrong side of the Augustan moral geometry, causing these atrocities against Indians and black slaves, repose the forces of capitalism, industrialism, and imperialism that rose to supremacy during the Enlightenment thanks to the scientific revolution of the time. "Newton is my Deity"—Dixon's refrain (e.g., page 116)—evokes the worship of science and technology that would produce marvels like the Jesuit telegraph in Canada, but put them (as in *V.* and *Gravity's Rainbow*) at the service of power-hungry, conspiratorial oppressors. Aligned with Newton on this dubious side of the Augustan moral geometry are other rationalist figures such as Linnaeus (430), Fermat (336), Herschel (769), Gibbon (349), the Encyclopedists (359), and the Royal Society.

In this reverse geometry the purported triumphs of the Age of Reason actually reflect moral turpitude. The imperialist version of this moral corruption is Clive of India's rapacious administration, and its economic exponent is Adam Smith, whose Invisible Hand brings down some venomous sarcasm from the author vis-à-vis "the well-guarded, and in the estimate of some, iniquitous,

Iron-Plantation of Lord and Lady Lepton" (411). Their spokesman,
Mr. LeSpark, stayed

> safe inside a belief as unquestioning as in any form of Pietism [that
> he] . . . goeth likewise under the protection of a superior Power,—not,
> in this case, God, but rather, Business. What turn of earthly history,
> however perverse, dare interfere with the workings of the Invisible
> Hand? Even the savages were its creatures. . . . (411)

Although he admits that "a considerable Sector of the Iron
Market [is], indeed, directed to offenses against Human, and of
course Animal, flesh" (412), LeSpark fails to acknowledge the invisible labor force behind the Invisible Hand. Instead it is the
narrator Cherrycoke who delivers the fundamental reproach that
Pynchon means to evoke in every mention of the Mason-Dixon
Line: "What is not visible in his rendering . . . is the Negro Slavery . . . the inhuman ill-usage, the careless abundance of pain
inflicted, the unpric'd Coercion necessary to yearly Profits beyond
the projectings even of proud Satan" (412). Even Mason and Dixon
themselves are divided by their Line, with their names ironically
reversed from their subsequent historical meanings: it is Mason
who beds with slave girls in South Africa and otherwise condones
slavery, while Dixon—whose name evolved into "Dixie"—enacts
his Quaker abolitionism to the extent of risking life and limb in
the Baltimore slave-market episode (700). This discrepancy is one
reason why, "at the end of the eight-Year Traverse, Mason and
Dixon could not cross the perilous Boundaries between themselves" (689). But back in England, it is Dixon who thinks nothing of putting his surveyor's skills at the service of the Enclosures
movement, helping rich aristocrats expropriate common lands
from the poor (754), while it is Mason who sides passionately with
the weavers' rebellion against capitalist expropriation (313). The
Line thus not only separates Mason and Dixon; it marks off
schizoid divisions within each psyche.

One might therefore say that *Mason & Dixon* is a giant prose
version of Robert Frost's "Mending Wall," with the Line standing
in for the wall and the Enlightenment furnishing the dubious
rationale for wall-building. "He had slic'd into Polygons the
Common-Lands of his Forebears," Pynchon says of Dixon's jour-
neyman work with Enclosures; "He had drawn Lines of Ink that
became Fences of Stone" (587). Despite some local benefits of the
Line in confirming property ownership and political boundaries,

nothing good can finally be said of it. As early as page 8, the Reverend Cherrycoke calls the project "brave, scientifick . . . and ultimately meaningless." Later, the Line is described dismissively as having "the width of a Red Pubick Hair" (296) and as comprising "a Conduit of Evil" (701). It comes in the end to stand for every manner of artificial division and social hierarchy, from constructing the map of empire to maintaining the Great Chain of Being within which "Ev'ryone lies . . . each appropriate to his place in the Chain. . . . We who rule must tell great Lies, whilst ye lower down need only lie a little bit" (194).

The Line, then, represents a misbegotten rationalist undertaking that affords Pynchon book-length opportunity to expound his antirationalist theme. To a considerable extent, he accomplishes this end through playful magic realism motifs such as the giant cheese, the mechanical duck, and the Jesuit telegraph. Another tactic is to highlight the inhuman brutality of the times in episodes like the Tyburn hanging or scalp-taking on the frontier (111, 681). But probably the most sustained attack on rationalism comes about through the religious motifs that pervade the novel. Initially set in the Advent season of 1786, *Mason & Dixon* employs every manner of religious reference to indicate the prevalence of the nonrational: ghostly visitations, a golem tale, the Giant Beaver creation myth (620), a Wesleyan revival in Newcastle (100), a Whitefield revival in Philadelphia (261), a rendition of "Havah Nagilah" at George Washington's home (285), and various biblical applications: for example, Philadelphia as "Sodom-on-Schuylkill" or "the most licentious Babylon of America" (355, 356). This is not to say that religion is treated uncritically. At one point Christianity is implicated in "ev'ry Crusade, Inquisition, Sectarian War, the millions of lives, the seas of blood" (76), and even the genteel Reverend Cherrycoke lapses into "speculation upon the Eucharistic Sacrament and the practice of Cannibalism" (384). But the bulk of the Reverend's narration posits a Christian counterpoint to the Age of Reason's rationalist complacies. "Of course, Prayer was what got us through," he declares about the *Seahorse* episode (30), and his "Unpublished Sermon" turns the science of astronomy into a divine allegory: "As Planets do the Sun, we orbit 'round God according to Laws as elegant as Kepler's. . . . We feel as components of Gravity His Love, His Need, whatever it be that keeps us circling" (94).

The main converts of the novel are of course its pair of central figures. In the closing pages of *Mason & Dixon,* Mason comes to realize two fallacies in his Age of Reason philosophy. One is that the struggle for order, lucidity, and progress epitomized in the Line is nullified by the possibility of radical human evil. Mason's vision of evil gains ironic force against the backdrop of exuberance occasioned by Sir William Herschel's discovery of a new planet:

> The [Royal Astronomer Masklyne] had shar'd his delight with Mason over the new Planet. . . . Yet to Mason was it Purgatory. . . . What fore-inklings of the dark Forces of Over-Throw that assaulted his own mind came visiting? . . . There may be found, within the malodorous Grotto of the Selves, a conscious Denial of all that Reason holds true. Something that knows, unarguably as it knows Flesh is sooner or later Meat, that there are Beings who are not wise, or spiritually advanced, or indeed capable of Human kindness, but ever and implacably cruel, hiding, haunting, waiting. . . . (769)

It is this undermining of Augustan faith in reason that causes Mason initially to forego a second expedition to see the Transit of Venus in 1768: "'Someone must break this damn'd Symmetry,' Mason mutters" (718). Likewise, he abandons astronomy in favor of astrology when he casts Dixon's horoscope (765).

During his Age of Reason phase, Mason's chief fallacy was to commit himself to reason, progress, and science—to the Transit of Venus and the Line—at the expense of his family. When he returned from St. Helena, only to set out immediately for America, his sister Anne reproached him about abandoning his children: "And the next time you see them? Years, again?" (202). Both Mason and Dixon make amends for this neglect in the closing pages. The lifelong search for a viable community in Pynchon's books thereby ends in the two travelers' commitment to the most ancient and deeply rooted of human communities, the biological family. In effect, the first Transit of Venus, in 1761, was a scientific expedition; the second, in 1768—after the Line is finished—bears out the allegorical meaning that the scientists had failed to recognize the first time: "to watch Venus, Love Herself, pass across the Sun" (61).

So Mason and Dixon both get married again, siring more children (as Thomas Pynchon himself has done in his fifties) while gathering their older offspring into the new family circle. Mason's renewed bond with his most father-hungry son, Doctor Isaac, best epitomizes this strategy. As though to compensate for those missing years of fatherhood, Mason reverts with the grown-up Isaac to an early stage of child-rearing: "As they lie side by side in bed, Mason finds he cannot refrain from telling his Son bedtime stories about Dixon. 'He was ever seeking to feel something he'd hitherto not felt'" (763–64). Of course Mason is speaking of himself as well as Dixon in that last statement, with family feeling as that long-missing sentiment: "The Boy he had gone to the other side of the Globe to avoid was looking at him now with nothing in his face but concern for his Father" (768). So Mason additionally tells his own family story, how that earlier transit of Venus—Mason's romance with Rebekah—led to his earlier family-formation: "At some point, invisible across the room, Doctor Isaac will ask, quietly, evenly, 'When did you and she meet? How young were you?'" (767).

Thus, in the end, this epic quest narrative narrows its focus to the wisdom of that genuine eighteenth-century mock-epic, Voltaire's *Candide:* Mason and Dixon were to hoe their own gardens. (Voltaire is mentioned on page 372.) But in a perverse final twist of the plot, Mason gets the better garden. The Pynchonesque black humor of history decrees that it is Dixon the would-be American who ends up in an English cemetery, while Mason the would-be Royal Society member expires in Philadelphia, soon to be the American capital city, under the solicitous gaze of that quintessential American man, Benjamin Franklin. It is a measure of his growth that Mason accepts the new identity that Franklin has arranged to confer upon him: "Upon Rebekah's Tomb-Stone he has put 'F.A.S.' [Fellow of the American Society] after his own Name. So it means much to him" (761). It means much also that after Mason's death his and Rebekah's two sons, William and Dr. Isaac, choose enthusiastically to "stay, and be Americans" (772), though Mason's new wife and younger children go back to England. In this transition from father to sons, Pynchon's closure appears to grant greater weight to the ameliorative promise of America than to the tragic patrimony of the Line—the invectives of *Slow Learner* notwithstanding.

As for the Enlightenment, Pynchon's dimming action figures to have no more lasting effect than the paltry assaults of Foucault and the critical theorists a generation ago. One reason for this result is that the neoclassic writers did the job first and better, in (for example) the satires of Swift, Johnson, and Hogarth as well as the skeptical inquiries of Rousseau and Godwin. Indeed, they brightened the Enlightenment by so criticizing it, adding their luster to the permanent brilliance of Gibbon, Pope, Mozart, Adam Smith, and similar eminences, including those flawed vessels of Enlightenment wisdom, Pynchon's cameo characters Washington and Jefferson. But if he shared the failure of Foucault and company to effectively dim the Enlightenment, Pynchon had one vital advantage over those ideological comrades in arms: unlike them, he is a first-rate artist. When the ephemeral politics of our age have boiled away, what will remain in *Mason & Dixon* is a richly stylized epic novel, peopled with a big cast of lively, uniquely drawn characters.

By conferring the immortality of art upon these figures, Pynchon achieves a victory of sorts over the true essence of chaos, which is not ideological but metaphysical, incorporated into the one-way arrow of time. Whether figured as the messed-up calendar with its missing eleven days (190, 554), or as the watch that gets swallowed into "acid and bile and [that] smells ever of Vomit" (325), time is the final adversary, a universal juggernaut that annihilates lives and meanings. In the encounter with Johnson and Boswell, near the end of the book, the Reverend Cherrycoke unmistakably stands in for Pynchon when describing the artist's salvage project against the power of Time:

> "I had my Boswell, once," Mason tells Boswell, "Dixon and I. We had a joint Boswell. Preacher nam'd Cherrycoke . . . a sort of Shadow ever in the Room who has haunted [me], preserving [my] ev'ry spoken remark."
>
> "Which else would have been lost forever to the Great Wind of Oblivion,—think . . . how much shapely Expression, from the titl'd Gambler, the Barmaid's Suitor, the offended Fopling, the gratified Toss-Pot, is simply fading away upon the Air, out under the Door, into the Evening and the Silence beyond. All those voices. Why not pluck a few words from the multitudes rushing toward the Void of forgetfulness?" (747)

Though "a few words" is hardly the right phrase for *Mason & Dixon,* these sentiments define the book's lasting achievement. "Slow Learner" may describe Pynchon the political/cultural critic, but there is nothing slow or unlearned about his artistic power at this sunset end of a grand career.

NOTES

1. William Faulkner, "Nobel Prize Address," 10 December 1950, in *The Harper American Literature,* vol. 2, ed. Donald McQuade, et al. (New York: Harper & Row, 1987), 1368.

2. Thomas Pynchon, *Slow Learner: Early Stories* (Boston: Little, Brown, 1984), 18–19. Further references will be noted parenthetically within the text.

3. Alexander Pope, "An Essay on Man" and "Intended for Sir Isaac Newton," respectively, *Alexander Pope: Selected Works,* ed. Louis Kronenberger (New York: Modern Library, 1948), 127, 330.

4. Thomas Pynchon, *Mason & Dixon* (New York: Henry Holt, 1997), 323. Further references will be noted parenthetically within the text.

The Sound of One Man Mapping:
Wicks Cherrycoke and
the Eastern (Re)solution

JOSEPH DEWEY

"Mason,—shall we argue Religious Matters?"
"Good Christ. Dixon. What are we about?"
—*Mason & Dixon*

Mason & Dixon is a tale, we are to believe, told one winter evening in December 1786, by a specific (if invented) narrator— Wicks Cherrycoke, an aging British parson who had accompanied Mason and Dixon as party chaplain on their historic survey twenty years earlier, a minister currently without a congregation, a minister without even a home, lodging temporarily at his sister's well-appointed Philadelphia residence.[1] Further, it is a tale told to a specific audience: Cherrycoke's extended family of sisters, in-laws, nephews, and nieces. Indeed, Cherrycoke can stay at his sister's home only as long as he is able to entertain his youngest relations with stories of his travels. The novel opens with the family gathering in the snug parlor against a descending dusk for another of Nunk Wicks's stories, this one, he promises, about America. But Wicks Cherrycoke has come to Philadelphia not to visit his family but rather to pay his respects at Charles Mason's grave, a site he has haunted since his arrival in the city weeks earlier.

But why filter the tale of the 1764–67 surveying expedition, a narrative line sufficiently rich in metaphoric and historic resonance, through the framing device of an invented minister imposing on the generosity of his sister's family in affluent post-Revolution Philadelphia? Certainly, the frame forces upon the text an uneasy credibility, specifically the telling of this tale, nearly eight hundred pages complete with musical interludes, in the space of a single night—although, by dawn, despite a pipeline of caffeine that pumps throughout the night, the family has largely abandoned Cherrycoke for sleep. More problematic, however, such a frame takes Cherrycoke far from the probable range of his familiarity. For example, Cherrycoke recounts Mason's expedition to St. Helena; the first months of the American expedition before Cherrycoke joined; several sidetrips into Colonial America by both Mason and Dixon; and the duo's years in England following the expedition. Furthermore, Cherrycoke freely re-envisions the historic record of Mason and Dixon and introduces, without explanation, paranormal effects in the manner of Baron Münchausen, the era's most notable fabulator, whom Cherrycoke cites. These spectacle effects include talking dogs, an invisible robot duck, conversing clocks, a glowing severed ear, a valley of giant vegetables, a man who turns into a beaver, luminous ghosts, and a Quebec convent of anti-nuns trained in the arts of vice.

Why, then, opt for such a narrator? And why a minister? Why *this* minister recounting *this* tale to *this* audience? Wicks Cherrycoke makes a considerable impress on the narratives of Mason and Dixon—indeed, within the license of his fireside narration, Cherrycoke reinvents the expedition and freely fashions the emotional lives of both central figures. His is the voice we hear. Mason and Dixon, to borrow a phrase Mason applies derisively to Cherrycoke, are merely the shadows he casts. But why?

Within the best tradition of the ministry, Cherrycoke holds forth at such tedious length to teach—to teach a particular audience a particular lesson perceived to be critical to its spiritual health, a lesson (again all too often within the tradition of the ministry) lost to an inattentive, uninterested "congregation." The narrative presence of Wicks Cherrycoke turns *Mason & Dixon* into an explicitly religious novel that explores the damaged legacy of Christianity, the emerging muscle of the Enlightenment and, finding both systems wanting for largely the same reasons, turning to a most unexpected source—the mysticism of the East—for (re)solution.[2]

Like Christian philosophers back to Paul (whose meditation in Corinthians on corporeal resurrection Mason ponders), Wicks Cherrycoke is obsessed with mortality; he haunts graveyards, ruminates over the past, and accepts that, now past fifty, he approaches death—"beach'd upon these Republican shores—stoven, dismasted, and imbecile with age."[3] When Cherrycoke's initial sea voyage, aboard the *Seahorse* that is carrying Mason and Dixon to Sumatra to observe the transit of Venus, is interdicted by a French pirate ship, Cherrycoke is exposed in the ensuing battle to the unnerving immediacy of mortality—he performs awkwardly as ship's doctor amid the carnage of running blood and splintered bone. Cherrycoke wants death as the West has always fashioned it: a neat, if inevitable absolute, a closing moment of translation as potent and as stirring as when the *Seahorse* much later slides across the Equator, quietly passing hemispheres, and for one hushed moment casts no shadow. Cherrycoke understands that denial of death's omnipotence is the play of children— that maturity brings with it a reasonable fear of its brutal intrusion. Yet he envies those he sees at a taproom, their cheery faces testifying to an ability to ignore the fact of inevitable closure that so haunts him.

In addition to being darkly morbid, Cherrycoke is quite alone, a Britisher in colonial America, a man literally without home, even his family back in England. Put off by his early run-in with the law, they pay him a generous stipend in return for his staying away. Throughout his own narrative, his presence is only awkwardly tolerated—he is an intruder, a nuisance, a "cherubick Pest" (434). Surrounded in his adopted America by aggressive minds bent on dominating the natural environment through the methodical application of science and by reckless entrepreneurs who ruthlessly pursue the satisfactions of the material life by exploiting that same natural environment, Cherrycoke is alienated from his own time, a man involved in oddly medieval theological speculations, attempting to locate the viability of the Christian directive, a man genuinely shocked by the rapacity, brutality, and preposterous decadence of those nominal Christians all around him. He is a Christian who has come to understand that doubt is the lot of any believer. Thus, as a minister, he sees himself as a shoddy impostor. He is a Christian adrift in the tick-tocking vastness of a cosmos that, since Newton a scant generation earlier, had been wholly restructured into a simple, albeit intriguing, clockwork. He is a Christian who feels not the reward of direction associated with a benevolent hands-on Creator but rather the fear that life is a ride in a driverless carriage across a "Prairie of desperate Immensity" (361). Alienated from the traditional joy premised by the Christian agenda, Cherrycoke acknowledges only a "dead Vacuum ever at the bottom" of his soul (356). He is a Christian, yes, but one locked within an interminable Advent season—his is a tale suspended in mid-December—awaiting with significant anxieties the redemptive promise of the Parousia.

Like Henry Adams a century later, Wicks Cherrycoke wrestles with the unsettling implications of the diminishing presence of Christianity. He probes its most imposing mysteries in unpublished sermons and in a spiritual daybook, wrestling there in deep privacy with questions—the "Thorns-and-Angels Stuff" (568)—that include the moral composition of angels, the implications of the Eucharistic sacrifice, the meaning of the Resurrection, the place of doubt within a Christian conscience. All the while he repackages the lambent mysteries of God's presence by awkwardly appropriating the harder-edged vocabulary of Newton's all-too-convincing logic, arguing that Heaven and Hell might be surveyed and measured or that the Nativity star may have been a passing comet or that God's love might best be understood as a cohesive energy much like Newton's gravity.

But Wicks Cherrycoke is too much of his age not to see that Christianity has lost its muscle—he acknowledges that the revival energies of traveling preachers such as the legendary Whitefield or celestial phenomena such as the fiery comet that flares across the night skies over Cape Town surely excite the appropriate passion for reformation but that such promising reawakenings quickly wane. He observes among the Dutch settlers in South Africa that, by defining notions of sin, the Christian congregation comes merely to relish the dark energy of violation. Most distressing, he notes that the deep promise of the New World as stage vast enough for God's final triumph had quickly lapsed into a simple mercenary enterprise, an empire of death and trade.

Left without the reassuring certainties of the passing age of faith, Wicks Cherrycoke enters the narrative a fearful pilgrim as much in space—a Britisher adrift in America, homeless and rootless—as in time: aware of mortality, fearful of lapsing time. He searches for the consolations of faith, for its benediction of purpose, for its viability as antidote to his own finitude, and for its sense of the immediate environment as the profound gesture of creation rather than as either the bottomless resource bin so typical of the New World entrepreneurs or the elaborate math problem so typical of the Royal Academy that sponsors each of Mason and Dixon's enterprises. Cherrycoke is a tragic casualty, an inconvenience lost between great ages, searching for a workable deity, needing to verify, to touch the Christological experience, certain of its import but unavailable to its immediacy.

I

> I set sail . . . in the hope that Eastward yet might dwell some-
> thing of Peace and Godhead, which British Civilization, in
> venturing Westward, had left behind.
>   —Wicks Cherrycoke

As a young man in England, Wicks Cherrycoke is imprisoned for posting anonymous broadsides identifying those responsible for committing harsh (if legal) acts against the unempowered: foreclosures and evictions and seizures of property. It is a righteous stand, a defiance of the Christian world as it (mis)operates, an insistence of the vast difference between moral responsibility and legal right. Imprisoned "among the Rats and Vermin," Wicks Cherrycoke is seized by a blinding moment of illumination in which he understands that his self is a curiously immaterial entity, his name an awkward irrelevancy, and that he is in fact part of an embracing All, an epiphany, accompanied by strange lights and "Voices indecipherable," that he characterizes to his Philadelphia family years later as "one of those moments Hindoos and Chinamen are ever said to be having" (10).

It is a moment for which his jailers, not surprisingly, label Cherrycoke insane—they compel him either to sign on to a sea voyage for treatment or face commitment to Bedlam. Cherrycoke intuitively hungers to voyage to India but finds himself over the next several months—and, indeed, for the rest of his life—frustrated in his attempts to get to that "fearful and inexhaustible" East (86). But, in that prison moment, Cherrycoke, a minister shaken by the stark evidence of the failure of the Christian system, intuitively touches—but quickly (dis)misses—a (re)solution that rests not in the West but in that very inexhaustible and mysterious East that will elude Cherrycoke for the rest of his life.

That moment in jail aligns Wicks Cherrycoke with a complex tradition that assumes significant dimension within *Mason & Dixon*. That moment of unasked for, unanticipated revelation, more intuitive than intellectual, parallels in its argument and its intensity the Eastern tradition of the satori, the glimpse, the awakening—often at the darkest moment of pain and isolation— that reveals the absurd construction of the ego as untenable abstraction and the uplifting release of perceiving the wider embracing unity of a cosmos that is not some problematic gift crafted by a meddling, capricious deity or some vast, efficient machine bound by a system of laws but rather is an ever-growing organic entity, ceaselessly (incomprehensibly) moving with a luminescent logic of its own. Imprisoned for the crime of "Anonymity"—such a "crime" befits the Western tradition of hyper-egocentricity—Wicks Cherrycoke stumbles in a moment of awkward clarity onto the very path around the gridlock that Pynchon has long tested between the lingering pull of Christian mysticism and the push of contemporary science.[4]

Throughout Cherrycoke's narrative, characters will touch on the Eastern (re)solution—a freewheeling hybrid of Hinduism, Zen Buddhism, African tribalism, Native American primitivism, ancient Druidism, Quaker quietism, and the Taoist practice of Feng Shui—but the disciplined purity and deep conviction of such a resolution is dismissed as foolishly insane, dangerously simplistic, or blatantly heretical. Pynchon, then, offers in *Mason & Dixon* an antiparable in which the (re)solution is repeatedly dismissed; within the freewheeling paradox of Eastern thought, it is the solution that is both present and absent, like the koan posed by the mysterious stranger in the slouch hat who accosts Mason at the New York docks as the astonomer prepares to depart America after the surveying expedition. In a voice between "Mockery and Teasing," the gentleman, face obscured by the hat, asks Mason to which Falmouth he journeys and then suggests with pitched mystery that there is a "Falmouth invisible" (705), which, like the center of a circle, cannot be seen but can nevertheless be found with compass and ruler. With that, the stranger sidles off. That Falmouth invisible is akin to the novel's Eastern (re)solution—the resolution that is both in the narrative and yet absent, the calm center that the reader cannot find within any of the characters but can nevertheless locate.

Thus, Cherrycoke gives to his slumbering family (and to us) the narrative of the spiritual struggles of Charles Mason, a man who hungers for the transcendent experience long held to be the privilege of the Christian soul, a man who struggles by life's end (or at least within the life's end as cast by this narrator) to make his peace with the exotic wisdom that Cherrycoke himself cannot. Charles Mason, appropriately, begins a man torn. Professionally committed to decoding the very heavens and measuring the vast plane of the immediate into a reliable system of gridlines yet devastated by the death of his young wife, Mason pursues any evidence of an afterlife and the paranormal, seeking reassurance that the scientific reach is not our limit. He is haunted, like Cherrycoke,

by the dark intrusion of mortality. Like Cherrycoke, Mason is
alienated from his family, estranged from his father and from
his sons. And Mason is as well a man prone, as we shall see, to
unasked-for moments of clarifying—distinctly Eastern—wisdom, the implications of which he long discounts.

But to be misunderstood by the narrow Western mind is surely
no surprise. The Eastern solution is so fundamentally opposed to
Western assumptions that outright rejection or deep suspicion
or shallow derision have always been our safest, quickest responses. Consider its radical pre-Christian agenda that denies
validity to the cumbersome Western cataloging systems of time
and space; that denies value to the ego construction; that de-
mands tuning into the planet as a living organism that moves by
the sweet aimlessness of its own direction; that rejects the rituals
and doctrines of institutional religion; that denies the validity of
Cartesian opposition and insists that dualities from the simple
(up and down) to the complex (good and evil) to the metaphysical (life and death) are cooperative, not tensive; that asserts
enigmatically that the mental capacities must be challenged and
then voided in order, paradoxically, to reveal their true strength;
that restructures the cosmic "void" into a vast force-field, an
open-ended creative and pulsating energy webbing that finds its
most developed American expression in the most luminous moments of the Transcendentalists.

Although tying a narrative presence to its creator or speculating on the inclinations of a writer as (r)e(c)lusive as Pynchon is
surely reckless, much has been written about the fascination of
Pynchon's generation for the pull of Eastern mysticism.[5] His generation of disaffected, college-educated, middle-class white America turned in significant numbers amid the narcoleptic Eisenhower era and throughout the height of the counterculture to the
challenge of Eastern mysticism, fascinated by the possibilities of
interior exploration and disciplined detachment, frustrated over
the collapsing vision of the West—the erosion of community, the
destruction of our ecology, the heavy press of authority, the loss
of authentic experience and feeling, the worship of money, the
crass need for the ego, the thinning of Western religions into
empty codes of social conduct, and the brutalities promised by the
death-soaked rhetoric of the Cold War—and uninterested in the
social activism that characterized that generation's more public
and vocal response to such dissatisfactions (a stance suggested
by Cherrycoke's posting of handbills). Wicks Cherrycoke, then, is

a trained minister with the soul of a hippie, a Job in tie-dye, a man estranged from his own spiritual inclinations that pull him Eastward—a man deeply divided, as it were—who tells the only story he can: a story of lines and boundaries, real and imagined, that restrict, enclose, and ultimately strangle.

To understand the anxieties that motivate Cherrycoke's night-long recitation, consider his audience—the LeSpark clan, representatives of a generation Cherrycoke surely fears is already lost, a generation strikingly similar to the Eisenhower fifties that shaped Pynchon's counterculture sensibility: deeply materialistic, emotionally bankrupt, profoundly cynical, hypereducated, thoroughly mercenary and worldly, disturbingly joyless, spiritually dead.

During the long winter evening, we meet the young twins, munching cookies while demanding from their uncle lurid stories of frontier barbarism with touches of French women; three wealthy brothers-in-law—an arms dealer who admits to the pragmatism of selling to any side of a conflict, a lawyer with fanatical faith in the bloodsport of litigation, and a soap merchant who happily produces a vile product that degrades quickly into a viscous slime that actually leaves surfaces dirtier; a nephew, DePugh, enthralled as a college student by the aridity of numbers and by the mock-spiritualism of the Continental craze of mesmerism; another, the young woman Tenebrae, who mechanically embroiders for the long winter's evening, a beautiful form devoid of heart, a soulless artisan; and Ethelmer, educated just enough to reject with cynical insouciance the entire Christian edifice, a moral reptile who eyes the developed "nubility" (103) of Tenebrae with unpleasant randiness, who admits to paying a dollar on Saturday nights to laugh at the lunatics in a neighborhood asylum, and who eventually steals away from the didactic night-long narrative of his earnest uncle to read *The Ghastly Fop*, a sort of erotic comic book—a fact acknowledged by his uncle who goes so far as to introduce its characters into his own narrative. This clan evidences an era—indeed, a culture—in massive moral descent, whose deterioration, we are told during a lively discussion of contemporary musical tastes, is suggested by a young nation that will take as its national anthem a ribald British drinking song, whose bold chords Ethelmer plays on the family piano. Much as the narrative commences at dusk, at a time of diminishing illumination, to move into this clan is to descend into a disturbing darkness, suggested by their names: from Wicks (a steady if fragile illumination) to the LeSparks (the brief compensations of a moment's gaudy flashiness) to the young niece, Tenebrae (a gloomy, heavy darkness).

II

"I've ascended, descended, even condescended, but the List's not ended,—but haven't yet *trans*-cended a blessèd thing, thankee."

—Charles Mason

But what has fashioned such a generation?

Although it may sound incongruous, Cherrycoke's narrative finds the fanatical authoritarianism of high medieval Christianity and the radical curiosity of Newton's Grand Enlightenment sharing more than they oppose—and mutually responsible for the devolution of Western culture. Christianity and Enlightenment science resist the Eastern notion that we are placed "in" nature; rather both assume we are surrounded by brute fact, a grand, if hostile environment of inert matter. We are, thus, compelled by our vulnerabilities to assert domination, control over its sheer presence. In both traditions, we struggle with—not in—nature.

In the drama of Christian morality, we struggle against our base nature, the temptations to accept as sufficient the material, the immediate, the carnal—temptations often tested within Cherrycoke's narratives of many-corridored seraglios, groaning dinner boards, free-flowing libations, readily available hallucinogens, and ripping bodices. Cherrycoke inherits a drifting Christian system cautious of mystery and diminishing into metaphor, suggested by his ruminations over the doctrinal debate between the ancient notion of transubstantiation and the more contemporary, more conservative theory of consubstantiation. His generation of Christians carelessly borrows the sacred, subtle imagery of transubstantiation to expound on matters secular: as convenient metaphor to explain the colonies' right to representation in Parliament or to describe the architecture of the imported cuisine novelty, the sandwich. Like the Society of Jesus, which pursues a shadowy chase of the surveying expedition, Christianity has devolved from its transcendent premise into the cold simplification of authority and blind allegiance, into spiritless rituals and convoluted dogma, and into the joyless overlay of an afterlife posited by the melodrama of punishment and reward. Cherrycoke's abiding anxieties over the obsolescence of the Lamb of God, sacrificed yet triumphant, finds expression in two of Mason's experiences—presumably invented by Cherrycoke—that each centers on disquieting encounters with lamb carcasses: one, Mason's recollection of a queasy youth spent amid the greasy stench of oven-baking sheep, of "Mutton-fat vaporiz'd and recondens'd, again and again, working its way insidiously . . . into all walls" (86); the other, a more disturbing moment aboard ship when, bothered by a thudding as he tries to sleep, Mason ends up locked in the hold, which contains dozens of free-swinging lamb carcasses, stripped and skinned, meat later tossed overboard during a dockside riot, the slaughtered Lamb (Cherrycoke pointedly reveals) wasted.

But Cherrycoke stands as well on the very cusp of the glamorous age of science, which, for all its fanatical connection to the natural realm, exercises here only a mercenary possessiveness and aggressive curiosity that despoils the very natural world it explores. Like Christianity, Enlightenment science suffers from a loss of its transcendent premise. After all, the urge to take control of the Earth's abundance, that sense of responsible stewardship commanded by the Creator-God in Genesis, diminished into the compelling urgency of Newton's minions to map the world—the surrounding "it"—into subjection, to decode its abundant mysteries, to dis-enchant it by finding within its wheeling energies the discipline of laws and by impressing upon it the dubiously reassuring cross-stitchings of boundary lines and longitude and latitude until its exhilarating vastness is enclosed within the mesh of fine lines like some great animal caught within a flimsy scrimp of netting. Too fond of analysis, too suspicious of mystery, too enamored by the methodical process of explicating deep telluric forces, we commit our considerable energies to the (futile) business of mastering the horizontal plane.

It is thus from our vulnerabilities that we fashion the great passion play of Christ and that we encumber the skies with heaven; and it is from those same vulnerabilities that we inscribe the great grids of latitude and longitude and that we record the intricate measurements of days and weeks so central to Cherrycoke's narrative.[6] Within the sciences—as within Christianity—the cosmos is simplified into a battlefield, hostilities inevitable as long as we are held to be separate from nature and as long as we resolve to dominate and direct. Cherrycoke's narrative teems with those compelled by such raw, aggressive need. There are the cool professionals: Nevil Maskelyne, who joylessly pores over the mind-numbing labor of nightly observations; the curious: Dr. Franklin, a shabby magician whose clunking battery apparatus pales next to the stunning bolt of lightning from a passing thunderstorm; the exploitative: Lord Lepton, who manages, Kurtz-like, an iron mine in the heart of the Pennsylvania wilderness and who runs there a darkly forbidding pleasure dome; and the tinkerers: like Jacques de Vaucanson who, in ill-advised experiments into building a robot duck, unleashes, like Dr. Frankenstein, a monstrous mechanical fowl endowed with a sufficient degree of animal drives to understand its loneliness.

Nevertheless, Cherrycoke's America rests smugly certain that nature is a domesticated force—a darkling premise long shared by Pynchon. Even before Cherrycoke assumes narrative control, we are given the terraced architecture of the novel's opening sentences with their disturbing images of nature leashed: snowballs and sleds that make play of winter's fury; warm kitchens and stoked hearths that diminish winter's impact, suggested by the drifts outside that bury Philadelphia and by the ice fog that cottons the night sky; a house cat that mock-stalks beneath the furniture; huge stewing pots that teem with produce and stock; serving trays that are loaded with split fruits and sugary treats; and the furnishings themselves that are so elaborately carved— each evidence a nature domesticated and a humanity insulated and relishing its technology of control.

Indeed, the natural world subjected to such enslavement forms a critical element of Cherrycoke's narrative. The injunction Cherrycoke lodges against the open pornography of human enslavement in South Africa and in colonial America finds a most disturbing parallel in the great line Mason and Dixon chain across the American wilderness; in the systematic exploitation of the natural resources as conducted by those such as Lord Lepton (whose name suggests the atomic particle that fails to maintain a sufficient interaction in the field of freewheeling particle collisions and remains unbonded); in the abuse of natural resources from caffeine to marijuana, sugar to opium, by characters within the narrative. Even George Washington, whom Mason and Dixon meet during a Southern detour invented by Cherrycoke, is compelled by no loftier vision than the relentless appetite for wilderness. He dismisses as anarchy its deep organizing structures, its ecological soundness, as well as the civilizations of Native Amer-

icans that it had nurtured for centuries. But such rapacious development, the much-vaunted and very American pursuit of hap-
piness (the very phrase Dixon will give to Jefferson at a Williamsburg tavern), guarantees only that the New World will be cut with
property lines, its resources stripped and channeled into private
enterprises. America, Cherrycoke prophecies, will be measured
into simplicity. Thus, despite such apparent mastery (recall Cherrycoke working the creaking mechanism of the LeSpark orrery as
he explains, from the mock-omnipotent posture of a mock-deity,
the mechanics of the transit of Venus), we cannot find comfort in
our gaudy new sciences anymore than in our ancient religion.

III

> Being and non-being produce each other;
> Difficult and easy complete each other;
> High and low distinguish each other;
> Sound and voice harmonize each other;
> Front and behind accompany each other.
>   —Tao-te Ching

For his bored audience of slumbering auditors, each a sorry ex-
emplum of Western excess, Wicks Cherrycoke (re)fashions from
the historic figure of Charles Mason a parable of gradual enlightenment, of movement by the closing moments of his life to a distinctly Eastern resolution, the very solution Cherrycoke himself
long resists, one that centers on two notions: a re-enchantment
of the Earth as an animated creature and an overthrow of intellection, specifically the analytical system of oppositional logic
that has centered Western thought since Descartes, indeed since
Genesis.

Clearly, in the story of Charles Mason, Cherrycoke revels in the
sheer appeal of virid wilderness, the striking effect of an inchoate
nation still "meadow'd to the Horizon" (7). But appeal, of course,
is not sufficient. Unlike Western thought that assumes domination as imperative and the aesthetic pleasure over open land as
invitation to exploit (Dixon is crippled by a fear of unenclosed
space), the Eastern vision sees the Earth as a living entity, the
water, the mountains, the wilderness—and humanity itself—
aflow with a shared, potent animation. Characters do offer awe-
struck asides over apprehending this living earth—but, because
we are in the hands of a narrator finally uncertain over his own

inclination to the Eastern solution, it is never wisdom wholly accessible.

For instance, during his interment on the blasted isolation of St. Helena, Nevil Maskelyne comes to see the earth as a living, if slumbering, dragon, a notion that he attempts to explain to Mason, who quickly dismisses it as insanity. The epiphanic revelation does little for Maskelyne. Too deeply influenced by the Christian (melo)drama of Eden, Maskelyne cannot accept our place within such a vast webbing but rather dismisses humanity as little more than lice. And then there is the ghost of Rebekah who repeatedly counsels Mason to sink his affections deeply into the horizontal plane—ironic advice, of course, coming from a manifestation of the paranormal plane. And there is the considerable eloquence of Zhang, the refugee from *The Ghastly Fop* whom Cherrycoke interjects into his evening's narration. On the run from Jesuit fanatics, Zhang forcefully exhorts the surveying expedition about the living earth so deeply violated by their ugly vista. But Zhang cannot find his way to the detachment and serenity such wisdom premises within the Eastern tradition. Indeed, he finds far more immediate the threat of the Jesuits and ultimately turns into a running paranoid who simplifies the living wilderness into a contested geography. Pointedly, the expedition eventually is unable to distinguish Zhang physically from his Jesuit persecutor. We are left, then, with little to hope. Those most profoundly moved by the natural webbing of the wilderness—the Native Americans—are simplified into savages or shunted into irrelevancy, and Cherrycoke, a scant twenty years later, ruminates on a wilderness so completely lost.

Furthermore, Cherrycoke's narrative troubles the viability of oppositional logic and offers within the complex partnership of Mason and Dixon the decidedly Eastern notion that opposites generate each other within a larger field of endless flux; that apparent opposites are in fact complementary, dependent, and interactive; that polarity is only a convenient construction of the overreaching analytical mind. It is, perhaps, the critical cautionary point of Cherrycoke's night-long sermon that for the American experiment to succeed requires the Eastern sense of balance—a posture that is, ultimately, (in)accessible. Cherrycoke develops Mason and Dixon as the paradigmatic yin and yang: from religion to politics, from taste in food and women to their education and temperament, Mason and Dixon—as astronomer and surveyor representing the heavens and the earth—are polar opposites. And yet, as Cherrycoke offers in one of his more Eastern moments, when apart the twosome stumble, often get lost, perform inefficiently; together, they work efficiently, smoothly. It is that balance of oppositions that attracts Cherrycoke. When Cherrycoke closes the narrative of the American expedition, he invents a wild scenario had Mason and Dixon not abided the interdiction of the Native Americans some two hundred miles into the Pennsylvania wilderness. In it, Mason and Dixon retire to a coral island in the *middle* of the ocean, to live out their days tuned to flux and the "Ubiquity of Flow" (713)—a most Eastern posture of balance and interplay that is here, of course, a pronounced fantasy. Cherrycoke tries in the bluntest sort of way to bring their energies together. He conjectures Mason's deeper attachment to Dixon (a "passion . . . comparable to that occurring between Public School Students in England" [697]), a shocking joining that he knows Mason cannot, dare not act upon. Such interdiction only underscores how impossible is the yin-yang balance within the Western framework.

And yet balance alone succeeds—like the flowered wallpaper pattern one character contemplates that achieves a dimensional depth only when, under his gaze, the individual blossoms appear to divide and then slide into other blossoms. On St. Helena, Mason must perform identical observations from opposite sides of the island—one settled and crossed by narrow alleys and bustling markets, the other wild, open to the forbidding elements of wind and surf—and then balance them to arrive at error-free data. In the astronomical phenomena that Mason and Dixon track, the Transit of Venus, a heavenly object that is a mere point of light in the nighttime skies is exposed briefly against the clarifying backdrop of the sun to be a heavy, dense planet. In that terrible, exhilarating moment, Venus is revealed to be both light and matter. Cherrycoke understands that resolution cannot be found in the traditional logic of oppositions. Even the most significant of such oppositions—is and was, life and death—is routinely undermined by his narrative's residue of persistent paranormal ghosties and by the lurid evidence of the public hangings that both Mason and Cherrycoke attend in which those men dangling reveal prominent erections.

Balance, then, is the lesson Minister Cherrycoke wants to reveal by fashioning his Charles Mason. In his nightlong narrative,

Cherrycoke, like Mason asquint at his telescope, charts nocturnal illuminations of his own: those signal moments of Mason's satoris, each a gesture toward his life's closing epiphany and each, we presume, an invention of Wicks Cherrycoke. Mason's narrative is regularly blasted by strikingly intrusive moments of clarifying vision at right angles with Western thought. Early on, Mason, observing the skies for a comet shortly after the death of his wife, hears the plaintive cry of an owl and understands in a strikingly Zen-like moment that the sound is not an owl at all but rather the sound of mortality itself seeking expression through the instrument of the owl. Then, after a tumble from a horse, Mason hears a voice caution him against trusting too deeply in the resources of reason. Later, staring into the sudden brightness that sparks from the discharge of an entanked electric eel, Mason reels from the stunning perception "in the heart of the Electrick Fire" of a space beyond color, shape, "an Aperture into another Dispensation of Space, yea and Time, than what Astronomers and Surveyors are us'd to working with" (433). Much later, long after the American expedition, Mason surveys an evening sky and suddenly understands that the sky he has mapped for most of his life is little more than a two-dimensional dome. With electrifying force, the sky expands into a third dimension, a radical optical readjustment that convinces Mason that he begins only that night to understand the nature of sky, a moment that turns him, so late in life, away from the hard sciences entirely.

Mason's satoris are (as he explains to a doubting Dixon) unsummoned and unwanted. They are experiences that call on Mason to acknowledge a cosmic vastness unreachable by his zenith sector, to understand the limits of intellection itself, to reject notions of time and space as entrapments and artificial constructions, to participate in a dynamic and vital void and to accept its pulsing mystery—to acknowledge a world, in short, best described by the Eastern tradition. But, under Cherrycoke's narration, Mason long resists, too pulled by the persistent love of a dead wife, too empowered by his own technology, too convinced of the brutal intrusion of death, too enamored by the possibility premised by Christian notions of bodily resurrection (a doctrine that ironically Cherrycoke expounds while bent over having a mighty bowel movement in the forest). When Dixon advises him to relinquish his obsession with Rebekah, the melancholic Mason snaps (ironically) that he cannot live like "some Hindoo" in the "eternal Present" (166).

IV

To turn Eastward, is somehow to resist time and age,
to work against the Wind, seek ever the dawn, even
. . . defy Death.
                                        —Wicks Cherrycoke

How, then, will Cherrycoke teach the Eastern solution? If his invention Mason moves via the compelling urgency of inexplicable visionary moments, Cherrycoke's drifting audience needs considerably more prompting. What will be Cherrycoke's instrument of instruction?

Consider those dozens of intrusive narrative moments of pure invention. Dixon's teacher gives him a perpetual-motion watch that morphs mysteriously into a ticking vegetable, which one of the surveyors consumes hoping to secure immortality for at least part of himself, only to find the ticking a constant irritation until his son reaches down his throat to pull out the device, only to find it has grown teeth and violently resists such extraction. Or Zepho Beck who, under a full moon, transforms into a six-foot beaver with an enormous capacity for tree-gnawing. Or the valley of giant vegetables, with beets cut with entranceways like some vast mine. Or the darkling vortex in which Mason spends the eleven days dropped from the English calendar in 1752, days he spends wandering about a desolate landscape fraught by malevolent flying shapes. Or the monstrous worm that surrounds an English castle and devours any who challenge him but who is finally destroyed by a brave lord who makes a bargain with God to ensure victory, a deal that ironically compels him to choose between killing his own father or incurring the wrath of the bookkeeper-God. Or the journey into the frozen wastes of Norway to a great cave where Dixon descends into the Inner Earth and finds a race of philosopher-scientists who fear that when the earth is finally measured their kingdom will disappear. Or the two great clocks that admit, in animated conversation, that despite being transported across open ocean and feeling a deep attraction for its rolling pulse, neither knows exactly what "ocean" means.

Such narrative asides—and these are a mere sampling—are clearly fabrications that manipulate most baldly supernatural phenomena. They turn Cherrycoke far afield from what Mason labels him: his amanuensis. So twisted and absurd, such intrusive tales are to provoke thought in an audience Cherrycoke can see drifting away from him as the long night passes. It is an instructional tradition, not surprisingly, that reflects Cherrycoke's Eastern inclinations, specifically that most traditional Eastern narrative exercise known as the koan, a brief narrative that is less a story and more an open-ended riddle, a contradictory and often paradoxical situation that offers the willing and flexible mind an occasion for meditation and that allows the mind the opportunity to push past its limited power and to tap into a more intuitive response. Those koans mentioned above surely direct us to reconsider—but not resolve—paradoxes central to Cherrycoke's arching spiritual vision: time and its (im)potence; the role of the intellect and our (ir)resistible urge for the fleshly; the (un)winnable contest between the animal and the intellect; scientists' (ir)reverence for the earth they despoil; God's tormenting of the very creations he treasures. Unlike satire, so often as unambiguous as a lightswitch, koans frustrate the normative urge for neat closure and resist explication; and unlike the "joaks," often quite lame, that characters tell within Cherrycoke's narrative, koans are not occasions for comic relief but rather are posed as crises in intellection, as perplexing realities, contradictory and (ir)resolvable.

Indeed, paradoxes typical of koan-ish wisdom haunt Cherrycoke's rendering of the Mason and Dixon experience: the great boundary line itself means nothing and yet means everything, ugly and visible and yet potently abstract, both vista and symbol; the slaves in colonial America are everywhere (in)visible, the obscenity of the institution (un)acknowledged to the point that Cherrycoke, on Dixon's sidetrip southward, comments, "In all Virginia, tho' Slaves pass'd before his Sight, he saw none" (398); the gift of a New World itself is acknowledged as nothing less than a paradise by its legion of despoilers whose fervid push West methodically destroys the very paradise they hymn, a New World lost even as it is discovered. To explore each assertion is to challenge the intellect to abandon the effort to square it logically and only then to be flooded by the intuited perception of the validity of such (ir)resolvable paradoxes.

Cherrycoke, finally, maneuvers Mason toward a paradoxical position that is decidedly Eastern. When Mason returns to England, he first rejects the Royal Society, the learned assemblage that represents the science that pillages the earth for its secrets without reverence: he turns down an assignment to measure the magnetic pull of a Scottish mountain. And then, on assignment

in Ireland to measure yet another Transit of Venus, Mason performs rather an ancient ritual of dowsing and finds an underground well of the sweetest water. It is then that he is bowled over
by the satori in which he sees the stars overhead not as a map-
pable dome but rather as a living three-dimensional field of vast
energies. Relinquishing finally his morbid preoccupation with the
dead Rebekah, he remarries. Gazing into a mirror, he conceives
of a sense of Being given to the complexities of both sin and honor,
a marvelously contradictory yin/yang construction that is not only
of the intellect but decidedly blood-scented.

He then dreams of strange glyphs carved on the sides of massive rocks—signs he cannot decode, imposing a limit on his vast
intelligence. And as he prepares to die, he signals the reward of a
lifetime probing the difficult mathematics of astronomy that have
so disenchanted the night sky: he whispers to his young wife, "it
turn'd out to be simple after all" (772). Mason thus embraces a
cosmos so simple, so apparent, that it can never be understood.
He has moved to the Eastern (re)solution. But (within the framework of the controlling narrator) it is, of course, wisdom wasted
on his audience. The hovering Dr. Franklin encourages the dying
Mason to accept status as an adopted American, yet another tired
validation of boundaries. Mason's new wife wants only to comfort
him by blandly reassuring him, as she prays, that he is "safe"
(although he demonstrates an acceptance of a radical vision that
renders him anything but safe within the Christian tradition she
urges). And his sons promise only to pursue the mercenary rewards of life in America, to domesticate the magic of the "savages"
and to enjoy the bountiful fishing, both disturbing suggestions of
the same sort of menacing urge to control the primitive that so
dooms the American experiment. Mason's, then, is a koan delivered, like Cherrycoke's narrative, to an (in)attentive audience.

And so what we hear in *Mason & Dixon* is the sound of one man
mapping, Wicks Cherrycoke outlining, largely to himself, in a most
subtle and maddeningly indirect method, the Eastern solution
that has remained for him—like India itself—(in)accessible. It is
a resolution that, like the natural world as Mason finds it, is so
simple and yet so mysterious. And, in the end, Wicks Cherrycoke
prepares to depart in the company of the (r)e(c)lusive poet, Timothy Tox, a fanatic and visionary figure who finds fit company in
the dark religiosity of Cherrycoke, a renegade parson who cannot finally convince himself or his nodding audience of the validity of what his own beleaguered soul so stunningly intuited.

In a narrative crossed by bold yet invisible lines none runs finally as deep as the line that separates the narrator from the narrated, between Cherrycoke and narrative resolution itself, between Cherrycoke and the very answer he glimpsed in that prison cell long ago. In the Eastern tradition, the narrative of (Charles Mason's) salvation is as well the narrative of (Cherrycoke's) salvation denied. Of course, Pynchon, that "old hippie,"[7] understands the dark futility of Cherrycoke's intuited solution. Writing in the quietus of the twentieth century, Pynchon understands just how far the American experiment will fail to embrace the difficult vision of the Eastern mindset, the solution that, like the Falmouth invisible, is even today at once demonstrably everywhere and yet, sadly, nowhere.

NOTES

1. One of Cherrycoke's "descendants," Roger Cherrycoke, a psychic and spiritual medium, is on the staff of the White Visitation in *Gravity's Rainbow*. Surely, Wicks Cherrycoke, well on his way to reluctantly abandoning his religion but valiantly resisting relinquishing the spiritual dimension, prefigures this character with his unsettling power to summon visions of the Other World.

2. John A. McClure's assessment ("Postmodern/Post-Secular: Contemporary Fiction and Spirituality," *Modern Fiction Studies* 41 [1995]), that Pynchon is the most "exciting religious novelist of our time" (153), is echoed in a number of standard approaches to Pynchon's fondness for characters who quest for the transcendent realm. See, for instance, Dwight Eddins, *The Gnostic Pynchon* (Bloomington: Indiana University Press, 1990); Molly Hite, *Ideas of Order in the Novels of Thomas Pynchon* (Columbus: Ohio State University Press, 1983); Tom LeClair, *The Art of Excess: Mastery in Contemporary American Fiction* (Urbana: University of Illinois Press, 1988); John O. Stark, *Pynchon's Fictions: Thomas Pynchon and the Literature of Information* (Athens: Ohio University Press, 1980); Robert A. Hipkiss, *The American Absurd: Pynchon, Vonnegut and Barth* (Port Washington, NY: Associated Faculty Press, 1984); Thomas H. Schaub, *Pynchon: The Voice of Ambiguity* (Urbana: University of Illinois Press, 1981); Victoria Price, *Christian Allusions in the Novels of Thomas Pynchon* (New York: Lang, 1989); and Elaine B. Safer, *The Contemporary American Comic Epic: The Novels of Barth, Pynchon, Gaddis, and Kesey* (Detroit: Wayne State University Press, 1988). To varying degrees, each study centers Pynchon's fictions on the tension between the search for transcendence with its luminous logic of meaning and its apparently inevitable frustration. None directly explores the Eastern solution, although David Porusch ("'Purring into Transcendence': Pynchon's Puncutron Machine," in *The Vineland Papers,* ed. Geoffrey Green, Donald J. Greiner, and Larry McCaffery [Normal, IL: Dalkey Archive Press, 1994], 31–45) explores the dimensions of the karmic metaphors in *Vineland* and McClure cites the powerful pull of animism, transcendentalism, and Native American spiritualism in the same work. T. Coraghessan Boyle ("The Great Divide," review of *Mason & Dixon, New York Times Book Review,* 18 May 1997, 9) touches on this need in *Mason & Dixon* but scarely mentions Cherrycoke.

3. Thomas Pynchon, *Mason & Dixon* (New York: Henry Holt, 1997), 8. Further references will be noted parenthetically within the text.

4. Although specific anatomy of Eastern religions is beyond the scope of this essay, the definition followed here has been culled from a number of standard definitions of Eastern religions, most helpfully the work of Harvy Cox, *Turning East: The Promise and Peril of the New Orientalism* (New York: Simon & Schuster, 1977); Alan Watts, *The Way of Zen* (New York: Vintage, 1957; rpt., New York: New American Library, 1959); D. T. Suzuki, "The Meaning of Zen Buddhism," in *Selected Writings on Zen Buddhism,* ed. William Barrett (New York: Doubleday-Anchor, 1956), 3–27; Thomas Cleary, ed. and trans., *The Essential Tao: An Initiation into the Heart of Taoism* (San Francisco: HarperSanFrancisco, 1991); and Sarah Rossbach's *Feng-Shui: The Chinese Art of Placement* (New York: Dutton, 1983). Fritjof Capra's fascinating *The Tao of Physics: An Exploration of the Parallels between Modern Physics and Eastern Mysticism* (Boulder: Shambhala, 1975; rpt., New York: Bantam, 1977) probes ways in which the argument of contemporary quantum physics has come to approximate the ancient principles of Eastern mysticism, a provocative thesis if applied to Pynchon, himself a student of that very body of contemporary scientific thought.

5. Watts, Barrett (in his introduction to Suzuki's *Selected Writings on Zen Buddhism*), Capra, and Cox all make the same case for the interest of the counterculture in orientalism. Pynchon's deep ties to the counterculture have been suggested by Eddins and LeClair, who both see in Pynchon a variant of the counterculture's return to Nature; by Louis Menard ("Entropology," review of *Mason & Dixon, New York Review of Books,* 12 June 1997, 22–25) and Anthony Lane ("Then, Voyager," review of *Mason & Dixon, The New Yorker,* 21 July 1997, 97–100), who both acknowledge the Beat influence but do not cite any of the Eastern references in *Mason & Dixon;* in Porusch, McClure, and Deborah Madsen (*The Postmodernist Allegories of Thomas Pynchon* [New York: St. Martin's, 1991]) in their explorations of Pynchon's treatment of the lost hippie culture in *Vineland;* and by Pynchon himself who, in his chatty introduction to *Slow Learner* (Boston: Little, Brown, 1984), details the influence of the Beats on his early thought.

6. Cherrycoke dismisses the flimsy constructions of timekeeping through several narrative asides on the 1752 calendar reformation in which England simply dropped eleven days. The gap haunts Cherrycoke and Mason's generation because of its obsession with the limited realm of the immediate. Interestingly, when Mason, in a moment of barroom loquacity, directly addresses the working-class indignation over the lost days, he reassures a drunken gathering that the British government had, in fact, colonized the eleven days, that they hadn't been lost at all. Mason recounts a wild tale of the British enlisting a tribe of "Asiatick Pygmies" (196) who did not reckon time as the British and, in fact, had no fear of time. Again, the Eastern (re)solution is posed but only as a barroom fantasy.

7. Lane, "Then, Voyager," 100.

Reading at the "Crease of Credulity"

Bernard Duyfhuizen

> ... a sinister and wonderful Card Table which exhibits the
> cheaper Wavelike Grain known in the Trade as Wand'ring
> Heart, causing an illusion of Depth into which for years chil-
> dren have gaz'd as into the illustrated Pages of Books ... along
> with so many hinges, sliding Mortises, hidden catches, and se-
> cret compartments that neither the Twins nor their Sister can
> say they have been to the end of it.
> —Thomas Pynchon, *Mason & Dixon*

In conjunction with the release of the paperback edition of
Thomas Pynchon's *Mason & Dixon,*[1] Henry Holt, the novel's publisher, posted on its Web site a "Reading Group Guide" to the
novel. Among the suggested points for prospective book clubs to
discuss are two focusing on the transmission of the narrative in
Mason & Dixon:

- The events of the novel are narrated by the Reverend Wicks Cherrycoke, who tells the story of Mason and Dixon after dinner for the
  entertainment of his family. How does he gain access to the details
  of the events? How does he fill in the gaps of events he doesn't actually witness? Do his perspective and morality color the narrative?
  Is he reliable? Does the fact that he is trying to entertain a youthful audience account for the appearance of talking dogs, conversing
  clocks, and mechanical ducks?
- There are actually two narratives taking place simultaneously in
  Mason & Dixon: the story of Mason and Dixon and the framing
  narrative, set in the LeSparks' living room many years later, as the
  Reverend Cherrycoke tells his tale. How does the framing narrative
  serve the novel? How do the discussions, comments, and arguments
  by the framing characters affect the relation of the narrative? What
  undercurrents of tension can you identify in the framing narrative?
  How do they affect the "storytelling"?[2]

When I originally proposed this essay for this collection, many of
the same questions were going through my mind. In what follows, I'll endeavor to answer some of the questions posed, to pose

some new ones, and to suggest some larger implications of the narrative of transmission operating in *Mason & Dixon.*

First off, although it is his most extended use of a framing narrative, *Mason & Dixon* is not the first time Pynchon has used framing techniques. In *V.,* for instance, the "historical chapters," most of which Herbert Stencil orally narrates, inset a series of anecdotes about the lady V. within the base narrative set in 1956. In particular, chapter 3, in which narrative perspective shifts across seven characters and a camera-eye, and chapter 9, the retelling of Kurt Mondaugen's experiences in Southwest Africa, demonstrate Pynchon's use of framing techniques to destabilize the direct transmission of events in any form other than that of a mediated narrative representation.[3] As Steven Weisenburger has aptly shown, episode 14 of *Gravity's Rainbow* presents the reader with a complex set of framed perspectives that take the reader into the nightmare of Katje Borgesius's experiences at Captain Blicero's V-2 launch site, and then deeper into the nightmare of Franz van der Groov's extermination of the Dodoes.[4] And more recently in *Vineland,* Pynchon combines oral narration with the technologies of film, video, and databank production to provide Prairie Wheeler with a record of her mother's past life.[5]

It can also be safely assumed that Pynchon is more than casually aware of some of the classic frame narratives in the English tradition. Allusions to and echoes from Joseph Conrad's *Heart of Darkness* can be found in various places in Pynchon's writing. Moreover, in his essay "Is It O.K. to Be a Luddite?" he substantively cites the framing technique used in Mary Shelley's *Frankenstein* and in Horace Walpole's *The Castle of Otranto.*[6] The concern of *Mason & Dixon* with issues of the Gothic, the Frankensteinlike creation of Vaucanson's mechanickal Duck, and, as David Cowart has argued, the novel's general Luddite sensibility indicate the relation of Pynchon's 1984 essay to the composition of *Mason & Dixon.*[7] One might also imagine that Pynchon's interest in ghosts and communication with the "other side" would have made Emily Brontë's *Wuthering Heights* part of his reading list. Lastly, it is hard to imagine that Mason and Dixon do not belong to a literary genealogy that includes Don Quixote and Sancho Panza or Rosencrantz and Guildenstern. In all of these precursor frame narratives, the narrating frames are designed clearly to mark the dramatized transfer of story from one narrator to another, from one system of diegetic level and relationship with the core story to a different system of diegetic level and relationship. Moreover, although in novels within the framing tradition breakdowns do happen, often for significant reasons, in most cases novelists go to great pains to keep the frame boundaries distinct and to account for the process by which the full narrative has been constructed.

Pynchon has also taken great pains in constructing his narrative frames, but upon close analysis his frames seem to be designed to deconstruct themselves. The boundaries blur, the reader loses his or her sense of where the frame's edge separates one narrative from another. Reliability—not in Wayne C. Booth's sense of the term[8] but in the more pejorative sense of "How can we know this narrative is a faithful and true account of the events?"— and narrating authority are always at issue in Pynchon's texts. How does the reader gauge the "reliability" of a "Stencilized" narrative in *V.*? How does the reader account for the hypertext possibilities in the computer files Prairie accesses in *Vineland?* Who has authority over the status of the narrative finally transmitted? Is the reader forever caught in an infinite regress of transmissions?

In *Mason & Dixon* the narrative frame appears at the outset to be fairly conventional, but some 770 pages later we would all have to agree that Pynchon has turned classic frame narrative technique on its ear. With, I hope, tongue in cheek (is there a new hypertext equivalent to this cliché from oral culture?), the "Readers Group Guide" states, "The events of the novel are narrated by the Reverend Wicks Cherrycoke, who tells the story of Mason and Dixon after dinner for the entertainment of his family." "Entertainment"? The sheer size of the novel should alert us to the absurdity of this frame-tale conceit. As readers we suspend our disbelief in granting that Marlowe's tale in *Heart of Darkness* or the governess's manuscript in Henry James's *The Turn of the Screw* could be related in a single sitting, but it is hard to grant the same suspension of disbelief to the story of Mason and Dixon. Yet Pynchon dares the reader to do just that: in chapter 32 the LeSpark twins, Pitt and Pliny, are finally sent to bed (316); and the final chapter opens, "Now 'tis very late. Dawn is the next event to consider . . . " (758), and most of Cherrycoke's audience has drifted off to sleep.[9] The reader may find here sanction for having dozed now and again during reading, but the question is posed as to whether the reader drifts into "a poison'd Dream" of America or "the Innocence of Unconsciousness" (759).

Overlooked by the "Reading Group Guide" is the frame narration that contains Cherrycoke's narration. The narrating voice that opens the text at its outermost extradiegetic level comes from an undramatized narrator whose historical narrating situation is more likely the late twentieth rather than the late eighteenth century. This sort of narrator and narrating situation is what we usually find in Pynchon's texts. Cherrycoke's narration is, to follow Gèrard Genette's schematization of diegetic levels, an intradiegetic narration that shifts from a heterodiegetic to a homodiegetic to, on brief occasions, an autodiegetic relationship to the narrated events.[10] Furthermore, embedded in Cherrycoke's narration are numerous quoted narrations by Mason or Dixon and various inset narrations by minor characters such as Frau Redzinger, Nevil Maskelyne, and Armand Allegré. Throughout the text, however, the extradiegetic voice signals its presence when the narrative transmission requires some management (a narrative pointsman, we might say).

For the most part these narrative *interruptions* are brief parenthetical passages indicating some interjection by a member of the listening audience such as this first one in the text: "('Writing in your sleep, too!' cry the Twins.)" (14). Some of the *interruptions* are not as typographically marked, but as the context makes clear, Cherrycoke's narration has brushed against the extradiegetic narration:

"'Twas small work to come up with us, get to leeward,—from which the French prefer to engage,—and commence her broadsides, the *Seahorse* responding in kind, for an hour and a half of blasting! and smashing! and masts falling down!"

"Blood flowing in the scuppers!" cries Pitt.

"Did you swing on a rope with a knife in your teeth?" asks Pliny.

"Of course. And a pistol in me boot."

"Uncle." Brae disapproves.

The Rev[d] only beams. One reason Humans remain young so long, compar'd to other Creatures, is that the young are useful in many ways, among them in providing daily, by way of the evil Creatures and Slaughter they love, a Denial of Mortality clamorous enough to allow their Elders release, if only for moments at a time, from Its Claims upon the Attention. "Sad to say, Boys, I was well below." (37)

As his narrative resumes, Cherrycoke corrects his representation of his role in the attack on the *Seahorse,* but of more interest is the meditation on youth and the "Denial of Mortality." Although Cherrycoke may also hold this belief, this piece of narrative discourse must be grammatically and rhetorically attributed to the extra-diegetic narrator. For the reader, however, bits of the text such as this become part of a dialogic matrix of double-voiced narration that allows Pynchon to play with his text to produce complex effects. One of the most striking of these effects comes at *Mason & Dixon*'s close. Because part of Cherrycoke's narrating situation is his belated arrival for Mason's funeral, his narration of Mason's last days merges dialogically with the extradiegetic narrator's voice to form an elegiac yet ironic narrative of Mason's death and his sons' inheritance of America.

If the scene of Cherrycoke's narration is not without its problems, then the province of his narrated tale is likewise open to question. Cherrycoke claims his right to tell the story of Mason and Dixon because at different times his path crossed theirs, first during the time of the initial Transit of Venus and second when he joins their surveying party working on the Line. However, for long stretches of the narrative Cherrycoke is not a witness to the events, especially the closing "plot" frame of the second Transit of Venus and Dixon's last days. Nonetheless, he refers often to various "records" such as letters, field books both official and unofficial, the "Minute-Book" of the Royal Society (717), Mason and Dixon's published observations (691), and Mason's "hidden journal," in which at one point Mason muses, "Should I seek the counsel, God help me, of the cherubick Pest, Cherrycoke? He will take down ev'ry Word he can remember. (Might it prove of use, in any future Claims for Compensation, to be recorded, at what's sure to be impressive Length, as having sought Spiritual Assistance?)" (433–44).[11]

In chapter 76, Cherrycoke "speculates" (744) an encounter between Mason and Samuel Johnson, along with his trusty sidekick James Boswell, during his tour of the Hebrides.[12] Toward the end of their conversation, the speculation self-reflexively collapses on itself as Mason comments to Boswell, "'I had my Boswell, once, ... Dixon and I. We had a joint Boswell. Preacher nam'd Cherrycoke. Scribbling ev'rything down just like you, Sir'" (747). As with Boswell's narrative position, how much historical reliability is there in Cherrycoke's narration of Mason's comments? Johnson tellingly responds to this concern for the preservation of "ev'ry spoken remark,—"

"Which else would have been lost forever to the great Wind of Oblivion,—think," armsweep south, "as all civiliz'd Britain gathers at this hour, how much shapely Expression, from the titl'd Gambler, the Bar-maid's Suitor, the offended Fopling, the gratified Toss-pot, is simply fading away upon the Air, out under the Door, into the Evening and the Silence beyond. All those voices. Why not pluck a few words from the multitudes rushing toward the Void of forgetfulness?" (747)

We might well answer that this "pluck[ing] of a few words" has been the dialogic method of *Mason & Dixon* all along, that its man-ifold bricolage of voices has been writing a history recalled from the "Void of forgetfulness." Yet it is not that simple because the reader is still nagged by the problem of narrative reliability.

The question of reliability is foregrounded in the first chapter with Cherrycoke characterizing himself as "an untrustworthy Re-membrancer for whom the few events yet rattling with a broken memory must provide the only comfort now remaining to him" (8). Although he assists his "broken memory" by "producing a scarr'd old Note-book" (8), his listeners will occasionally challenge his narrative with charges of "no records" (171) or "no proof" (695) or "Parsonickal interpolation" (652). Cherrycoke at the outset of his narrative admits that the record he intended to keep in his Spir-itual Day-Book "'twas too often abridg'd by the Day's Fatigue" (14), and later in the narrative he admits to moments when no record survived (771), or when he "was not there" (345), or when Mason and Dixon "withdrew out of [his] hearing, so that regretfully [he] quite miss'd the Information" (652). Most of these challenges or admissions come in conjunction with fairly straightforward ele-ments of narrative; the more extreme fabulations such as the scenes with the Learn'd English Dog, the conversing clocks, the mechanickal Duck, Mason's journey into the eleven missing days, or Dixon's journey to a world in the interior of the earth go by with barely a murmur. As his readers have come to expect, Pyn-chon mixes his extensive historical research with outrageous fab-ulations, demanding that his readers confront a fictional world that is ontologically unstable. The frame structure of *Mason & Dixon* assists in this play of history and fabulation in that Cherry-coke becomes the filter for the narrative play, linking in a pas-tiche a series of set pieces, many of which display Pynchon's considerable powers. However, it is fair to question whether a narrative made of so many different narrating acts and levels of containment holds together sufficiently.

One of the more narratologically intriguing moments in the text surrounds the use of *The Ghastly Fop,* a fictional intertext of a serial narrative of dubious morals. *The Ghastly Fop* is first referred to by Dixon, while he and Mason are on St. Helena, as a "Grub-Street" product, "worth a dozen of any *Tom Jones*" (117). It is one of the texts read to the renowned Robert Jenkin's Ear (178), and once in America, Mason "guiltily [reads] from a ragged installment" (347). We learn a bit more about what sort of text *The Ghastly Fop* is when young Nathe McClean tries unsuccessfully to use its "erotick Pictures and Text" as a spur to masturbation. So far all the references have been brief and occur within the story of Mason and Dixon, but nothing prepares the reader for the next reference, and it takes a bit of reconstruction to straighten the narrating line.

Chapter 53 begins with an epigraph from one of Cherrycoke's *"Undeliver'd Sermons,"* which is full of Gnostic-inspired heresy, but when the narrative resumes, it begins with the narrative focus on an unidentified "she," and although the last chapter had closed with Mrs. Harland giving Mason and Dixon a Christmas hug, the style of this new chapter signals a shift to a different narrative register:

> She had found in her Kitchen, the Kitchen Garden, the beehives and the Well, a join'd and finish'd Life, the exact Life, perhaps, that Our Lord intended she live . . . a Life that was like a Flirtation with the Day in all its humorless Dignity . . . she was at her window, in afternoon peaceable autumn, ev'ryone else in town at the Vendue, Seth too, and the Boys, when They came for her,—as it seem'd only for her. The unimagin'd dark Men. The Nakedness of the dark and wild men. (511–12; ellipses original)

The reader discerns that the text has become a captivity narrative, but of whom? How does this tale relate to Mason and Dixon? Once it has been going for about nine pages, a parenthetical aside pegs Cherrycoke as the narrator: "(Tho' I was not present in the usual sense, nevertheless, I am a clergyman,—be confident 'twas an utterly original *moment musicale,* as they say in France)" (519), but five pages later the chapter ends with no further signals from the narrator and Mason and Dixon are still nowhere in sight. Moreover, it is difficult to see why Cherrycoke has drifted into this elaborate digression in the first place.

Chapter 54 continues the "Captive's" tale, but now the Captive herself becomes the narrator: "There came an evening during my novitiate when, after being fed but lightly, I was taken to a Chamber, and there laced into an expensive Corset, black as Midnight, imported, I was told, from Paris, from the very workshop of the *Corsetier* to the Queen" (525). Before this narrative can go too far, it is interrupted: "[Tene]Brae has discover'd the sinister Volume in 'Thelmer's Room, lying open to a Copper-plate Engraving of two pretty Nuns, sporting in ways she finds inexplicably intriguing" (526). You guessed it, it turns out we've been reading part of the *Ghastly Fop* series ("at least a Dozen Volumes by now"), which Ethelmer feels "oblig'd in Honor to read . . . all in Line" (527). Ethelmer and his cousin Tenebrae decide they can't leave the story hanging, so Ethelmer offers to read on, "And so off they minuet, to become detour'd from the Rev^d's narrative Turnpike onto the pleasant Track of their own mutual Fascination, by way of the Captive's Tale" (529). At this point not only Mason and Dixon, but also Cherrycoke has disappeared from sight and the extradiegetic voice narrates this scene of Tenebrae and Ethelmer's exchange about this inset text. Does the overt presence of the extradiegetic voice mean that this narrator has been in control since the chapter's beginning, insetting the Captive's narration and both narrating and insetting its continuation as we resume the tale of the finally named Eliza (529) Fields (531), and her escape from a Jesuit monastery in Canada with Captain Zhang, a Chinese Feng Shui master?

The narrating problem now is how to get back from this inset captivity narrative to Cherrycoke's narration. The classic logic of the frame narrative would call for Ethelmer and Tenebrae to finish their chapter of *The Ghastly Fop,* to close the book, and to return to Cherrycoke and his telling of Mason and Dixon's story. But before that can happen, Eliza and Captain Zhang "arrive at the West Line, and decide to follow the Visto east, and ere long they have come up with the Party" (534). In a wonderful bit of narrative slippage, *The Ghastly Fop* episode dialogically merges with the story of Mason and Dixon, and before another page goes by Cherrycoke has regained full control of the narration. There is, however, one more turn of the screw: Eliza apparently bears an uncanny resemblance to Mason's dead wife Rebekah, who has haunted him and the narrative throughout, but as with other red herrings in the novel, the narrative line of Eliza Fields dissipates as the picaresque tale of the survey forges on.

Although it is correct to say that *Mason & Dixon* traces a narrative line for its eponymous heroes, that line hardly resembles the "Visto" the two surveyors' project carved into the landscape

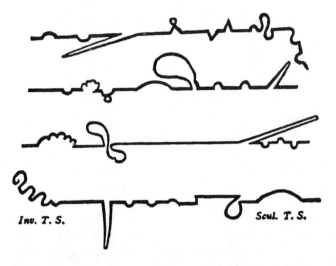

These were the four lines I moved in through my first, second, third, and fourth volumes.——In the fifth volume I have been very good,——the precise line I have described in it being this:

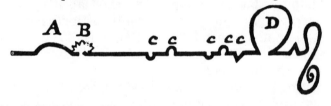

Laurence Sterne's sketches of the narrative lines of his novel *Tristram Shandy* (1760–1767).[13]

of America. Instead, it resembles the lines Laurence Sterne drew in volume 6, chapter 40 of *Tristram Shandy,* which just happened to be coming out in installments during the time Mason and Dixon collaborated on their different projects. But even this representation, fanciful as it is, assumes only a single "line" of narration, a single narrative voice. The narrative of *Mason & Dixon,* however, is so multivoiced that readers may be better off getting lost in its wilderness of narrators and voices than trying to carve a clear and straight Visto through its thicket of words. As with Pynchon's earlier novels, readers can trace in *Mason & Dixon* various narrative lines, but in the long run their experience more likely should resemble the experience of the children gazing upon and into that "worderful Card Table" cited in this essay's epigraph and on the novel's first page. As readers gaze into the "wonderful Card Table" of *Mason & Dixon,* they might find either a "Crease of Credulity" (496) or only "an illusion of Depth," but it will be a long time before they "can say they have been to the end of it."

NOTES

1. Thomas Pynchon, *Mason & Dixon* (New York: Henry Holt, 1997). References are noted parenthetically within the text.

2. "Reading Group Guide," *The New Novel from Thomas Pynchon,* Henry Holt. 20 May 1999 [http://www.hholt.com/pynchon/md_readinggde.html].

3. Thomas Pynchon, *V.* (Philadelphia: Lippincott, 1963).

4. Thomas Pynchon, *Gravity's Rainbow* (New York: Viking, 1973). Steven Weisenburger, "Hyper-Embedded Narration in *Gravity's Rainbow,*" *Pynchon Notes* 34–35 (1994): 70–87.

5. Thomas Pynchon, *Vineland* (Boston: Little, Brown, 1990).

6. Thomas Pynchon, "Is It O.K. to Be a Luddite?" *New York Times Book Review,* 28 October 1984, 1, 40–41. Although Pynchon's citing of *Manon Lescaut* in *V.* and "Under the Rose" (in *Slow Learner* [Boston: Little, Brown 1984], 101–37) is to Puccini's operatic adaptation, Abbé Prévost's novel is a classic example of narrative framing. For a more detailed account of framing and transmission techniques, see Bernard Duyfhuizen, *Narratives of Transmission* (Rutherford, NJ: Fairleigh Dickinson University Press, 1992).

7. David Cowart, "The Luddite Vision: *Mason & Dixon*" (paper presented at Beyond the Rainbow's End, International Pynchon Week Conference, London, June 1998).

8. Wayne C. Booth, *The Rhetoric of Fiction* (Chicago: University of Chicago Press, 1961). It would be the subject for a much larger study to consider Booth's notion of reliability as a measure of how reliably Pynchon's text represents the beliefs and values of the author. For Pynchon this is a particularly vexed question since he has made it all but impossible to access even a modicum of non-literary material upon which to base judgments about his beliefs and values. The problem is compounded in that as a satirist with such a strong command over his style and technique Pynchon always keeps the reader guessing as to when he (or if he ever) becomes literal and serious, when he comes out from behind the play of his fiction.

9. For Pynchon's readers the frame expands out from this border in *Mason & Dixon* since just as the novel's opening arced snowballs recall *Gravity's Rainbow,* so the opening "Now" of the passage quoted echoes *Gravity's Rainbow's* last line "Now everybody—" (760) as well as that earlier novel's third line "It is too late" (3); similarly "Dawn" echoes the American mornings framing *Vineland,* and the Christmastide setting of the narration recalls the Christmas Eve opening of *V.*

10. Gérard Genette, *Narrative Discourse,* trans. Jane Lewin (Ithaca: Cornell University Press, 1980).

11. Although some of these records are pure fabulations, more than a few readers who have begun to look into the quotation of historical documents in *Mason & Dixon* are finding many cases in which Pynchon is working directly

from the records produced by Mason and Dixon. See, for instance, the account of the Lancaster massacre reported in *The Journal of Charles Mason and Jeremiah Dixon,* ed. A. Hughlett Mason (Philadelphia: American Philosophical Society, 1969), 66. However, as Stacey Olster ("'A Patch of England, at a three-thousand-Mile Off-set': Representing America in *Mason & Dixon*" [paper presented at Beyond the Rainbow's End, International Pynchon Week Conference, London, June 1998]) has shown, one of Mason's favorite words for qualifying the precision of his measurements is "dubious"—one imagines Pynchon smiling each time a "dubious" measurement was recorded.

12. As Brian McHale has argued (*"Mason & Dixon* in the Zone, or, A Brief Poetics of Pynchon Space" [paper presented at Beyond the Rainbow's End, International Pynchon Week Conference, London, June 1998]), this speculated encounter between Mason and Samuel Johnson fits in a pattern of the narrative subjunctive that opens the fictional space for the imagined or fantastic scenes.

13. Laurence Sterne, *Tristram Shandy,* ed. Howard Anderson, Norton Critical Editions (New York: Norton, 1980).

Historical Documents Relating to *Mason & Dixon*

David Foreman

Introduction: "A Game"

There is a game among Thomas Pynchon's readers. In order to cope with the enormous amount of scientific, historical, pop-cultural, and artistic references in Pynchon's novels (some of them of dubious accuracy), the reader must ask at some point, "Is this true or is he making this up?" As C. E. Nicholson and R. W. Stevenson have written, "the reader becomes a demon in Pynchon's world, struggling to sort the facts."[1]

To compound these difficulties, Pynchon's novels often present imagined events and people as if they are true. For instance, in *The Crying of Lot 49* Pynchon creates *The Courier's Tragedy,* a production that has all the earmarks of a seventeenth-century drama. It is, in fact, apocryphal. Conversely, Pynchon can make the truth seem like fiction. In *Gravity's Rainbow,* the narrator is concerned with elaborate paranoid connections, among them the far-reaching power exerted by the German chemical cartel, IG Farben, in Europe and America before and during the war. In the context of the surreal comedy of *Gravity's Rainbow,* such speculations cannot be taken too seriously. However, "the truth is even more stupendous";[2] a reader who follows up on Pynchon's details might find Richard Sasuly's 1947 book *IG Farben* and discover that much of Pynchon's apparent invention is genuine.[3] As Thomas Moore has pointed out, Pynchon's details "have a maniacal way of proving to be true."[4] Investigation of the author's sources reveals a surprising degree of factual basis to his fiction. Readers who play "the game" often find a wide range of documented evidence to support Pynchon's historical and scientific information.

In my investigations of *Mason & Dixon,* I have indulged in "the game." This research grows out of my attempt during the summer of 1997 to read Pynchon's novel. In order to understand various topics discussed by the author, I found that I continually had to refer to secondary sources on astronomy and history. Before I had finished the first half of the book, I had already read four other books as supplements to my understanding of Pynchon. My primary concern in this paper is to sort out "the truth" from imagination. I will employ two kinds of sources in my investigation: primary historical documents and secondary interpretations of this information.

The most important surviving document relevant to Pynchon's novel is *The Journal of Charles Mason and Jeremiah Dixon,* and I will concentrate on this text for my analysis of primary sources. Additional records to keep in mind include the letters exchanged between the surveyors and their employers in Pennsylvania and Maryland and correspondence with their professional colleagues in the Royal Society and in the eastern colonies. Scientific essays by Mason and Dixon concerning their work in America were published in the Royal Society's *Philosophical Transactions.*[5] Nevil Maskelyne's interpretation of their data, also published in *Philosophical Transactions,* offers further insight into the pair's activities in the colonies.[6] In the archives of the states of Maryland and Pennsylvania, as well as the holdings of Britain's Royal Society, there exist additional sources that give us a broader view into the process of drawing the line and the lives of the men and women involved: payroll and expenditure records of the surveying party plus the scientific instruments they used.[7]

As for secondary historical analyses, much of what is available on the topic was published from the 1920s through the 1960s. Of special interest is the large number of articles written by Thomas D. Cope.[8] Cope can be credited with keeping Mason and Dixon's work in America alive in our historical imagination. He published over twenty articles about Mason and Dixon as a professor of physics at the University of Pennsylvania from 1939 to 1956. I will also concentrate on several other contributions to our knowledge of the Line, its architects, and their contemporaries, contributions I feel may have influenced Pynchon.

Beyond these technical details, which ask for identification as either fact or fiction, there remains a greater question to be resolved. How does this preponderance of information, some of it true and some of it invented, affect the reader's interpretation of the history of Mason and Dixon or of history in general? What is the relationship between "the facts" and fiction? These questions are among the topics I will address in this paper. My primary goal is to examine the historical documents currently available to us concerning Charles Mason and Jeremiah Dixon and to see in what ways these sources are possibly used by Pynchon in his novel.

THE JOURNAL OF CHARLES MASON AND JEREMIAH DIXON

One of the most important documents in relation to Mason and Dixon is *The Journal of Charles Mason and Jeremiah Dixon*. The original document resides in the National Archives, Washington, DC, having reached this site by a very circuitous route. It was carried with Mason during his entire travels in America, from New York to Williamsburg to Dunkard Creek and through the swamps of Delaware. In 1860, the original journal showed up in Halifax, Nova Scotia, "flung amidst a pile of waste paper into a cellar of Government House."[9] How *The Journal* arrived at this precarious location is not known. It was eventually purchased from Judge James Alexander of Halifax in 1877 and deposited in the National Archives. Not until 1969 was *The Journal* made widely available to the public in an edition other than the Archives' microfilm version. This edition, published by the American Philosophical Society, is a transcription of the original by A. Hughlett Mason (no relation to Charles Mason) of the University of Virginia.[10] Most likely, Pynchon used this version, widely available in most academic research libraries, as the basis for his research.

A. Hughlett Mason reports that *The Journal* was written in a single hand and is signed "C: Mason," evidence that it was Charles Mason who wrote the entire diary.[11] *The Journal* includes the notes on work carried out by Mason and Dixon on behalf of the Penn and Calvert families along their territories' mutual border. The document is full of mathematical scribblings, geometric diagrams, and, most prominently, notations of astronomical information routinely recorded by the surveyors. Mason also recorded detailed notes of their terrestrial progress, making numerous references to the "Post Marked West In Mr. Bryan's Field," the starting point for the Pennsylvania-Maryland border. At times, for many days in a row, the only notation is the ubiquitous "continued the line." In addition to official notes of Mason's and Dixon's work on the boundary line, there occasionally appear brief asides penned by Mason. These include accounts of the landscape, descriptions of Mason's trips to Lancaster and New York City, and tiny observations such as the following from 6 July 1766:

"measured three leaves on one Stem of a Hickory, Each of which was 17 inches in length and 12 inches in Breadth."[12]

Other copies of *The Journal* exist. One "fair copy" is in the Hall of Records of the State of Maryland. A second "fair copy" is owned by the Historical Society of Pennsylvania. Each is an edited version of Mason's notes, composed by the astronomer himself and given to the proprietors of Maryland and Pennsylvania upon completion of the survey. According to Hubertis M. Cummings, the Pennsylvania "fair copy" is "devoid of most of the drawings executed by Mason during the survey and cleared of all his personal meditations."[13] Pynchon makes use of these other versions of *The Journal*. The Rev. Cherrycoke "produces and makes available to the Company his Facsimile of Pennsylvania's Fair Copy of the Field-Journals of Mason and Dixon, 'copied without the touch of human hands, by an ingenious Jesuit device.'"[14] Cherrycoke's use of this "Facsimile" is not entirely accurate; nor is his apparent use of a photocopier. Throughout *Mason & Dixon,* sections from Mason's *Journal* are quoted, entries that we may assume are quoted by Cherrycoke as part of his narration. If we are to assume that Cherrycoke is using Pennsylvania's "Fair Copy" as the basis for his references to the *Journal,* then it is not possible for him to have access to the personal passages available only in the original document. Such entries were removed by Mason when he compiled the "fair copies." Pynchon's use of quotations from *The Journal* by Cherrycoke is not consistent with the contents of Cherrycoke's version of the journal.

In spite of this apparent narrative inaccuracy, Pynchon displays an awareness of the differences between the original notes of Mason and the "fair copies" given to the proprietors of the Colonies. Knowledge of this bibliographic discrepancy is made evident in Pynchon's description of Mason's trip to New York City. In the original *Journal,* Mason describes being thrown from his horse in front of a group of boys, a passage that Pynchon reproduces:

> Met some boys just come out of a Quaker Meeting House as if the De(vi)l had been with them. I could by no means get my Horse by them. I gave the Horse a light blow on the Head with my whip which brought him to the ground as if shot dead. I over his Head, my hat one way wig another and whip another, fine sport for the boys.[15]

Pynchon adds that "in the Foul Copy, he [Mason] writes, 'for ye D—l and the Boys,' but this does not appear in the Fair Copies the Proprietors will see" (*Mason & Dixon* 408). Curiously, Pynchon points out the differences in the versions of *The Journal,* noting that the "fair copies" given to the proprietors do not include the personal reflections that Mason recounts in the original *Journal.* Is the narrative voice in this passage that of Cherrycoke, displaying an extensive textual knowledge of the various journals, even though we are led to believe that he is only in possession of a "fair copy"? Or is it the omniscient narrator within whose story the narration of Cherrycoke is nested? There seems to be a collapsing of the narrative knowledge of Cherrycoke, in possession of the "fair copy," and of a larger narrative authority, one who quotes from the original *Journal* and who is aware of the differences in the various documents. The use of *The Journal* throughout the novel, combined with Cherrycoke's apparent possession of the inferior "fair copy," creates an unstable narrative authority, making it unclear who is controlling the telling of the story. We might also look at this problem as casting doubts about Pynchon's knowledge of the different primary sources. Are the inconsistencies due to an intentional mixing of voices with different levels of bibliographic awareness, or are they due to the Pynchon's inability consistently to differentiate between the various versions of Mason's journal?[16]

We should also note that in his description of Mason's trip to New York City, Pynchon adds a third journal to the bibliographic record, the "Foul Copy," in which Mason writes his additional remarks: "for ye D—l and the Boys." This phrase does not appear in the original *Journal.* It is an amendment to Mason's observation provided by Pynchon. Later there is mention of a fourth document, a "hidden Journal that he [Mason] gets to so seldom it should be styl'd a 'Monthly'" (*Mason & Dixon* 433). This, like the "Foul Copy," is an invention of the author, there being no evidence of alternative journals in which Mason apparently wrote his genuinely personal thoughts.

As the use of the previous *Journal* entry illustrates, what apparently caught the attention of Pynchon is not the plethora of scientific information, but the incidental impressions related by Mason about his experiences in America. In his introduction to *A "Gravity's Rainbow" Companion,* Steven Weisenburger tells us that "Pynchon's eye seems preternaturally alert for moments of personal testimony, comments often buried in footnotes or beneath heaps of technical data and objective detail."[17] *Mason & Dixon* corroborates Weisenburger's observations. When Pynchon quotes from *The Journal,* he zeroes in on the moments of personal reflection offered by its author. One such instance of this is the surveyors' experience of a thunderstorm on 25 May 1765 at 25 miles, 75.5 chains west of the Post Marked West in Mr. Bryan's Field. *The Journal* reads:

> May the 25th in the Evening a storm of Thunder and Lightning: about sun set I was returning from the other side of the river, and at the distance of about 1.5 Mile the Lightning fell in perpendicular streaks, (about a foot in breadth to appearance) from the cloud to the ground. This was the first Lightning I ever saw in streaks continued without the least break through the whole, all the way from the Cloud to the Horizon.[18]

Pynchon modifies this observation, writing, "less formally, he comes running into Dixon's Tent, just as Dixon is lighting his Evening Pipe. 'Did you see that?'" (462).

This passage helps us locate one source for the distinctive upper-case punctuation of nouns in the novel. Pynchon replicates the language of *The Journal.* Additionally, Pynchon quotes verbatim almost the entire passage from *The Journal,* lifting observations of the lightning from Mason's personal record and then offering his speculation as to what "really happened." Much of the action of the novel follows a similar pattern. The narrator, Rev. Cherrycoke, will cite a particular passage from *The Journal* and the subsequent narration will elaborate on Mason's documented observations.

As Cherrycoke reports the surveyor's journey across the Allegheny Mountains, he tells of their visit to a cave in South Mountain on 22 September 1765. The text of Pynchon's novel includes a long quote from *The Journal.* Again, it is lifted almost verbatim:

> The entrance is an arch about six yards in length and four feet in height, when immediately there opens a room 45 yards in length, 40 in breadth and 7 or 8 in height. (Not one pillar to support nature's arch): There divine service is often (according to the Church of England) celebrated in the Winter Season. On the Sidewalls are drawn the Pencil of Time, with the tears of the Rocks: The Imitation of Organ, Pillar, Columns and Monuments of a temple; which with the glimmering faint light; makes the whole an awful, solemn appearance: Striking its Visitants with a strong and melancholy reflection: That such is the abodes of the Dead: thy inevitable doom, O stranger; Soon to be numbered as one of them.[19]

In Pynchon's text, Cherrycoke's audience pauses to consider Mason's elaboration. Ethelmar remarks, "They handed that *in?*" (497). Pynchon "catches" Mason in one of his more poetic entries, an uncharacteristically impressionistic description of a cave. The personal passages of Mason in *The Journal* are very few in comparison to the enormous amount of technical information. In the majority of these personal passages, the viewpoint is one of a detached, objective, and distanced observer.

We, as readers in the late twentieth century, can also find reason to pause at this moment in the text. Interestingly, we see that Charles Mason has engaged in one of *Gravity's Rainbow*'s conventions, the use of the second-person pronoun. The preponderance of "you" in *Gravity's Rainbow* has a wide range of effects on the reader. Mason's use of the second-person pronoun ("thy" in "such is the abode For the Dead: *thy* inevitable doom, O stranger . . . ") is similar to Brian McHale's description of "you" found in a modernist or late-modernist context. McHale writes that "*you* retains a connotation of the vocative, of direct appeal to the reader, which imparts to these texts a slightly uncanny aura, as I think any reader would attest."[20] Appropriately, Cherrycoke's audience pauses, just as we too may pause when confronted with such an ominous appeal to our mortality.

Pynchon plays with both Mason's melancholic poeticism and with the literary weight of his use of the second-person pronoun. Outside the pages of *The Journal,* but within the pages of *Mason & Dixon,* Mason continues his personal reflections: "he will whisper later that Night, unable to quit the Fire 'nor Winter's Freeze, need bother us, snug in the Earth . . . those Ceilings! high as Heaven . . . '" (497). Pynchon adds that "all the way back to the Visto, Mason is seiz'd by Monology. 'Text,—' he cries, and more than once, 'it is Text,—and we are its readers, and its Pages are the Days turning'" (497). Pynchon grants Mason the insight of Derrida, two hundred years in advance.

We can add further evidence of Pynchon's attentive eye. Throughout *The Journal* the names of landowners whose property the line crosses are mentioned. Enoch Morgan (6/4/65), Daniel Camel (6/26/65), Elias Hoarisch (7/31/65), Wm. Pewsey of the Delmarva Peninsula (11/30/66), Mr. Spear (8/16/67), and the Pynchonianly dubbed Mr. Stumblestones of Wills Creek Valley (6/20/66, later referred to as Tumblestones on 11/22/67) all populate *The Journal.*[21] On 10 April 1765, only three miles and 49 chains from the Post Marked West in Mr. Bryan's Field, Mason writes that the line "went through Mr. Price's House."[22] The passage is innocuous at first glance, but if one examines the prepositional phrase of the entry, the language indicates that the line went *through* the house, bisecting Price's home. Pynchon comments on the situation by writing, "Takes them less than a week to run the Line thro' somebody's House" (446). Mr. and Mrs. Price themselves question the surveyors as to the true course of the line, "then producing some new-hackl'd Streaks of Hemp, and laying them down in a Right Line according to the Surveyor's advice,—fixing them here and there with tacks, across the room, up the stairs, straight down the middle of the Bed, of course . . . " (446).

Pynchon uses Mason's journal as a source for direct quotes on many occasions in *Mason & Dixon,* most often picking up on one of Mason's more personal interpretations of the landscape and the people around him. In the instances of Pynchon's citations of the "Field-Book," we can generally rely on the narrator's authenticity. Direct quotations are faithful to the original. However, Pynchon is not entirely accurate in his employment of temporal details, as we learn in chapter 63.

Pynchon records that a full moon rose above the Visto on 5 August 1766, while the surveyors retraced their steps back eastward towards the "Post Marked West In Mr. Bryan's Field" (621). In *Mason & Dixon,* Pynchon writes about the effect this monthly astronomical event has upon Zepho Beck. Zepho is a were-beaver, or as Pynchon writes, he suffers from "Kastoranthropy" (619). Zepho and the Swedish axeman, Stig, have arranged a duel reminiscent of John Henry's legendary competition with a steam-driven tunneling machine. Each will attempt to carve part of the Visto out of the forest, Stig with an ax and Zepho with his teeth. In Pynchon's text, just after the duel has begun, we find that "Mason looks at Dixon. Dixon looks at Mason. 'The Eclipse!' both cry at the same time. They have only now remember'd the Eclipse of the Moon, due to start later tonight" (622).

According to the record of Mason and Dixon, an eclipse occurs on 5 August. However, Mason's journal states that "The Sun Eclipsed," not the moon as Pynchon reports.[23] Later that month, a lunar eclipse did occur, fifteen days later. Pynchon is accurate about the fact that an eclipse takes place, but he alters the date of the two kinds of eclipses. Interestingly, there is no regular record of the phases of the moon in *The Journal,* so it would have been just as easy for the dates of the full moon to be altered as it is for the dates of the eclipses to change. In order for the joke to work—

Zepho turns into a beaver on the night of the full moon, but he turns back into a human when the moon is eclipsed—there must be a coincidence of the two celestial events, the full moon and the lunar eclipse. Why did Pynchon not switch the dates around so that the full moon coincided with the 20 August lunar eclipse? Instead of reporting the wrong kind of eclipse on 5 August, he could have fudged the facts by relocating the full moon to 20 August. Is this alteration intentional or is it truly a mistake, a misreading of *The Journal* by Pynchon? Such are the difficulties encountered by players in Pynchon's "game." Within the text itself, there is no disruption as the result of this factual inaccuracy. The joke works and the casual reader is unaware.

Another temporal problem in Pynchon's text involves a difficulty that arises in comparison to *The Journal*. On page 614 of *Mason & Dixon,* Pynchon notes that "they set a Post at 165 Miles, 54 Chains, 88 Links from the Post Mark'd West and, turning, begin to widen the Visto, moving East again, Ax-blows the day long. From the ridges they can now see their Visto, dividing the green Vapors of Foliage that wrap the Land." This is followed by a passage from *The Journal,* a passage that Pynchon does not date, but which can be found on 7 July 1766, as the surveyors stand atop Sidelong Hill. On page 616, Pynchon writes that "On June 14th, they stand atop the Allegheny Divide." He follows this with a long passage from *The Journal,* a passage that comes directly from the entry on 14 June 1766. If we assume that the pagination of the text corresponds to the flow of time, then the two passages create problems of temporality and of topology. Pynchon places the episode from July before the episode from June. The visit to Savage Mountain on 14 June must necessarily predate the visit to Sidelong Hill on 7 July because, if the party is moving east, they must first encounter Savage Mountain. Savage Mountain is approximately 25 miles west of Sidelong Hill. Pynchon's positioning in the text of Mason's impressions from Sidelong Hill before Savage Mountain is a reversal of their movement.

SECONDARY SOURCES

To claim that Pynchon "sticks to the facts" is an overstatement. For each shred of evidence in favor of the novel's historical authenticity, there is a moment of anachronism and absurdity. Terriers converse in English. Dixon flies. Frontiersmen transform into rodents, and timepieces talk to each other about the weather. It is difficult to stake a claim for Pynchon's veracity in light of such transgressions. This conflation of truth and fantasy has the effect of calling into question the nature of history and historiography. If we continue our reading of Pynchon with possible source documents in mind, we find that his manipulation of history and his distortion of historical fact are not wholly inconsistent with traditional historical interpretations of Mason and Dixon. Pynchon takes his case to greater extremes, but there is nonetheless evidence of creativity in the secondary historical documents. Again, I think it is valuable to consider Weisenburger's observation about Pynchon's eye, this time, as it relates to secondary sources.

In 1945, Thomas D. Cope wrote in the Pennsylvania Academy of Science's *Journal* that "the story of the work Mason and Dixon in the Middle Colonies from 1763 to 1768 is largely a 'lost chapter' of Pennsylvania history because writers have persisted in viewing it from an inappropriate frame of reference, the local or regional one, and in entangling it with border issues that are completely irrelevant."[24] Cope entreats his historical and scientific contemporaries to alter their take on the work of the two in order to see their true significance:

> to see the work of Mason and Dixon in its full significance one must view it from London of the early 1760's . . . one must attempt to see them as they appeared to James Bradley . . . one must know them as they were known by Dr. John Bevis and Daniel Harris . . . and one must associate with the master craftsmen-scientists of London who designed and made instruments of precision.[25]

In 1997, Thomas Pynchon has carried out Cope's proposal, taking it to a greater extreme. Just as *Gravity's Rainbow* is more than a story about a guy named Slothrop who gets erections when V-2 rockets hit London, so too is *Mason & Dixon* more than a book about two astronomer/surveyors etching a Visto through the North American wilderness. Pynchon expands the scope of his history to include examinations of the perspective of science in the 1760s, raising questions concerning the problem of longitude, the Transit of Venus, and the worldview that demanded their investigation. He incorporates the setting of late-colonial America, placing Mason and Dixon in encounters with Revolutionary American heroes and thereby addressing the philosophical and sociological questions which surround America's break from British colonial rule. As any reader of *Gravity's Rainbow* may recognize, Pynchon highlights the persistent presence of economics (the Dutch East India Company), conspiracy paranoia (Jesuit telegraphy), historical apocrypha (George Washington smoking pot), and the presence of the supernatural (the Glowing Indian, the Golem, and the Black Dog). In light of the historical significance of the Mason and Dixon Line as the boundary between North and South, we must also consider the question of slavery.

EVIDENCE OF JEREMIAH DIXON

An event from Jeremiah Dixon's life that Pynchon picks up for use in his novel is Dixon's encounter with an American slave owner. H. W. Robinson reports the story thus:

> Dixon came upon a slave driver mercilessly beating a poor black woman. Going up to him he said: "Thou must not do that!" . . . Then righteous wrath overcame his Quaker principles. He was a tall and powerful man, and an imposing figure, so without more ado he seized the slave driver's whip and with it gave him the sound thrashing that he richly deserved.[26]

Pynchon incorporates this scene into his novel when Mason and Dixon are in Maryland measuring a degree of latitude for the Royal Society. Dixon is approached in a saloon by a Slave-Driver who mentions an auction the next day. Dixon later sees the man in the street, beating a slave and, in a re-enactment of Robinson's scenario, Dixon thrashes the Slave-Driver (696–700). In both the historically documented Dixon and in Pynchon's character, "Dixon kept the whip as a trophy and took it back with him to Cockfield, where it was long regarded as a family treasure."[27]

Pynchon plants clues that indicate that Dixon's actions are not necessarily motivated by a sense of justice but instead are an act invested with more personal motives. During the pair's stay in South Africa, Austra, a black servant at the home of the Vroom family, is surreptitiously offered to the Vroom's guests in order that she may reproduce a light-skinned child who will be sold as a slave (65). She later appears at Lepton Castle in America as a slave serving drinks (419, 427). Before Dixon confronts the Slave-Driver, the text notes that Dixon's initial confrontation with him in a saloon the day before the beating is accompanied by these considerations: "Dixon . . . raises his brows amiably, at the same time freezing with the certainty that once again he is about to see a face he knows. Someone from the recent past, whose name he cannot remember. 'A fine young Mulatto gal'd be just your pint of Ale I'd wager, well tonight you're in luck, damme 'f you're not" (696). The memory, adjacent in the text to the mention by the Slave-Driver of the mulatto girl, subtly summons the presence of Austra. Is Austra among the women being abused? The text is not clear, but her presence is linked to Dixon's actions, casting the shadow of Dixon's sympathies towards Austra over the slave being beaten.

For the Pynchon canon, this scene carries greater weight. The reader of Pynchon's 1964 novel, *V.*, will recall a similar passage involving the German colonists in Southwest Africa. Pynchon describes scenes of terrible brutality by Germans to Africans, horrible beatings, rapes, and torture: "he bent her back over a rock and while they held her he first sjamboked her, then took her. She lay in a cold rigor; and when it was over he was astonished to find that at some point during it the women had, like good-natured duennas, released her and gone about their morning's labor."[28] In *Gravity's Rainbow,* the brutality is not as vivid, but the humiliating attitude on the part of the Germans toward Africans is still evident. In *Mason & Dixon,* a similar attitude of abuse and exploitation is presented in the relationship between the Africans and the colonists, particularly in the Vroom family's use of Austra to mother light-skinned children who will "fetch more upon the Market" (65).

A student of Pynchon's work may see something redeeming in Dixon's thrashing of the Slave-Driver. Colonialism and the racist exploitation that attends it are never endorsed as "good" in Pynchon's novels, but neither is it clearly labeled as "evil." It is difficult to pin down any didacticism of this sort in Pynchon's work as a whole, especially as it applies to this topic. However, Pynchon's portrayal of Dixon's thrashing carries with it an air of moral censure, a castigation that is dictated by the necessities of Dixon's documented history. Like the scenes of brutality in *V.*, the narrative dwells on the situation and its characters self-consciously. There remains the question of how we are to approach the violence in *V.*, how we should react to it. Similarly, the question remains as to how we are to look at Dixon's thrashing, what emotional investment we are to assume. Without arriving at a clear answer to either of these problems, we can at least sense that there is a dialogue between the two. Dixon's beating somehow is a reply to the violence the reader witnessed in *V.*

Relevant to the matter at hand is Pynchon's portrayal of Jeremiah Dixon as it is rooted in an article written by H. W. Robinson in 1950 for the American Philosophical Society, published in their *Proceedings.* In many instances, Pynchon incorporates details specific to Robinson's essay. One aspect of Dixon's character noted by Robinson is his dress. Robinson tells us that "there is a family tradition and it has appeared in print on many occasions that Dixon wore military uniform from 1760 until his death consisting of a long red coat and a cocked hat."[29] In Pynchon's novel, Dixon's attire is noted in our first encounter in London with the protagonists: "Dixon is . . . wearing a red coat of military cut, with brocade and silver buttons and a matching three-cornered hat" (16). Later, as the surveying party penetrates deeper into the West, the Youghiogeny ferryman, Mr. Ice, comments on Dixon's attire: "Forgive me, Sir, if I stare. Yours is the first Red Coat to be seen in these parts since Braddock's great Tragedy,—the only ones out here with the Opportunity to wear one, being the Indians who from the Corpses of the English soldiers, took them" (661).

Robinson claims that Dixon's apparent use of a military uniform "must be wrong, as his name does not appear on any army lists and he was never in any way connected with the army."[30] Dixon's red coat, a style of dress so heavily associated with the British army, was a misunderstood coincidence. Dixon "adopted as ordinary dress a long red coat and—as many people of the period did—a cocked hat. This has led historians to assume that he either held commissioned rank or wore military uniform without permission. A 'long red coat and cocked hat' had no significance."[31] Pynchon not only incorporates Dixon's attire into his text; he also brings in the misunderstanding among historians considering its significance. Mr. Ice considers it a military uniform, but Dixon claims it is "a means . . . of not being innocently mistaken for an Elk" (661).

Robinson's text is further used by Pynchon in his incorporation of the surveyor's "family weakness."[32] In spite of his Quaker heritage, Dixon still has his corporeal desires, particularly for alcohol. As Robinson notes, "the following entry appears in the Quaker Minute Book of Raby, under the date October 28, 1760:—Jery Dixon, son of George and Mary Dixon of Cocksfield disowned for drinking to excess."[33] Pynchon's Dixon exhibits this predisposition to drink at the beginning of the novel as he and Mason decide that since they will soon be on a ship and out of port, they should pursue their "last chance for civiliz'd Drink" (18). As the two prepare for their first trip along the Maryland-Pennsylvania border, they gather provisions. Later, at a Philadelphia apothecary shop, Dixon orders one hundred cases of laudanum, apparent proof of alcohol's status as a gateway drug for other, more powerful intoxicants (267).

A look at Dixon's preference for spirits further establishes the links between Robinson's article and Pynchon's characterization. Robinson states that "this was the period when drinking gin was at its height and it may be that the habit acquired by both father and son undermined their health so much as to lead to their early deaths."[34] Pynchon not only refers to Dixon's early death; he also notes his taste for spirits. Again, in the first scene of the two protagonists' initial encounter, we find that Dixon has a predilection for liquor: "'Grape or Grain, but ne'er the Twain' as me Great-Uncle George observ'd to me more than once. . . . Of the two sorts of drinking Folk this implies, thah' is, Grape People and Grain People, You will now inform me of Your membership" (17–18). Mason establishes his inclinations by saying that "Oh, I'll drink wine if I must" (18). Pynchon could merely be interpreting a common understanding of eighteenth-century drinking habits, but it is likely that his information is based on Robinson's article.

Robinson's article comes with the disclaimer that there is some confusion as to Dixon's character, a difficulty that is partly the result of similarities in the names of members of the larger Dixon family. Pynchon avoids these confusions, in particular the tempting assumption that Dixon "was one of the inventors of *coal gas,*" a fact that could lead to an elaborate connection to the IG Farben chemical cartel so prominent in *Gravity's Rainbow.*[35] Weisenburger tells us that the use of coal tar by William Perkins and August Wilhelm von Hoffman established the economic foundation for both Imperial Chemicals, Inc. and for IG Farben.[36] According to Robinson, it was Jeremiah's brother, George Dixon, who invented coal gas. In my readings of the novel, I did not perceive any hint of such a connection between the two ideas, a ripe topic for speculative improvisation that is appropriately not explored.

I will not go so far as to state that Pynchon relied completely on H. W. Robinson's work as the basis for his portrayal of Jeremiah Dixon, though it is not unheard of for Pynchon to rely on such a narrow basis for his facts. In the case of his use of historical information concerning the Soviet campaign against illiteracy used in the author's description of Tchitcherine's experiences in Kirghizistan, Pynchon apparently relied heavily upon Thomas G. Winner's *Oral Art and Literature of the Kazakhs of Russian Central Asia* for this section of *Gravity's Rainbow*.[37] H. P. Hollis's 1934 article, "Jeremiah Dixon and his Brother," contains additional information about Dixon's family. An important detail not repeated by Robinson in his article is Hollis's description of William Emerson, the man who taught Dixon to fly, as "an eccentric character."[38] Robinson merely refers to Emerson as "the celebrated mathematician of Hurworth, County Durham" and makes no mention of his peculiarities.[39]

Another important source for Pynchon's characterization of both Dixon and Mason is a document that predates the Civil War. In 1854, John H. B. Latrobe delivered an address, "The History of Mason and Dixon's Line," to the Historical Society of Pennsylvania. Latrobe retells the origins and development of the political squabbles between the Penn and Calvert families. In a moment of "very idle speculation," Latrobe attempts to determine the character of the surveyors by analyzing the signatures that appear in Mason's journal. Mason, claims Latrobe, "from these small hints . . . was a cool, deliberate, pains taking man, never in a hurry; a man of quiet courage, who crossed the Monongahela with fifteen men, because it was his duty to do so."[40] In contrast, Dixon's signature is not the consistent, uniform mark of his partner:

> All he seems to have cared to do was to put something on paper that would indicate his presence. . . . Occasionally, his signature is very small; again, it is as large and sprawling as a schoolboy's; from all which, I infer that he was a younger man, a more active man, a man of impatient spirit and a nervous temperment, just such a man as worked best with a sobersided colleague.[41]

Edward Bennett Mathews repeats Latrobe's observations about Mason and Dixon in his 1909 history of the boundary dispute,[42] as does Earl Schenk Miers is his 1965 essay, *Border Romance*.[43] In *The Stargazers,* a novel remarkably similar to Pynchon's work in many respects, Barbara Susan Lefever also portrays the two according to Latrobe's design. Lefever's Mason is the older, strong-willed, advice-dispensing astronomer. Dixon is less restrained. In Lefever's novel, Dixon gives in to temptation while in Cape Town, succumbing to "the young South Sea Islander with the

long flowing hair."[44] Pynchon's contribution to Mason's and
Dixon's story is a reiteration of the personalities as they were
originally invented by Latrobe's graphological analysis and sub-
sequently perpetuated by later historians. Pynchon's Mason, the
sober and uptight straight man, and his Dixon, reckless and "ever
seeking to feel something he'd hitherto not felt," have been characterized as such a complementary pair since before the Civil
War (764).

THOMAS D. COPE

If we look closer at the body of work on Mason and Dixon sup-
plied by Thomas Cope, we find that he, like Charles Mason in his
Journal or Latrobe in his *History,* is in the habit of peppering
his objective observations with personal conjecture and embel-
lishment. In one such instance, Cope draws links between the
architecture of the Great Pyramids of Egypt and the Mason and
Dixon Line.

The boundary line between Pennsylvania and Maryland was
defined according to methods that relied on astronomy. Mason
and Dixon were hired to undertake the job because of the accuracy with which they carried out their observation of the Transit
of Venus in 1761 at Cape Town. Because of the difficulties posed
by trying to draw a line parallel with the latitudinal lines of the
globe, lines that are actually segments of an arc, astronomy was
essential to drawing an accurate boundary. Previous colonial
surveyors, not well trained in the sciences of astronomy or surveying and using poor equipment, had failed on three occasions
to accurately draw the tangent line from the middle point of the
Delmarva Peninsula tangent to a circle surrounding the New
Castle courthouse ("They were provincials; what could one expect
of them?" writes Cope in their defense.[45]) Attempts to establish
the Maryland-Pennsylvania boundary were met with disappointment as well. The expense of these failures forced the Penn and
Calvert families to hire Mason and Dixon, two proven experts in
their trade. Mason and Dixon, using astronomical observations
to determine their latitude and longitude on the earth, accurately
measured the tangent line, the east-west line between Maryland
and Pennsylvania, and three other smaller geographic segments
in North America using these techniques. Cope draws attention

to the possibility that similar procedures were employed to build the Great Pyramids:

> It was claimed a century ago that the Pyramid of Cheops at Gizeh, Egypt contains in its design evidence that the architects of that structure were guided by the pole which was then near a bright star in the head of the Dragon. A recent writer on the Pyramids ... still maintains that the orientation of the Pyramids at Gizeh is so consistent as to suggest that the architects who planned the structures were guided by the pole of the heavens as it was among the stars when the pyramids were built.[46]

Cope's body of work represents his attempt to bridge the historical gaps between Mason and Dixon and their counterparts in England and America. In this passage, Cope extends the genealogy beyond their scientific colleagues and immediate predecessors to the architects of the Great Pyramids.

Both Cope and Pynchon have perceived the significance of astronomy to the work of the Mason and Dixon Line, and both authors have included speculation about the role of the Pyramids in a greater human scheme. Cope ties the two together according to a common scientific use of the predictable mechanisms of the heavens. Pynchon's connections are far more radical, tying the two projects together according to a deliberate plot designed to control the earth's energy. In Pynchon's rewriting of the line, Captain Shelby leads Mason and Dixon to a sight, directly in the path of the boundary, where a mound stands. Pynchon indicates that this pyramid is unlike its Egyptian predecessors in that it does not contain the corpses and treasures of buried kings: "it was broken into years ago, perhaps by some larcenous Fool who had it confus'd with a Pyramid" (599). The mound is described by Dixon as a Leyden Battery, a device designed to "Accumulate Force," presumably harnessing the energy of ley lines (599). Captain Zhang expands upon Dixon's speculation about the mound and its placement on the line, saying that it is part of a larger network of lines and points through which *Sha* may flow. Zhang refers to "Extra-terrestrial Visitors" as the beings who have drawn the lines, a network to which the surveyors are contributing; "they came from the sky, they prepar'd to emplace these Webs of right lines upon the Earth, then without explanation they went away again" (601). Earlier statements by Mr. Everybeet further implicate the Pyramids as part of a grand network of "Tellurick-energy," saying that "the fam'd Egyptian Pyramids, whose ever-mystickal Purposes, beyond the simply funerary, are much speculated upon" (547). Everybeet's idea is consistent with common myths about the Pyramids. Perhaps they are supernatural in origin, placed upon the earth by aliens for a purpose beyond our ken.

In several articles, Cope speculates as to the last years of Mason's life. After having lived in England for eighteen years, Charles Mason returned to Philadelphia in the autumn of 1786. He died there, leaving his widow and eight children in America. Before his death, it is reported that Mason left in the hands of Benjamin Franklin "an astronomical project that Mason was eager to lay before Dr. Franklin. No information about the nature of the project has been found."[47] Pynchon picks up on this mystery, indicating that Mason has detected something in the heavens that he must disclose to Franklin: "'Tis a construction . . . a great single Engine, the size of a Continent . . . Day by day the Pioneers and Surveyors go on, points are being tied in . . . '" (772). Mason speaks in riddles ("'Ah, you old Quizzer,'" Franklin says to him), and for the reader of Pynchon's and Cope's work, a mystery reamains as to what exactly it was that Mason wished to communicate to Franklin (772).

H. G. DWIGHT

Another secondary text that may have influenced Pynchon is a 1926 article by H. G. Dwight published in the *Yale Review*. Dwight's approach to Mason and Dixon is less formal than Cope's. He is unabashed about offering his conjecture as to what may have happened "between the lines" of Mason's *Journal*. Like Pynchon, Dwight picks out the passages in *The Journal* that are Mason's personal observations. He also provides tongue-in-cheek commentary that Mason "trotted through what twenty-five years later was to become the District of Columbia, uttering never a syllable about it."[48] Also, "If he held his tongue about Franklin and Washington and George Mason and Patrick Henry, to say nothing of that young Thomas Jefferson who rode in his tracks to Annapolis ten years before writing the Declaration of Independence, he may not have disapproved of their rough ways."[49] Pynchon creates encounters with Franklin, Washington, and Jefferson in his novel, seeming to take up the suggestions of Dwight. It is a stretch to try to argue convincingly that Pynchon was indeed influenced by this brief article, but what I think is most important about its presence is that it indicates the nature of historical interpretation. Dwight reports the facts as found in *The Journal,* but he does so by mixing it with his personal disappointment in the taciturnity of Mason, of the astronomer's ignorance of the spirit of the times, and with a refreshing irreverence.

We can also gather from Dwight's article the significance of Mason and Dixon to American history. Dwight's attitude is appropriately light. Mason was in the midst of burgeoning political upheavals but seems wholly unaware of the events such as the Stamp Act. Dwight's article helps locate Mason and Dixon on the margins of American history, as the men from whom the North-South boundary derives its name, but who imprint no greater influence on history. Traditionally, Mason's and Dixon's work has been the subject of interest among engineers rather than political historians. This marginal position in history occupied by Mason and Dixon is consistent with Pynchon's penchant for such situations. Pynchon has written about other such events and persons in "Under the Rose" (the Fashoda crisis), *V.* (the Herero uprisings), and *Gravity's Rainbow* (the V-2 program and IG Farben).

MASON AND DIXON AND HISTORIOGRAPHY

Dwight's playful attitude toward history lacks the seriousness of "real" historical studies. He abandons the objective viewpoint of the detached historian. In this transgression, we find that Dwight (and Cope in his instances of speculation) illustrates Linda Hutcheon's point that "the provisional, indeterminate nature of historical knowledge is certainly not a discovery of postmodernism."[50] Dwight recognizes the gaps in the historical record of Mason's *Journal,* and he helps us to see that history is a matter of perspective. Mason can evidently inhabit pre-Revolutionary America without commenting upon what our retrospective sense of history tells us must have been obvious—the revolution was stirring. It was less than a decade away.

Pynchon accomplishes the same tweaking of our sensibilities about history as does Dwight, but on a grander scale. As the reader sinks his teeth into the text, he or she is confronted by personalities directly from our history, people whom he or she knows to be "real." Documents purporting to be authentic, such as *The*

Pennsylvaniad, The Journal of Charles Mason and Jeremiah Dixon, and the works of Cherrycoke, add to this apparent authenticity. Inevitably, the reader must ask, "Is this true or is this made up?" Depending upon the insistence of our questioning, we soon discover that some of the purported facts are real and some are imagined.

If the reader engages in a very close comparison between the historical record and Pynchon's interpretation, he or she finds that, yes, there are many instances in which the author takes great pains to stay loyal to the truth of history, to the real events. David Seed has pointed out that in traditional historical fiction, such a device is employed in order to add verisimilitude to the author's elaborations: "that dates back at least to Walter Scott, who used it as a strategy to increase the authenticity of his fiction."[51] Traditionally, the facts buttress the fiction. In the case of *Mason & Dixon,* the opposite is true.

Mingled with Pynchon's attention to the historical record is a constant flaunting of anachronisms. Blatant slips from the real are represented by the invasion of figures such as Popeye the Sailor in the Allegheny Mountains, or his companion, the Rabbi of Prague, whose greeting to the surveyors—"the Fingers spread two and two, and the thumb held away from them likewise, . . . Live long and prosper"—is apparently out of place (485–86). Mr. Edgewise uses a Thermos to keep his coffee warm (356). Considering the constant barrage of anachronisms both minor and hilariously blatant, Seed's idea concerning traditional historical fiction does not apply to *Mason & Dixon.* Just the opposite occurs. Instead of the facts adding authenticity to the fantasy, the fantasy corrupts the facts and disrupts the whole retelling of history, infecting it with the uncertainty of fiction.

Linda Hutcheon contributes to our understanding of the interplay between fact and fiction: "historiographic metafiction refutes the natural common-sense methods of distinguishing between historical fact and fiction. It refuses the view that only history has a truth claim, both by questioning the ground of that claim in historiography and by asserting that both history and fiction are discourses."[52] By blurring the boundary between history and fiction, Pynchon forces us to see history as a construction. If we view the novel with this in mind, we find that the novel is in fact a discourse, a telling of the story of English men of science by Rev. Cherrycoke. The good Reverend himself echoes Hutcheon's claims about historical discourse as part of the epigraph of chapter 35:

Her Practitioners [History's], to survive, must soon learn the arts of the quidnunc, spy, and Taproom Wit,—that there may ever continue more than one Life-line back into a Past we risk, each day, losing our forebears in forever,—not a Chain of single Links, for one broken Link could lose us All,—rather, a great disorderly Tangle of Lines, long and short, weak and strong, vanishing into the Mnemonick Deep, with only their Destination in common. (349)

The historian is like the gossip or the barroom comedian. The practice of history is in the style of the telling, not really in the facts. History as merely fact is a tenuous disassociation with the past at risk of being cut. Cherrycoke seems to indicate that the closer one sticks to the facts, the less relevant history becomes.

Should this lead us to believe that as history develops from a mere mimesis of facts to a self-conscious process of retelling that it will eventually lose its factual basis? Will history become entirely a fiction? I do not think this is true, and the evidence as presented in Pynchon's novel seems to support my view. Even though history is essentially a discourse, "the facts" still are important. In spite of the absurdities of the novel, there truly is a fidelity to the historical record. It is the temporal and cultural anachronisms, the invasion of twentieth-century concepts into *Mason & Dixon,* which offer truly valuable insight into the operation of "the facts." Hutcheon writes that "the meaning and shape are not in the 'events,' but in the systems which make those past events into present historical 'facts.'"[53] The invasion of Americans into the western lands, the colonies' break from England—these are among the systems of history that Pynchon addresses in his novel. The importance of Mason's and Dixon's tracing of the line across the earth is the basic "fact" of the novel. As the surveyors' endeavor is juxtaposed against the anomalies of Pynchon's bizarre interjection of the supernatural and the slightly out-of-place, the Line takes on elements of metaphor, allegory, and symbolism. The Line and its creation inform us about how it was constructed in the 1760s, how we reconstruct it from the twentieth century, and how our sense of history is constructed as well.

CONCLUSION

I found an in-depth study of the historical background of *Mason & Dixon* to be very rewarding. These investigations have allowed me to get a good grasp on the topology of Mason's and Dixon's journey that Pynchon builds upon as well as the scientific data and concepts that Pynchon employs. I believe that understanding these concepts allows for a fuller understanding of Pynchon's texts. Drawing direct links, really indulging in "the game," is a habit that is full of pitfalls, but it is nonetheless valuable. Pynchon gives us a great knotting-into, and part of the pleasure of reading *Mason & Dixon* is the unwinding of the various trails that tie into the text. Much of my work is speculation, guessing at the path of the author's research, hoping to get close to a source document to help explain a baffling passage. Considering the relatively thin body of available knowledge concerning Mason and Dixon, we can be reasonably assured that "the game" we play has been played before and that at times we are walking in the investigative footsteps of Pynchon.[54]

NOTES

1. C. E. Nicholson and R. W. Stephenson, "'Words You Never Wanted to Hear': Fiction, History, and Narratology in *The Crying of Lot 49*," in *Tropic Crucible: Self and Theory in Language and Literature,* ed. Ranjit Chatterjee and Colin Nicholson (Singapore: Singapore University Press, 1984), 304.

2. Thomas Pynchon, *Gravity's Rainbow* (New York: Viking, 1973), 647.

3. Richard Sasuly, *IG Farben* (New York: Boni and Gaier, 1947).

4. Thomas Moore, *The Style of Connectedness: "Gravity's Rainbow" and Thomas Pynchon* (Columbia: University of Missouri Press, 1987), 6.

5. Charles Mason, "Observations for Determining the Length of a Degree of Latitude in the Provinces of Maryland and Pennsylvania in North America," in *Philosophical Transactions of the Royal Society,* 1768; reprint *Philosophical Transactions of the Royal Society of London* 58 (1768): 274–328; Charles Mason and Jeremiah Dixon, "Astronomical Observations, Made in the Forks of the River Brandywine in Pennsylvania, for Determining the Going of a Clock Sent Thither by the Royal Society" *Philosophical Transactions* 58 (1768): 329–30. Both articles cited by Mark Skertich, "'This Palpable Disregard of the Plain Provisions of Nature': The Role of the Royal Society in the Mason-Dixon Survey" (master's thesis, West Virginia University, 1993), 100.

6. Nevil Maskelyne, "The Length of a Degree of Latitude in the Province of Maryland and Pennsylvania Deduced from the foregoing of Operations," *Philosophical Transactions of the Royal Society* 58 (1768): 323–25; cited by Skertich, "This Palpable Disregard," 99.

7. For an exhaustive bibliography of primary sources and an extensive list of secondary sources published before 1909, see Edward L. Burchard and Edward B. Mathews, "Manuscripts and Publications Relating to the Mason and Dixon Line and Other Lines in Pennsylvania, Maryland, and the Virginias," in *Report on the Resurvey of the Maryland-Pennsylvania Boundary* (Harrisburg, PA: Harrisburg Publishing, 1909), 205–403.

8. I credit Mark Skertich ("This Palpable Disregard") for introducing me to Cope's work and for providing an extensive bibliography of secondary sources.

9. George W. Corner, preface to *The Journal of Charles Mason and Jeremiah Dixon,* ed. A. Hughlett Mason (Philadelphia: American Philosophical Society, 1969), vii.

10. Ibid.

11. A. Hughlett Mason, introduction to *The Journal of Charles Mason and Jeremiah Dixon,* 1.

12. Charles Mason and Jeremiah Dixon, *The Journal of Charles Mason and Jeremiah Dixon,* 130.

13. Hubertis M. Cummings, *The Mason and Dixon Line: Story for a Bicentenary 1763–1963* (Harrisburg, PA: Commonwealth of Pennsylvania, 1963), 113.

14. Thomas Pynchon, *Mason & Dixon* (New York: Henry Holt, 1997), 554. Further references will appear parenthetically within the text.

15. Mason and Dixon, *The Journal,* 67.

16. Even Mason and Dixon scholars are confused about the number of versions of *The Journal.* A. Hughlett Mason's introduction to his 1969 transcription reports the existence of Mason's original in the National Archives and the "fair copy" owned by the State of Maryland, but he does not mention the "fair copy" owned by Pennsylvania (1). In the bibliography to his study of the Mason and Dixon Line, Hubertis M. Cummings lists the original in the National Archives and the "fair copy" owned by Pennsylvania, but he does not mention the "fair copy" owned by Maryland (113). Burchard and Matthews's bibliography provides the most detailed record of the journal, including information about the contents and origins of Mason's notebook and both "fair copies" (351).

17. Steven Weisenburger, *A "Gravity's Rainbow" Companion* (Athens: University of Georgia Press, 1988), 8.

18. Mason and Dixon, *The Journal,* 87.

19. Ibid., 111.

20. Brian McHale, *Postmodernist Fiction* (London: Metheun, 1987; rpt., New York: Routledge, 1991), 223.

21. Mason and Dixon, *The Journal,* 91, 93, 99, 149, 179, 129, 191.

22. Ibid., 81.

23. Ibid., 130.

24. Thomas D. Cope, "A Frame of Reference for Mason and Dixon," *Proceedings of the Pennsylvania Academy of Science* 19 (1945): 80.

25. Ibid., 80–82.

26. H. W. Robinson, "Jeremiah Dixon (1733–1779)—A Biographical Note," *Proceedings of the American Philosophical Society* 91 (1950): 273.

27. Ibid., 273.

28. Thomas Pynchon, *V.* (Philadelphia: Lippincott, 1963; rpt., New York: Harper, 1990), 272.

29. Robinson, "Jeremiah Dixon," 273.

30. Ibid.

31. Ibid.

32. Ibid.

33. Ibid.

34. Ibid.

35. Ibid., 272.

36. Weisenburger, *A "Gravity's Rainbow" Companion,* 95.

37. Brian McHale, class discussion, West Virginia University, Morgantown, WV, October 9, 1997.

38. H. P. Hollis, "Jeremiah Dixon and His Brother," *Journal of the British Astronomical Association* 44 (1934): 296.

39. Robinson, "Jeremiah Dixon," 272.

40. John H. B. Latrobe, *The History of Mason and Dixon's Line* (Philadelphia: Historical Society of Pennsylvania, 1855), 41.

41. Ibid.

42. Edward Bennett Mathews, "History of the Boundary Dispute between the Baltimores and Penns Resulting in the Original Mason and Dixon Line," in *Report on the Resurvey of the Maryland-Pennsylvania Boundary,* 185.

43. Earl Schenck Miers, *Border Romance: The Story of the Exploits of Charles Mason and Jeremiah Dixon* (Newark, DE: Spiral Press, 1965), 20–21.

44. Barbara Susan Lefever, *The Stargazers* (York, PA: Printing Express, 1986), 128.

45. Thomas D. Cope, "When the Stars Interrupted the Running of a Meridian Line Northward Up the Delaware Peninsula," *Proceedings of the American Philosophical Society* 100 (1956): 565.

46. Ibid., 566.

47. Thomas D. Cope, "The Astronomical Manuscripts which Charles Mason Gave to Provost The Reverend John Ewing during October 1786," *Proceedings of the American Philosophical Society* 96 (1952): 423.

48. H. G. Dwight, "The Mason and Dixon Line," *Yale Review* 15 (1926): 694.

49. Ibid., 701.

50. Linda Hutcheon, *A Poetics of Postmodernism: History, Theory, Fiction* (New York: Routledge, 1988), 88.

51. David Seed, *The Fictional Labyrinths of Thomas Pynchon* (Iowa City: University of Iowa Press, 1988), 128.

52. Hutcheon, *A Poetics of Postmodernism,* 93.

53. Ibid., 89.

54. I wish to thank Brian McHale for being a great teacher and encouraging me to work further on this essay. I also thank Cheryl Torsney for proofreading and suggesting important revisions.

Plucking the American Albatross:
Pynchon's Irrealism in *Mason & Dixon*

JEFF BAKER

ABOUT THREE-QUARTERS OF THE WAY INTO *GRAVITY'S RAINBOW,*
Slothrop finds himself in the Zone reflecting upon his American
ancestry, and especially on his first American ancestor, William.
A hog drover who comes to love his pigs and the preterition they
symbolize for him, William Slothrop eventually writes an essay
inspired by his animals' "nobility and personal freedom." Titled
On Preterition, as the narrator describes it, the tract argued for
a kind of spiritual democracy in which the distinction between
the elect and preterite falls away into a community of equals, a
democratic culture that no longer makes the distinction between
souls.[1]

On the very next page, the descendant Tyrone is inspired to
ask—"Could he [William] have been the fork in the road America
never took, the singular point she jumped the wrong way from?
Suppose the Slothropite heresy had had time to consolidate and
prosper? Might there have been fewer crimes in the name of Jesus, and more mercy in the name of Judas Iscariot? It seems to
Tyrone Slothrop that there might be a route back—."[2]

William's attempt to "elevate" the preterite bespeaks a concern
with a particular kind of democratic culture that I have elsewhere
argued is central to both *Gravity's Rainbow* as well as to the sixties' revolutionary mentality that characterizes the large majority of Pynchon's work.[3] Tyrone's desire to "find some way back" to
that mythical fork in the road attests to the fact that, in choos-
ing the commercial, imperialistic death structures of Europe and
of Them, America has somehow forsaken the promise, the "gift
from invisible powers,"[4] which it was supposed to have represented. In light of what I've been arguing for some time now to
be among Pynchon's primary philosophical and ethical concerns,
the publication of *Mason & Dixon* this year seemed, at first blush,
to be corroboration on a large scale of my reading of Pynchon's

fiction. After all, even the novel's reviewers have described the book as one that "explores the underside of the American colonial enterprise, and European imperialism in general, to unravel the historical roots of the racial and social dislocations that haunt his other works and contemporary America." Or, as reviewer David Cohea puts it, *Mason & Dixon* explores the boundaries of the known and the thinkable in order to travel "200 years into our past to examine the darker wellsprings of the American soul" with a view toward examining how America "lost—or sold" its freedom.[5]

In truth, the novel sets about to explore the very "fork in the road America never took" that Slothrop laments in *Gravity's Rainbow.* In *Mason & Dixon,* Pynchon does indeed examine the roots of the American Revolutionary War, just as one might have expected from the decidedly activist author of *Gravity's Rainbow* and *Vineland,* only to find a gang of merchants and slave owners who would justify their own self-serving greed with the overblown rhetoric of universal law, egalitarianism, and democratic freedom.

Take, for example, the Sons of Liberty, whose primary spokesman in *Mason & Dixon* is the irrepressible Captain Volcanoe. We first meet the Sons of Liberty in the novel after the pair have separated to explore the colonies individually. Called upon to repair the Sons' telescope, Mason must resort to pretending to be a Frenchman in order to allay the patriots' suspicions and outright hatred of the British. In fairness, Pynchon's portrayal of the Sons of Liberty as primarily economically motivated is indeed accurate. One of the Sons explains the group's rancor: "'It goes to the Heart of this,' snarls the half-breed, Drogo. 'All the Brits want us for, is to buy their Goods. The only use we can be to them, is as a Herd of animals much like the Cow, from whose Udders, as from our Purses, the contents may be periodically remov'd. . . .'"[6] This hatred of all things British is reinforced by the group's willingness toward violence against the offending parties. Captain Volcanoe, in fact, wants his telescope fixed for spying, not star-gazing, the better to get the drop on any British soldiers who might be happening to pass his way, and the narrator describes the telescope's view as "a field marshal's dream" (403).

In point of fact, there really was a group during the Revolutionary period known as the Sons of Liberty, or "the Liberty Boys,"[7] and their opposition to British rule was indeed based upon defending their economic interests in the colonies, as is clear from the writings of Silas Downer, a member of the Rhode Island Sons.

In a 1765 *Providence Gazette* article written by Downer, the patriot wrote that

> a new System of Government, with Relation to the Colonies hath lately been conceived by those at the Helm, and certain Principles adopted, as deleterious in their effect on our Bodies Politic, as Arsenick if administered, would be to the Body natural. You, my countrymen, already feel some of the Effects of this horrid Policy. Men of War, Cutters, Marines with their Bayonets fixed, Judges of Admiralty, Tide-Waiters, Land-Waiters, with a whole Catalogue of Pimps, are sent hither, not to protect our Trade, but to distress it.[8]

In truth, the British presence in colonial trade had been oppressive for decades throughout the 1700s prior to the uprisings of the Sons of Liberty and other revolutionary groups. The Board of Trade in Britain had been established in 1696 to oversee trade in the colonies, and the board set about almost immediately to limit the kinds of trade, as well as the means of trade there. Among the various prohibitions and limitations placed upon colonial trade were the Woolen Act of 1699, the Hat Act of 1732, and the Iron Act of 1750. In addition, as historian Louis Hacker writes,

> the axe of disallowance descended regularly. As early as 1705 a Pennsylvania law for building up the shoe industry was disallowed; in 1706, a New York law designed to develop a sail-cloth industry was disallowed; in 1706, 1707, and 1708, laws of Virginia and Maryland, providing for the establishment of new towns, were disallowed on the grounds that such new communities must invariably lead to a desire to found new manufacturing industries and that their existence would draw off persons from the countryside where they were engaged in the production of tobacco.[9]

Thus, the issue of taxation without representation raised by the Sons of Liberty in *Mason & Dixon* is one that had culminated after literally years of intrusion into colonial trade. Moreover, their argument in the novel that someone like Ben Franklin being granted representation in Parliament would help allay their feelings of injustice toward the king and toward England is of course completely accurate historically (*Mason & Dixon,* 404–5). By the time of the Stamp Act crisis of 1766, at which time Mason chances to meet Volcanoe and his crew, a furor had arisen among the Sons across the thirteen colonies in protest, which an anonymous

Providence Gazette article from 1766 outlining the Sons' complaints regarding the Stamp Act, suspected to have been written by Silas Downer, made clear.[10]

All of this history seems straightforward enough, and Pynchon, as usual, has his facts right. But as is so often the case in Pynchon's writing, it's what the narrator *doesn't* tell us that ends up being the most important information with regard to the novelist's various critiques of Western society, politics, economics, and culture. And what we don't see in the novel is the Sons of Liberty's reliance upon the rhetoric of democracy to foment popular discontent among the colonial citizenry and to justify their obviously economic rebellion against the British government—rhetoric that future president of the United States John Adams was calling at this time "those democratic principles which have done so much mischief in this country."[11]

For example, in New York, threats levied by the Sons at the British and their representatives read: "Pro Patria—The first Man that either distributes or makes use of the Stampt Paper let him take Care of his House, Person, & Effects. [Signed:] Vox populi— We dare."[12] Evident here is the clear assertion that the "voice of the people" lends authority to the Sons of Liberty and their threats. However, it is also clear that this authority was never clearly given by the people themselves but was simply rhetoric that masked a much more mercenary aim, which of course was the proprietary interests of the local merchants and their unwillingness to bow any longer to the Board of Trade's dictates. In New York, many of the Sons were, in fact, merchants, and the minutes of one of their meetings lays out their complaints against the Stamp Act—all mercantile[13]—though the rhetoric employed throughout the meeting raises a democratic hullabaloo about the freedom of the "vox populi."

Perhaps most interesting of all in light of the democratic rhetoric that was increasingly employed to justify the imminent revolution in the colonies was the fact that, according to historian Jesse Lemisch,

> the family patterns, the religious, social, and educational homogeneity of the House of Commons were duplicated in the [colonial] House of Burgesses. An examination of six pre-Revolutionary legislatures shows that the "economic elite" comprising the top 10 percent of the population held 85 percent of the seats.
>
> Even the town meeting was not in fact the hotbed of democracy of popular myth: Samuel Eliot Morison has called "political democracy"

in colonial Massachusetts a "sham," and a recent study has detailed the devices which the powerful used to control the town meeting.[14]

Thus the democratic rhetoric employed to stir public opinion during the Stamp Act and the Revolutionary period was, by and large, a smokescreen on the part of the ruling elites to mask their own proprietary self-interest in rebelling against the British and their taxation upon colonial trade. In point of fact, democracy was not the issue at all, though it became the rallying cry of groups like the Sons of Liberty in their efforts to undermine British rule in the colonies. Perhaps most inexplicable and offensive, though, was the revolutionary rhetoric of slavery employed by the Sons of Liberty (and many other revolutionaries) to justify the growing colonial rebellion. For example, a song quoted, in part, in Dawson's history of the New York Sons included these stanzas:

I.

In Story we're told, How our Fathers of old,
Brav'd the Rage of the Winds and the Waves,
And cross'd the Deep o'er, To this Desolate Shore,
All because they were loth to be **SLAVES;** *Brave Boys,*
All because they were loth to be SLAVES.

II.

Yet a strange Scheme of late, Has been form'd in this State,
By a knot of political Knaves,
Who in Secret rejoice, that the Parliament's Voice,
Has condemn'd us by **LAW** to be **SLAVES;** *Brave Boys,*
Has condemn'd us by **LAW** to be **SLAVES.**

✳ ✳ ✳

XII.

With the Beasts of the Wood, We will ramble for Food,
And lodge in wild Desarts and Caves
And live Poor as Job, on the Skirts of the Globe,
Before we'll submit to be **SLAVES;** *Brave Boys, &c.*

XIII.

The Birthright we hold, Shall never be Sold,
But sacred maintain'd to our Graves;
Nay, and ere we'll comply, We will gallantly die,
For we *must not* and *will not* be **SLAVES;** *Brave Boys*
We *must not* and *will not* be **SLAVES.**[15]

Perhaps the greatest irony of the revolutionary rhetoric that was employed by citizens, merchants, and politicians alike during this period, evident in the above Sons of Liberty song, is manifested in the continual references to the fact that the colonies believed themselves to be increasingly enslaved by the British, yet the very trade that the colonists were attempting to protect had, as its economic foundation, the practice of slavery and the slave trade. Certainly, in *Mason & Dixon,* Pynchon emphasizes this aspect of the conflicts that characterized the birth of the United States more than any other. Slavery, in fact, permeates the novel, and its grim aspect is evident long before the surveyor and the astronomer reach the colonies.

No sooner do Mason and Dixon arrive in Cape Town than they are accosted by the Dutchman Bonk, whose primary concern is that the pair have come to spy on the Dutch slave trade (59). And of course it isn't long after that when Mason experiences the slave girl Astra's nocturnal visit, during which she explains to the astronomer the nature of his desirability: "All that the Mistress prizes of you is your Whiteness, understand? Don't feel disparaged,—ev'ry white male who comes to this Town is approach'd by ev'ry Dutch Wife, upon the same Topick. The baby, being fairer than its mother, will fetch more upon the Market,—there it begins, there it ends" (65).

The "great Worm of Slavery" (147) lays behind the entire economy at Cape Town, and at St. Helena as well, so it seems odd, to some degree at least, when Mason and Dixon are so surprised to see it in the colonies. After all, during this period of unprecedented imperialistic expansion, as the narrator explains, "Commerce without Slavery is unthinkable" (108). Yet Dixon is somehow flabbergasted to find slavery such a booming business in America, as his comments to Mason reveal: "Ev'rywhere they've sent us,—the Cape, St. Helena, America,—what's the Element common to all? . . . Slaves." Dixon continues:

> "Ev'ry day at the Cape, we lived with Slavery in our faces,—more of it at St. Helena,—and now here we are again, in another Colony, this time having drawn them a Line between their Slave-Keepers, and their Wage-Payers, as if doom'd to re-encounter thro' the World this Public Secret, this shameful Core. . . . Pretending it to be ever somewhere else, with the Turks, the Russians, the Companies, down there, down where it smells like warm Brine and Gunpowder fumes, they're murdering and dispossessing thousands untallied, the innocent of the

World, passing daily into the Hands of Slave-owners and Torturers, but oh, never in Holland, nor in England, that Garden of Fools . . . ? Christ, Mason."

" . . . No matter where in it we go, shall we find all the World Tyrants and Slaves? America was the one place we should *not* have found them." (692–93)

This notion of American exceptionalism that Dixon displays is of a piece, however, with the duality of mind among the colonists themselves upon the issue of slavery. As one historian has put it, "The very term 'slavery' was among the most frequent in the revolutionary vocabulary. The war was seen as essentially a battle against political servitude. Some were able to talk in the same breath of their own slavery and that of their Negroes without being fully aware of the implications of what they were saying."[16] Thus, the Sons of Liberty's revolutionary song is simply indicative of this strange form of blindness that allowed colonists to speak of their own servitude to England without ever considering the hypocrisy of their position vis-à-vis the issue of Negro slavery.[17]

Similarly, when Pynchon has Dixon describe himself as a "Traveling man, traveling West!" (287) to Colonel Washington, thereby allaying the American's Sino-Jesuit paranoia, Pynchon reveals an insider's knowledge into that secret fraternal brotherhood long speculated to have been at the heart of all of the major revolutions of the eighteenth century—the Freemasons.[18] Dixon's exclamation, in fact, describes a controlling metaphor in Masonic cosmology, in which "Each of us," the Masonic mythos claims, "has come from the mystical 'east,' the eternal source of all light and life, and our life here is described as being spent in the 'West' (that is, in a world which is the antipodes of our original home, and under conditions of existence as far removed from those we came from and to which we are returning, as is West from East in our ordinary computation of space)."[19]

The Freemasons even had a song dedicated to this metaphor of East and West as spiritual journey, a stanza of which goes as follows:

> From East to West the soul her journey takes;
> At many bitter founts her fever slakes;
> Halts at strange taverns by the way to feast,
> Resumes her load, and painful progress makes
> Back to the East.[20]

While trite and perhaps otherwise unremarkable, Pynchon's choice in identifying the "East/West" Masonic metaphor as Dixon's shibboleth certainly accretes another layer of meaning upon Mason and Dixon's already symbolically overdetermined Line and their personal odyssey in creating it. Perhaps more significant, though, is the very mention of the Freemasonry movement in the novel at all, which occurs not only here, but later, when the narrator actually delivers a brief history of Freemasonry's evolution from a guild-related artisan's society to a more social and "speculative" order in the early eighteenth century (290).

For any writer purporting to excavate the roots of democracy in America, there is good reason to examine the Freemasons, who were a powerfully influential force upon the building of the new government and in eventually educating the post-Revolution citizenry in democratic and ethical principles.[21] Benjamin Franklin was the grand master of a lodge in Philadelphia,[22] and George Washington himself first became a member as early as 4 November 1752.[23] Some forty-one years after his initiation into the society, Washington presided as Grand Master at the ceremonial Masonic dedication of the nation's capitol building on 18 September 1792.[24] More to the point, however, with regard to the beginnings of American democracy is the question, just how democratic was the Freemasonry movement in the colonies, circa 1750 through 1780? The answer should not surprise many Pynchon fans.

This society, among which a majority of the American founding fathers claimed membership, according to historian Steven Bullock, "was not a middle-class order that embraced a wide range of members. Instead, membership was restricted almost exclusively to men of rank. . . . In this project," Bullock continues, "colonial Masons recreated the fraternity in their own image. American gentlemen found connection with kings and nobles and with enlightened ideas and images nearly irresistible."[25]

> As their balance between social hierarchy and merit suggests, Masons did not imagine a world of complete equality. Indeed, they implicitly supported social distinctions. The fraternity's special clothing, its emphasis on charity, and its processions all proclaimed high standing. The closed nature of the group, along with its high fees, excluded men without adequate financial resources.[26]

Thus, while colonial Masonry may have "helped blunt and buffer the divisive forces of ethnicity, religion, and nationality . . . it did so, ironically, by reinforcing the crucial eighteenth-century social division, that between gentlemen and others."[27]

If Pynchon were merely reconstructing the birth of America and the contradictory elements that both comprised it and have remained with us to the present day, certainly there is much suggestion in the novel to point the way to an historical critique of this revolutionary rhetoric with regard to the hypocritical practices of the colonists. There is much evidence indeed to suggest that America was in fact "a gift from invisible powers" that had been spurned in favor of the "European Death-structures" of trade and power, and, in that refusal, America has brought upon itself all of the ills of our present reality. Mason, in fact, speculates about the legacy that slavery alone will impose upon the new nation:

> "Acts have consequences, Dixon, they must. These Louts believe all's right now,—that they are free to get on with Lives that to them are no doubt important,—with no Glimmer at all of the Debt they have taken on. That is what I smell'd,—Lethe-Water. One of the things the newly-born forget, is how Terrible its Taste, and Smell. In Time, these People are able to forget ev'rything. Be willing but to wait a little, and ye may gull them again and again, however ye wish,—even unto their own Dissolution. In America, as I apprehend, Time is the true River that runs 'round Hell." (346)

If one were attempting to read the novel as historical critique, then an earlier narrator's comment would seem to sum up the essence of that critique: "Small numbers of people go on telling much larger numbers what to do with their precious Lives,— among these Multitudes, all but a few go on allowing them to do so" (153). Indeed, this observation is merely a continuation of the examination of North Atlantic culture, politics, onto-epistemology, and loci of power that Pynchon so grandly undertook in *Gravity's Rainbow* and so wistfully lamented in *Vineland*. In *Gravity's Rainbow,* as Slothrop slowly plucks and strips his "albatross of self," the one "ghost-feather" he continually passes over is the one that represents "America": "Poor asshole," the narrator comments, "he can't let her go."[28] Similarly, in *Mason & Dixon,* Cherrycoke exhibits the same attachment: "I was back in America once more," he says, "finding, despite all, that I could not stay away from it, this object of hope that Miracles might yet occur, that God might yet return to Human affairs, that all the wistful Fictions necessary to the childhood of a species might yet come true . . . a third Testament . . . " (353).

Just so, it might be argued, is Pynchon unable to wrest himself from the notion of American exceptionalism: plucking the albatross of America, he seems himself unable to let go of the "ghost feather" that we ought, in the end, to have done better. From his earliest work, he has been preoccupied with the notion of America as that "gift from invisible powers" that has never lived up to its promise. Indeed, Pynchon's writing has demonstrated these concerns as early as "Entropy," which indicts Wall Street and the "mind of Moloch" during the political horse-latitudes of the American fifties. His critique of America continued with his more radical treatment of such countercultural concerns as two separate and unequal "Americas" in *The Crying of Lot 49,* which, as Oedipa's odyssey through the labyrinthine W.A.S.T.E. system reveals, exist in a land where the "chances [were] once so good for diversity."[29]

Pynchon then sounded an escalating countercultural critique with the publication of *Gravity's Rainbow,* in which the selfish indifference of the "glozing neuters," numb to the "System's" repressive practices, calls to mind the "good Germans" of an earlier debacle but also represents the "great silent majority" of the Nixon era during the Vietnam War. His critique continued in *Vineland,* where the writer's activist impulse is reduced to an almost wistful recollection of a sixties' radical and anarchic mentality, which points up, in its portrayal of a Reagan-era fascism not only accepted but *embraced* by an overwhelming majority of Americans, the lamentable failure of America to live up to its promise as a new beginning that might have been untainted by the "death structures" of trade and politics.

As a writer of and about the sixties, Pynchon, one might argue, has continued his critique with the publication of *Mason & Dixon,* revealing once and for all that America's claim to democracy, liberty, and freedom was a sham from the start. And, further, one might extrapolate that the American Civil War and the radical revolution of the sixties have been the only attempts toward real change that the U.S. has ever seen. Such an argument becomes all the more grim in the face of an unpromising future for participatory democracy in the United States. Because of a generation of "baby boomers" whose radicalism in the sixties seems to have shifted from "'*J'accuse*' to Jacuzzi,"[30] America shows no great signs of ever realizing the promise that it once held for sixties radicals.

Yet the novel's scope clearly ranges beyond "the dwindling promise of our American enterprise—which dwindling, in *Mason & Dixon,* begins at the outset of the forcible colonization of our continent, at the very moment we survey this land."[31] It is a novel obviously concerned with more than simply "the 'world-making' activity represented by the Line. Establishing the Line presents a metaphoric locus for exploring the colonial enterprise as it refashions the new Eden of America into legal and land development parcels, imposing the worst forces of the past on virgin land that had seemed to promise a fresh start"[32]—though the book is certainly concerned with this historical dimension of the birth of the United States.

Any reading of the novel that hopes to capture the gist of the book's real genius must account for a narrative that appears to imitate the diction, punctuation, and capitalization practices of an eighteenth-century style, but that nonetheless tears the fabric of that pseudohistoricity with cartoon-like irruptions and hippie-ish anachronisms. How does one account for the appearance of a character such as the Rabbi of Prague whom Dixon encounters and who, by way of greeting, flashes Mr. Spock's Vulcan blessing to "Live Long and Prosper" (485)? How again does one explain the appearance of a character whose description seems disturbingly akin to that of the cartoon character Popeye on the very next page (486)? Why is Benjamin Franklin wearing psychedelic purple-lensed glasses and giving late-night concerts with a couple of groupies in tow (294)? Why is George Washington smoking dope with our heroes and Martha bringing munchies for them afterwards (278; 280)? Perhaps most inexplicably, how does a character like Captain Zhang materialize into the purportedly "historical" narrative out of Tenebrae's dream after she falls asleep in 'Thlemer's room as he reads to her the Jesuit Abduction scenes from *The Ghastly Fop* (511–53)? Moreover, when Zhang appears like a deus ex machina near the end of the novel to provide a very New Age sort of explanation of Feng Shui and a most anachronistic assessment of the Line's consequences for American history (615), are we supposed to take anything in the story the least bit seriously?

On the most obvious of levels, the very absurdity of such narrative irruptions as Captain Zhang, the Learnèd English Dog, Vaucanson's mechanickal Duck and the French cook Armand's tale, vegetables flying out of the magnetic ground and sticking to the iron plough somewhere near York, Pennsylvania, the Octuple

Gloucester, and the journey to the giant vegetables not only allow Pynchon to call attention to the hallucinogenic and allegorical qualities of the narrative: they also reveal, in our very characterization of them as impossibly absurd and humorous, just how completely successful was the victory of the Enlightenment project in its reduction of possibilities to certainties. In this sense, the creation of the Line is merely symbolic of the victory of reason over magic, of certainty over possibility: "Does Britannia, when she sleeps, dream?" the narrator asks.

> Is America her dream?—in which all that cannot pass in the metropolitan Wakefulness is allow'd Expression away in the restless slumber of these Provinces, and on West-ward, wherever 'tis not yet mapped, nor written down, nor ever, by the majority of Mankind, seen,—serving as a very Rubbish-Tip for subjunctive Hopes, for all that *may yet be true*,—Earthly Paradise, Fountain of Youth, Realm of Prester John, Christ's Kingdom, ever behind the sunset, safe till the next Territory to the West be seen and recorded, measur'd and tied in, back into the Net-Work of Points already known, that slowly triangulates its Way into the Continent, changing all from subjunctive to declarative, reducing Possibilities to Simplicities that serve the ends of Governments,—winning away from the realm of the Sacred, its Borderlands one by one, and assuming them unto the bare mortal World that is our home, and our Despair. (345)

Here, the trope of America assumes symbolic weight far heavier than merely a lost opportunity for democratic practice—it becomes representative, instead, of the loss of magic, and of salvation—it becomes an allegory for modernity in all its Newtonian permutations. The great tragedy of modernity is the completeness of reason's victory, and Pynchon would counteract this gray reality with a narrative that turns its back on reason's certainty. In *Mason & Dixon,* Pynchon is attempting nothing less than to throw off the yoke of history and of realism, and therefore mere historical critique is but one of his concerns; the narrative offers us the possibility of magic in a reason-weary world. It offers us an alternative to the Disney-esque hyperreality of a realism that has become, in the words of contemporary American writer Curtis White, a State Fiction, and, in so doing, reinforces the activist mentality of the radical sixties that has characterized most of Pynchon's work.

In a 1992 article titled "Fiction's Future," Curtis White wrote about a publishing collective he helped start called Fiction Collective Two (FC2): we are confronted by "a situation," he writes, "in which a fictional discourse becomes part of a broader ideological confrontation, a situation in which a given literary aesthetic becomes a State Fiction. . . . Language and certainly literature are always the site of social dialogue or struggle. So one chooses not to write Realism because one chooses not to be in complicity with the state form which has appropriated it."[33]

This is not a new view of the power relationships between fiction, narrative, and politics for White. In a 1984 article about Italo Calvino's fiction, White wrote that

> the confrontation between realism and "experimentalism" is not only a narrow, provincial, literary dispute, it is also part of a broader ideological battle between not necessarily but factually combative epistemologies. Realism has become a State Fiction, a part of the machinery of the political state. It is through the conventions of Realism that the State explains to its citizens the relationship between themselves and Nature, economics, politics, and their own sexuality. This massive epistemological exercise takes place every day, right before our eyes on television, in the movies, in *Time* magazine, in the simple-minded, relational rhetoric of politicians, and so on.[34]

Neither is this an especially new view of either politics or narratology more generally—Pynchon makes essentially the same point both explicitly and stylistically in *Gravity's Rainbow,* in *Vineland,* and now in *Mason & Dixon.* And the point is that, as long as we are living in the realism of the material world, the state holds the upper hand. Where no magic is possible (or even permissible), then the *material*—in the form of television, high-tech movies, and soulless rock and roll—constitutes the overhyped reality of an all-too-corporeal existence.

In *Vineland,* Pynchon's much-beloved Mucho Maas helps the hapless antihero Zoyd Wheeler come to terms with the death of sixties magic. Mucho opines: "But acid gave us the X-ray vision to see through [the state's power over life and death], so of course they had to take it away from us." To which Zoyd replies: "Yeah, but they can't take what happened, what we found out." Mucho explains: "'Easy. They just let us forget. Give us too much to process, fill up every minute, keep us distracted, it's what the Tube is for, and though it kills me to say it, it's what rock and roll is becoming—just another way to claim our attention, so that beautiful certainty we had starts to fade, and after a while they have us convinced all over again that we really are going to die."[35]

The death of magic. The absence of doubt. Or, as Mason's sarcasm in a conversation with Maskelyne would have it, "So will the Reign of Reason cheerily dispose of any allegations of Paradise" (134). This is why the radical fiction writer, dedicated as he or she must be to the irruption of irreality, so "values the beauty of the new and 'monstrous.'" And the point of this irrealism is precisely, as one of Calvino's characters would say, to "explode" the barrier "between monsters and nonmonsters" so that "'everything is possible again.'"[36]

Mason & Dixon is irrealist fiction: The novel "levels" its various narrative codes, such as "history," "fiction," "cartooning," "song," "science fiction," "fantasy," "sermon," "personal recollection," and "cultural critique," and thereby assigns each code the same ontological status within the larger narrative structure. Thus, the novel's ontologically reductionist narrative coding renders *Mason & Dixon* Pynchon's deepest foray thus far into the disassembly of realist narrative strategies in the career of a writer who seems to have thoroughly enjoyed blowing up both readerly and writerly narrative expectations. In this way, too, the narrative coding embodies the democratizing principle that underlies the novel's egalitarian message, at the same time reinforcing the ontological status of the "irrational" and "irreal" phenomena embedded within the quasi-historical fabric of the narrative. Thus the narrative absurdities of *Mason & Dixon* set about returning the known simplicities back to the subjunctive from whence they came, and the novel does so in an act of narrative subversion that repudiates reality in favor of the monstrous possibilities of the irreal.

On the other hand, realism, and the rationalized narrative structures that derive from it, are symbolized in *Mason & Dixon* by the lifeless linearity of the Visto, which in turn symbolizes the Enlightenment's Grand Narrative of Science that actually produces it. Thus while Pynchon draws characters like Maskelyne who attempt to find transcendence and apotheosis through pure mathesis (134), he also gives us Mason, who finds the future Royal Astronomer's single-minded, reasoned approach to divining the essence of God through science "a walking cautionary Tale."

We have seen Pynchon in this antirational, anti-Enlightenment, antirealist mode before, of course—in *Gravity's Rainbow,* for example, where the Rocket stands as the culmination of Reason's achievement, which gives the illusion of apotheosis by apparently transcending nature's own "Telluric splendor." Like Slothrop, Blicero, and Enzian, Franz Pökler has been inculcated with this dream of transcendence above the phenomenal world, and looks to the Rocket for the security that he so desires. He finds "safety among the indoor abscissas and ordinates of graphs" of Rocket mathematics.[37] Pökler's utopian impulse toward transcendence is symbolized ingeniously by the very calculus he employs in the designing of the Rocket.

Yet Pökler's actions reveal that the "problem" with such abstracting, idealizing systems is not only that they are unable to subsume the entire range of living experience, but that they also directly affect and shape the human beings who employ such systems in order to manipulate and control their world. Pökler's capitulation to his own system's metaphor is evident in his willingness to employ his calculus's "succession of stills" upon his own daughter Ilse's summer visits in order to maintain his illusion of security and peace.

The narrator tells us that Pökler once knew "all of Ilse's cryings, her first attempts at words, the colors of her shit, the sounds and shapes that brought her tranquillity."[38] But by the time of "Ilse's" first visit to Peenemünde, the engineer admits that he can no longer tell if the girl is his own daughter or not. Nonetheless, because he is overwhelmed with a "strong inrush of love" upon seeing her, he allows himself to believe that she is his daughter. Then, just as he had once pieced together the plot-lines of films that he had only watched in bits and pieces while dozing off during the intervals, and just as he has accepted the pornography of movement by which his calculus represents the Rocket's parabola in a flash of successive frames, so Pökler begins the six-year process of piecing together a daughter out of each summer's successive "still" of her visit to him:

> So it has gone for the six years since. A daughter a year, each one about a year older, each time taking up nearly from scratch. The only continuity has been her name, and Zwölfkinder, and Pökler's love— love something like the persistence of vision, for They have used it to create for him the moving image of a daughter, flashing him only these summertime frames of her, leaving it to him to build the illusion of a single child.[39]

Thus, Pökler has been subsumed by the very "mathesis" by which he had hoped to "transcend." With this realization, Pökler quits the game, and tells "Ilse" that she doesn't have to come back next year.[40] Upon his renunciation of the "system" that had kept him isolated from the misery that surrounded him, Pökler is finally able to see what the work of his own hands and mind had helped to create:

> The odors of shit, death, sweat, sickness, mildew, piss, the breathing of Dora, wrapped him as he crept in staring at the naked corpses being carried out now that America was so close, to be stacked in front of the crematoriums, the men's penises hanging, their toes clustering round and white as pearls . . . each face so perfect, so individual, the lips stretched back into death-grins, a whole silent audience caught at the punch line of the joke . . . and the living, stacked ten to a straw mattress, the weakly crying, coughing, losers. . . . All his vacuums, his labyrinths, had been the other side of this. While he lived, and drew marks on paper, this invisible kingdom had kept on, in the darkness outside . . . all this time. . . . Pökler vomited.[41]

In Pynchon's brutal description of Dora, with its now familiar images of Nazi death camp atrocities, he has pointed up the kind of inhuman savagery that those like Pökler are able to allow to occur (and even *participate in*) so long as they rely on their idealizing systems to both justify and overlook such vicious oppression, torture, and murder.

And this, I think, is at least part of the essence of Pynchon's critique in *Mason & Dixon*: participation in the system for whatever reason is tantamount to tacit acceptance and even approval of the system's horrible effects. And this is why Dixon, toward the end of the novel, beseeches Mason: "Didn't we take the King's money," he asks, "as here we're taking it again? whilst Slaves waited upon us, and we neither one objected, as little as we have here, in certain houses south of the Line" (693). With grim insight into their complicity with the system, Dixon here raises the question of the pair's guilt in simply going along with the status quo. Like Pökler's complicity with the Nazi system and its implications for an entire generation of "good Germans," Mason and Dixon's guilt in this modern allegory is shared, in the end, by each of us. Or, another way to phrase the issue from a more contemporary point of view, as Curtis White has done regarding the failure of the sixties generation to live up to its ideals, might sound like this: "you don't have to live in the 'belly of the beast' to benefit from the beast's reign."[42]

In the end, *Mason & Dixon* stands as an indictment of all who fail to challenge the crippling and exploitative effects that lay behind the comfortability of their lives. Even the tale's narrator, the Reverend Cherrycoke, is shown to be a hypocrite, for he must rely on the good graces of arms dealer LeSpark (411) in order to enjoy the comfortable perch from which he spins his tale. Just as Mason and Dixon's Line comes to represent the "Bad History" that Zhang so presciently foresees, so must we recognize that Pynchon's allegory subsumes the very world in which we live and our complicity with its horrid underbelly. It is certainly true that the surveyor and the astronomer are sympathetic characters, yet it is the very fact of their amiability and sympathetic nature that renders them such powerfully negative examples. Pynchon's tale of their Line is filled with numerous descriptions of how painstakingly the two work to get the measurements just right (cf., 461). Yet there is never any examination as to *why* they should be surveying the Line at all—or to what purpose it will be put. Dixon's willingness to upbraid and whip the Slave-Driver notwithstanding, the two are every bit as complicitous as any slaveholder in the novel, for they are willing to enjoy the benefits of the system while complaining about its horrible injustices. Indeed, here is a lesson for any with stomach enough to listen, and courage enough to hear. If we don't leave this novel with at least a vague feeling of uneasy guilt, then we haven't read it nearly as carefully as it has been written.

Perhaps as importantly, the novel indicts our culture's terrible loss of magic and imaginative play, and its resulting dependency upon reason and its narrative counterpart, Realism. For, like Cherrycoke, it's Mason and Dixon's very literal-mindedness allows them to participate in the system, thereby enjoying its effects, while hypocritically maintaining the luxury of criticizing its immorality. In the end, it is no mistake that so many of the novel's anachronistic narrative irruptions derive from the culture of 1960s America. In addition to the obvious parallels between the American Revolution of the late eighteenth century and the attempted radical revolution of the sixties, Washington's penchant for hemp and Franklin's tinted granny glasses allow Pynchon to indict both revolutionary generations on the charge of complicity with the system. And if the wacky, hallucinogenic irruptions undermine narrative realism and the politics that accompany it, they also remind us that, at various times in our history, there have been generations who had a chance to really make a difference—

to make America that "gift from invisible powers"—but who sold out to the forces of trade and politics.

And this brings us to a central question, I think, in Pynchon's writing from *Gravity's Rainbow* to the present. Were the sixties a bust? Were the efforts of sixties radicals, in the end, a failure? SDS radical-turned-university-professor Todd Gitlin's answer, decidedly, is no. "To put it briefly," he writes, "the genies that the Sixties loosed are still abroad in the land, inspiring and unsettling and offending, making trouble. For the civil rights and antiwar and countercultural and women's and the rest of that decade's movements forced upon us central issues for Western civilization—fundamental questions of value, fundamental divides of culture, fundamental debates about the nature of the good life."[43]

Surely those genies are loosed here in Thomas Pynchon's latest novel *Mason & Dixon,* which successfully raises the same essential debate—that is, how to be? *Mason & Dixon*'s irrealism stands as a force for undermining a narratively and politically oppressive realism. The novel is also an indictment of an entire generation's complicity with the unfair and often inhumane effects of our culture of late capitalism. In the end, Pynchon's personalization of these issues in his intimate and sympathetic portrait of Mason and Dixon begs the toughest of questions—one raised, in fact, by Foucault in his introduction to Deleuze and Guattari's *Anti-Oedipus,* where he discusses the need to examine and overcome "the fascism in us all, in our heads and in our everyday behavior, the fascism that causes us to love power, to desire the very thing that dominates and exploits us."[44]

But each of us, of course, must come to terms with this issue as best we can. Yet it is significant that Pynchon leaves us with something new in *Mason & Dixon,* something we've never seen before in his fiction and which helps shed some light upon how we might best attempt to answer Foucault's charge. Toward the end of the novel, Mason is visiting the now-Royal Astronomer Maskelyne, surveying the discovery of a new planet through the telescope, when he sees—"outside the world"—a procession of evil, which vision helps the astronomer to understand that:

There may be found, within the malodorous Grotto of the Selves, a conscious Denial of all that Reason holds true. Something that knows, unarguably as it knows Flesh is sooner or later Meat, that there are Beings who are not wise, or spiritually advanced, or indeed capable of Human kindness, but ever and implacably cruel, hiding, haunting, waiting,—known only to the blood-scented deserts of the Night. (769)

Beyond reason and consciousness, Pynchon suggests, evil does exist in the world. And if this darkness dwells "a little over the Line between the Day and its annihilation," somewhere between "the number'd and the unimagin'd," then surely some equal and opposite force must counterbalance it in the universe—within some space unavailable to reason, within some magical zone beyond realism, though lost as it might be in the gray victory of the Enlightenment project. Perhaps in Pynchon's irreal fiction there exists a possibility of some small redemption, of some "kind Underground" that might yet provide "At least one moment of passage . . . to be found for every street now indifferently gray with commerce, with war, with repression . . . finding it, learning to cherish what was lost, mightn't we find some way back?"[45]

NOTES

1. Thomas Pynchon, *Gravity's Rainbow* (New York: Penguin, 1973), 555. As the narrator puts it, *On Preterition* "had to be published in England, and is among the first books to've been not only banned but also ceremonially burned in Boston. Nobody wanted to hear about all the Preterite, the many God passes over when he chooses a few for salvation. William argued holiness for these "second Sheep without whom there'd be no elect. You can bet the Elect in Boston were pissed off about that" (555).

2. Ibid., 556.

3. Jeff Baker, "A Democratic Pynchon: Counterculture, Counterforce and Participatory Democracy," *Pynchon Notes* 32–33 (1993): 99–131. See also Jeff Baker, "Amerikkka Uber Alles: German Nationalism, American Imperialism, and the 60s Anti-war Movement in *Gravity's Rainbow*," *Critique* 40, no. 4 (1999): 323–41.

4. *Gravity's Rainbow*, 722.

5. Bernard Duyfhuizen, "Worth the Wait," review of *Mason & Dixon, News and Observer* [Raleigh, NC], May 4, 1997, G4; David Cohea, "Pynchon Charts America's Divided Soul," *Orlando Sentinel,* May 4, 1997, F6.

6. Thomas Pynchon, *Mason & Dixon* (New York: Henry Holt, 1997), 402. Further references will be noted parenthetically within the text.

7. Henry B. Dawson, paper read before the New York Historical Society on 3 May 1859, reprinted as *The Sons of Liberty in New York,* Mass Violence in America series (New York: Arno and the *New York Times,* 1969), 40–41.

8. Quoted in Carl Bridenbaugh, *Silas Downer, Forgotten Patriot: His Life and Writings* (Providence: Rhode Island Bicentennial Foundation, 1974), 21–22.

9. Louis M. Hacker, "An Economic Interpretation," in *The American Revolution: How Revolutionary Was It?,* ed. George Athan Bilias, 2d ed. (New York: Holt, Rinehart, and Winston, 1970), 34.

10. Bridenbaugh, *Silas Downer,* 32–34. In part, the anonymous article read: "Americans absolutely determined never to submit to the loss of their Liberties,

nor to suffer the Stamp Act to take place. . . . formed themselves into corresponding societies, in all the Colonies and Places of note on the Continent, from South Carolina to New Hampshire, duly informing each other of the Situation of their respective public Affairs, and engaging, in Case of Necessity, to contribute all necessary Assistance to each other, to the Hazard of their Lives and Fortunes. They likewise generally determined, that in Case the Stamp Act should not be repealed by a certain Time, to carry on all Kinds of Business without Stamps, everywhere, as some Places, to their Honor, had already done, particularly in Rhode Island and Providence Plantations, (where the Example was first set) . . . " (23–24).

11. A. J. Beitzinger, *A History of American Political Thought* (New York: Dodd, Mead, 1972), 141.

12. Dawson, 82.

13. Ibid., 84–85.

14. Jesse Lemisch, "The Revolution as a Mass Movement," in *The American Revolution: How Revolutionary Was It?,* ed. George Athan Bilias, 2d ed. (New York: Holt, Rinehart, and Winston, 1970), 104.

15. Dawson, 76–77. This song is of course echoed in *Mason & Dixon,* in the Revolutionary song which Mason encounters somewhere in Virginia:: "Let us go to the Wall, / Let us march thro' the Pain, / Americans all, / Slaves ne'r again" (571).

16. Duncan J. MacLeod, *Slavery, Race and the American Revolution* (Cambridge: Cambridge University Press, 1974), 16–17.

17. Of course, not all of the colonists were quite so blind, as a sermon by Baptist Preacher John Allen in 1774 indicates: "Blush ye pretended votaries for freedom!" he admonished, "ye trifling patriots! who are making a vain parade of being advocates for the liberties of mankind, who are thus making a mockery of your profession by trampling on the sacred natural rights and privileges of Africans; for while you are fasting, praying, nonimporting, nonexporting, remonstrating, resolving, and pleading for a restoration of your charter rights, you at the same time are continuing this lawless, cruel, inhuman, and abominable practice of enslaving your fellow creatures" (quoted in MacLeod, *Slavery, Race and the American Revolution,* 16). Allen's rhetoric is echoed in *Mason & Dixon* by Cherrycoke's scathing criticism of Virginia slaveholders (275).

18. Margaret C. Jacob, *Living the Enlightenment: Freemasonry and Politics in Eighteenth-Century Europe* (New York: Oxford University Press, 1991), 10.

19. W. L. Wilmshurst, *The Meaning of Masonry* (London: Rider; rpt. of 5th ed., New York: Bell, 1980), 29.

20. Ibid., 48.

21. Steven C. Bullock, *Revolutionary Brotherhood: Freemasonry and the Transformation of the American Social Order, 1730–1849* (Chapel Hill: University of North Carolina Press, 1996), 138, 149.

22. Ibid., 47.

23. Ibid., 104.

24. Ibid., 137. Such "coincidences" proliferate as one examines the historical record of this period. For example, one of the interesting places of convergence where the Newtonians and Whigs who constituted the majority of Freemasons in England during the late seventeenth and early eighteenth centuries had first begun to have social discourse was, of all places, within the Royal Society. As Jacob writes,

By 1660 and the Restoration of monarchy in England and by 1663 and the establishment of the Royal Society under royal charter, the social version of scientific learning that prevailed during the 1640s . . . had given way to an increasingly entrepreneurial notion of scientific practice. Scientific learning became the work of great and enterprising minds at work in isolation, while the social purpose of science was linked solely with discoveries to improve trade and commerce, to build empire abroad and to promote material prosperity at home. (Jacob, *The Radical Enlightenment: Pantheists, Freemasons, and Republicans* [London: George Allen and Unwin, 1981], 74.)

Newton's *Principia* was published in 1687, and Jacob suggests that there is reasonable evidence that Newton himself benefited from championing his worldview as supportive of the newly established monarchy, of capitalistic self-interest, and of empire building through his influence upon the Royal Society (Jacob, *Radical Enlightenment,* 91). In any case, by the eighteenth century there is a clear historical relationship between Freemasons and the Royal Society in England (Jacob, *Radical Enlightenment,* 117). Into this world of secret societies, political intrigue, and empire building blunder the hapless Mason and Dixon, whose occasional paranoid speculations regarding the Royal Society's willingness to use them for whatever mercenary ends might suit the powers-that-be are, if anything, too mild and unsuspecting.

25. Bullock, *Revolutionary Brotherhood,* 51.

26. Ibid., 26.

27. Ibid., 59. Masons attending Boston celebrations between 1768 and 1770, for example, were recorded as follows—more than 60 percent were merchants, and another 14 percent were professionals of some sort. Fewer than 10 percent were artisans. These figures obviously support Bullock's argument that the society was indeed exclusionary (ibid., 59). For his part, Ben Franklin believed that men were motivated, in large measure, purely by self-interest alone. As one historian put it, Franklin, a "Newtonian and a Deist . . . saw nature ruled by law, but in contrast to the prevailing Shaftsburian optimism . . . declared ruefully: 'Whatever may be the Musick of the Spheres, how great so ever the Harmony of the Stars, 'tis certain there is no harmony among the Stargazers; but they are perpetually growling and snarling at one another like strange Curs'" (Beitzinger, *History of American Political Thought,* 182). In the place of any unrealistic expectations regarding democratic home rule, Franklin instead believed in "the ideal of promotion of the public good through leadership of the wise and good. It [would be] the task of these men, if common opinion [stood] to the contrary, to convince 'common People' that their interest [would] be promoted by desirable changes" (Beitzinger, *History of American Political Thought,* 185).

The author of the Declaration of Independence (and Freemason), Thomas Jefferson, also believed in a similar "natural aristocracy" (Beitzinger, *History of American Political Thought,* 274), though his view of "common people" was, if anything, more harsh by far than Franklin's unflattering portrait. He believed that urban workmen, for example, were "the panders of vice and the instruments by which the liberties of a country are generally overturned." This view, argues another historian, "suggests the narrow limits of [Jefferson's] faith in the ability of what he unashamedly called 'the swinish multitude' to govern itself" (Lemisch, "The Revolution as a Mass Movement," 105).

28. *Gravity's Rainbow,* 623.

29. Thomas Pynchon, *The Crying of Lot 49* (New York: Harper and Row, 1966), 181.

30. Todd Gitlin, *The Sixties: Years of Hope, Days of Rage* (New York: Bantam, 1987), 433.

31. Rick Moody, "Surveyors of the Enlightenment," *Atlantic Monthly,* July 1997, 110.

32. Duyfhuizen, "Worth the Wait," G4.

33. Curtis White, "Fiction's Future," *ANQ: A Quarterly Journal of Short Articles, Notes, and Reviews* 5 (1992): 251.

34. Curtis White, "Italo Calvino and What's Next: The Literature of Monstrous Possibility," *Iowa Review* 14, no. 3 (1984): 138.

35. Thomas Pynchon, *Vineland* (New York: Penguin, 1990), 314.

36. Curtis White, "Italo Calvino," 134.

37. *Gravity's Rainbow,* 399.

38. Ibid., 418.

39. Ibid., 422.

40. Ibid., 430.

41. Ibid., 433.

42. Curtis White, *The Idea of Home* (Los Angeles: Sun & Moon, 1992), 143.

43. Gitlin, *The Sixties,* xiv.

44. Michel Foucault, introduction to *Anti-Oedipus: Capitalism and Schizophrenia,* by Gilles Deleuze and Felix Guattari, trans. Robert Hurley, Mark Seem, and Helen R. Lane (Minneapolis: University of Minnesota Press, 1983), xi.

45. *Gravity's Rainbow,* 769.

Plot, Ideology, and Compassion in *Mason & Dixon*

THOMAS H. SCHAUB

I

Several years after the rumors of a book about Mason and Dixon first began to circulate, Pynchon wrote in the introduction to *Slow Learner:*

> Except for that succession of the criminally insane who have enjoyed power since 1945, including the power to do something about it, most of the rest of us poor sheep have always been stuck with simple, standard fear. I think we all have tried to deal with this slow escalation of our helplessness and terror in the few ways open to us, from not thinking about it to going crazy from it. Somewhere on this spectrum of impotence is writing fiction about it—occasionally, as here, offset to a more colorful time and place.[1]

Here are posed for us the terms of aesthetics and politics so central to criticism and theory in recent decades, but they are posed here in such a way as to allocate to the realm of power alone the power to do something, while the writing of fiction exists only on a spectrum of impotence between forgetfulness and insanity. While *Mason & Dixon*'s place on that spectrum has yet to be determined, the following discussion begins an inquiry into the aesthetic mode of the novel's relation to politics and the power to do something.

This region between forgetfulness and insanity, it may be recalled, is the region occupied by Oedipa Maas, what she comes to feel is the quasi-paranoid position of "relevance." Many readers have thought the saving grace of Oedipa's example to be her pursuit of meaning, projected or found remaining uncertain. It was this very uncertainty, among other devices, which created the interactive text sensitizing and radicalizing the reader. In this way,

Pynchon's fiction has always been an overdetermined instance of Peter Brooks's definition of plot: "the organizing line and intention of narrative . . . best conceived as an activity, a structuring operation elicited in the reader trying to make sense of those meanings that develop only through textual and temporal succession."[2]

In *Mason & Dixon,* this sense of plot is entirely missing, for meanings do not develop "through textual and temporal succession."[3] Instead Pynchon gives us a sequence of fables, each of which illustrates similar or related meaning, giving us a textual and temporal repetition of theme. Doubt and uncertainty, the mainstays of Pynchon's narrative torque, are in *Mason & Dixon* less structures of the condition of meaning than the fabulist's comment upon his own art, comments transposed into an eighteenth-century key, as here in a passage from Wicks Cherrycoke's book, *Christ and History:*

> Doubt is the essence of Christ. The final pure Christ is pure uncertainty. He is become the central subjunctive fact of a Faith, that risks ev'rything upon one bodily Resurrection. . . . Wouldn't something less doubtable have done?[4]

The reader can't help wondering at this point if Cherrycoke expresses an aspect of the writer's poetics, uncertainty providing the subjunctive condition of fiction's sacral mystery. With *Mason & Dixon,* Pynchon has jettisoned his use of the detective genre, the central figure in search of V. or Tristero or the rocket, and with this abandonment he has dispensed with the epistemological doubt that he had used to bedevil and provoke his readers. More accurately, from a narrative point of view this doubt remains but is transformed (or solved) by an intermediary storyteller—Wicks Cherrycoke—a device that makes clear from the get-go the contingency of what follows.

In *Mason & Dixon,* by sharp contrast with his earlier novels, the status (as well as the meaning) of the allegory is always in sight, while doubt itself becomes a recurrent theme, rather than the experience of the reader, who never works very hard to identify Pynchon's intentions or (for example) the meaning of that Line which Mason and Dixon are surveying: "we were putting a line straight through the heart of the wilderness," Cherrycoke recalls (8). The Line and its analogues spoil a good night of romance: "Imagine you're out late on a Spring night, riding along, with your Sweetheart, and Evening trembling with Promise, all the night an Eden" and all at once you blunder "sheep-eyed upon yet one more bloody Mill,—a river turn'd to a Race" (313). At another point, the Visto cuts a swath between husband and wife, leaving one in Maryland and the other in Pennsylvania. Dixon has made a living converting "common" ground to "private" property, and after his father's death sought a "mapped World he could escape to" (242). Mill-races, enclosures, maps, lines, and clocks are evidence, Cherrycoke tells his audience, that chartered companies are now "the form the World has begun to take" (252).

> Let Judges judge, and Lawyers have their Day,
> Yet soon or late, the Line will find its Way,
> For Skies grow thick with aviating Swine,
> Ere men pass up the chance to draw a Line.
>
> (257)

Through Captain Zhang, this propensity for the drawing of straight lines helps develop the ecological allegory of the novel. Zhang declares the Line "acts as a Conduit for what we call *Sha*, or, as they say in Spanish California, Bad Energy. . . . Ev'rywhere else on earth, Boundaries follow Nature,—coast-lines, ridge-tops, river-banks,—so honoring the Dragon or *Shan* within, from which Land-Scape ever takes its form. To mark a right Line upon the Earth is to inflict upon the Dragon's very Flesh, a sword-slash, a long, perfect scar" (542). Zhang's declaration is further evidence that Pynchon may have been working on *Mason & Dixon* during the writing of *Gravity's Rainbow* because it echoes a description late in the earlier novel: "You can look up and see a whole slope of cone-bearing trees rushing up darkly away from one side of the road. Trees creak in sorrow for the engineered wound through their terrain, their terrenity or earthhood."[5] This ecological mood begins to affect Dixon, too. By the time he encounters the American surveyor Shelby, he is put off by Shelby's "love of complexity" for whom the "pure Space" of America merely "waits the Surveyor" (586), and Dixon is made melancholy by Shelby's rabid pleasure in converting space to lines and angles. Because—and this is the last of my examples—"for as long as its Distance from the Post Mark'd West remains unmeasur'd, nor is yet recorded as Fact, may it remain, a-shimmer, among the few final Pages of its Life as Fiction" (650). The "America of the Soul" is ever "an Interior unmapp'd" (511)!

Writing itself is a kind of mapmaking, and nowhere more so

than in the genre of the Novel, with its claims to represent the past more faithfully than history itself. Given this implicit analogy between author and surveyor, however, Pynchon has his narrator sharply distinguish his own procedure from a history that claims to be a record of fact. In *Christ and History,* by Wicks Cherrycoke, the good reverend insists there must be "more than one life-line back into a Past we risk, each day, losing our forebears in forever"; unlike the technique of surveying that cuts a straight line, this one is "not a Chain of single Links, for one broken Link could lose us All,—rather, a great disorderly Tangle of Lines, long and short, weak and strong, vanishing into the Mnemonick Deep, with only their Destination in common" (349). This passage from Cherrycoke's book helps to clarify the analogy between Christic doubt and novelistic fiction implicit in the passage from this book that I quoted earlier, for here fabulist history—the novel—is a tangle of lifelines through which lives of the past are resurrected.

In the effort to write without bounds, to write extravagantly, Pynchon might remind readers of the conclusion to *Walden,* where ever-restive Thoreau expresses his impatience with a single understanding of life. "As if," Thoreau wrote,

> Nature could support but one order of understandings. . . . As if there were safety in stupidity alone. I fear chiefly lest my expression may not be extravagant enough, may not wander far enough beyond the narrow limits of my daily experience, so as to be adequate to the truth of which I have been convinced. . . . I desire to speak somewhere without bounds. . . . In view of the future or the possible, we should live quite laxly and undefined in front, our outlines dim and misty on that side. . . . The volatile truth of our words should continually betray the inadequacy of the residual statement. Their truth is instantly translated . . . the words which express our faith and piety are not definite; yet they are significant and fragrant like frankincense to superior natures.[6]

Similarly in *Mason & Dixon,* when Uncle Ives, speaking for the impulses of the Age of Reason, remonstrates with Wicks that what we need are facts, the "whole Truth," Wicks replies, "Who claims Truth, Truth abandons. History is hir'd, or coerc'd, only in Interests that must ever prove base. She is too innocent, to be left within the reach of anyone in Power,—who need but touch her, and all her Credit is in the instant vanish'd, as if it had never been" (350). Cherrycoke's solution to this difficulty requires forms of circumspection: "She needs rather to be tended lovingly and honorably by fabulists and counterfeiters, Ballad-Mongers and Cranks of ev'ry Radius, Masters of Disguise to provide her the Costume, Toilette, and Bearing, and Speech nimble enough to keep her beyond the Desires, or even the Curiosity, of Government" (350).

This last extended metaphor, of the fabulist doffing the disguise of (historical) truth, exactly reverses the strategy of *The Crying of Lot 49* in which Oedipa stumbles upon "the languid, sinister blooming of The Tristero" through a process of striptease—"As if the breakaway gowns, net bras, jeweled garters and G-strings of historical figuration that would fall away were layered as dense as Oedipa's own streetclothes in that game with Metzger . . . as if a plunge toward dawn indefinite black hours long would indeed be necessary before The Tristero could be revealed in its terrible nakedness."[7] And yet, as I have been trying to argue, there is neither striptease nor disguise (nor boundlessness) in *Mason & Dixon*. Instead of a "disorderly Tangle of Lines" we have ever before us a parable of the construction of the West misread by the Age of Reason and mystified as discovered "fact."

This play with the eighteenth century's familiar distinction between fact and fancy seems to be the bass line that the reader hears beneath the by turns comic and melancholy melody of *Mason & Dixon*'s progress. At the close of the novel, in which Cherrycoke imagines the deathbed scene between Mason and his second wife, with Benjamin Franklin attending, Mason unwittingly theorizes Pynchon's postmodern history in the language of deism, by which the eighteenth century managed to conflate Newtonian mechanics with a faith in God:

> "'Tis a Construction," Mason weakly, "a great single Engine, the size of a Continent. I have all the proofs you may require. Not all the Connexions are made yet, that's why some of it is still invisible. Day by day the Pioneers and Surveyors go on, more points are being tied in, and soon becoming visible, as above, new Stars are recorded and named and plac'd in Almanacks." (772)

But even the sympathetic irony implicit in this account of Mason's deathbed optimism has already been extracted from the Line and allegorized earlier in the novel when the character Nathe writes his school friend that the path of the Line "speeds its way like a Coach upon the Coaching-Road of Desire, where we create continually before us the Road we must journey upon" (459). That which Mason imagines latent, awaiting discovery and proof, record and name, is just what Mason says, "a construction." This is a familiar moral to readers of Pynchon's novels, who may recall the closing sentences of the Advent scene in *Gravity's Rainbow:* "you must create [the path] by yourself, alone in the dark."[8]

The conversion of common to private, of nature to commerce, of openness to enclosure, of wholeness to division, of pure space to lines and angles, and of unmapped soul to recorded Fact: of all these things the Line is the symbol. Wonder ye then at the party of surveyors?

II

Cherrycoke deserves more direct attention at this point because I have rather shamelessly been reading this narrator as a mildly distorted conduit for our author himself. There are reasons for doing so, given Cherrycoke's impeccable credentials. Perhaps most significant is the disappearance of the outside narrator into the voice of Cherrycoke. The novel begins with third-person narration ("Snow-Balls have flown their Arcs"), while the voice of Reverend Cherrycoke makes its appearance three pages later ("'It's twenty years,' recalls the Rev^d" [7]). Yet this standard nesting collapses by the end of the first chapter, where Cherrycoke's voice appears suddenly without quotation marks: "Tho' my Inclination had been to go out aboard an East Indiaman (the Rev^d continues), as that route East travers'd notoriously a lively and youthful World of shipboard Dalliance" (10). Nesting of narrators and narratives continues inside Cherrycoke's narrative voice, but at this point his becomes the outer narrative frame, displacing the mediating ground between character and author. In fact, Pynchon gives us the parenthetical to make sure we haven't missed the deletion of quotation marks. Removing those marks, I am suggesting, bestows a new authority upon Cherrycoke, or, at the very least, the reader is now turned over, as it were, to the good "Rev^d," and put in the care of his story.

As a storyteller resurrecting the past, Cherrycoke places himself within a three-part division of historians: mere chronologists, whose work is the business of lawyers; the compilers of testimony, the whole truth, which is the goal of historians; and remembrancers, whose memories "[belong] to the People" (349). Cherrycoke calls himself an "untrustworthy Remembrancer" (8), and *Mason & Dixon* is surely a novel for the people, as antigovernment as any Idaho militiaman, restless with any account settling into the rigid appearance of fact. Like the story of Dixon whipping the slave driver, though it does not appear in official histories, family stories are perfected "till what survives is the pure truth, anneal'd to Mercilessness, about each Figure, no matter how stretch'd" for it is "part of the common Duty of Remembering,— surely our Sentiments,—how we dream'd of, and were mistaken in, each other,—count for at least as much as our poor cold Chronologies" (695–96). We must, insists Cherrycoke, "place our unqualified Faith in the Implement, as the Tale accompting for its Presence" (695).

Though Pynchon's manipulation of the discourse of fact and fancy may and should be considered an aspect of his faithfulness to historical period (as is Uncle Ives's being scandalized by young ladies reading novels), there is no mistaking the accuracy of the term "fabulist," as described here by Cherrycoke, for characterizing Pynchon's narrative strategy. The creation of in-your-face "irresponsible narratives, that will not distinguish between fact and fancy" (351) has long been Pynchon's forte. These aesthetic swipes at power always have their moral, too: Oedipa constructs meaning and relevance through the act of metaphor, and Slothrop can turn any corner to find himself inside a parable. As Maxwell's Demon is a metaphor of Oedipa's search for meaning, and the Rocket of Western man's death-wish, so here the surveyors' Line is a metaphor of the construction of "the West" by the Age of Reason. The author of *Mason & Dixon* is a kind of Learnèd Dog, a "tail-wagging Scheherazade" offering "Provisions for Survival in a World less fantastik" (22), just as Cherrycoke earns his room and board by keeping the children entertained.

Thus when Cherrycoke tells his listeners of Dixon's encounter with the Rabbi of Prague—a staging device for yet another moral—who tells Dixon that the New World exists not for wealth but is a secret body of knowledge that may be read East to West "much as a Line of Text" (487), we know pretty well that this secret body of knowledge is none other than the novel itself, which is the reading of that Line. The implications of this irony, as Richard Rorty has written, "go all the way down,"[9] for the cutting of this Visto (the making of the Line as well as our reading of it) is ever the creation of what Cherrycoke terms the "subjunctive fact of a Faith" (511)—or of the novel's fabulation.

Even "humanity" itself, like the novel, is a creature of this age in which the modern subject is formed in discourse. This major theme in the novel is the best reason yet for giving Cherrycoke the authority here attributed to his character. For among the other items in his dossier is his status as ghost, returned like Banquo from the dead, a "shade with a grievance" (8) and resurrected storyteller, to narrate or resurrect stories from the past. Cherrycoke is an enemy of the state, having committed the crime of anonymity by leaving unsigned "Accounts of certain Crimes . . . committed by the Stronger against the Weaker" (9), including not only evictions and assize verdicts but also the crime of "enclosure" by which Dixon has been making a living and which the book seems to say is an English activity carried over into the spaces of America. (Under the pressures of Vietnam, Pynchon had expressed this view with the more highly charged language of apocalypse: In America "Europe had found the site for its Kingdom of Death."[10])

In naming names—Pynchon's Cold War origins remain central—without giving his own, Cherrycoke discovers that his "name had never been his own," just as Slothrop discovers his penis was never his own but belongs to the government as the means of calling him out, subjecting him:

> It took me till I was lying among the Rats and the Vermin, upon the freezing edge of a Future invisible, to understand that my name had never been my own,—rather belonging, all this time, to the Authorities, who forbade me to change it, or withhold it, as 'twere a Ring upon the Collar of a Beast, ever waiting for the Lead to be fasten'd on. . . .
> (10)

This Althusserian fable is the paradigmatic fable of the story that Cherrycoke has to tell about the assembly of the nation from the pure space of America—or, more pointedly, about the way that Old World institutions (enclosure and slavery, to name two) reproduced themselves in the newly discovered land.

From this viewpoint, one might understand *Mason & Dixon* to be not only an historical novel but also an historical-novelistic answer to Althusser's question, "What, then, is the reproduction of the conditions of production?"[11] Althusser argues that these conditions are reproduced through repressive state power and its control over ideological state apparatuses such as the church, the schools, or in the case of Pynchon's novel the Royal Society. ISAs, in turn, "function by 'ideology,'" which cannot exist "except by the subject and its subjects" who are (necessarily, tautologically) constituted as subjects by ideology.[12]

In a futile effort to speak outside this recognition, Pynchon has created voices of the nonhuman, like Learnèd Dog, who comment on their role in defining the subject's humanity. For self-protection, then, the Learnèd Dog acts as humanly as possible, "nightly delaying the Blades of our Masters by telling back to them tales of their humanity" (22). This may be another of Cherrycoke's qualifications, since, having died, he too is nonhuman and knows the ideological formation of the modern subject (the individual) in story—ideas, illusions, imaginary representations.[13] Coming at this construction from a different angle (or story) are the people from the East hired by Macclesfield, people who "remain'd as careless of Sequences in Time as disengaged from Subjects, Objects, Possession, or indeed anything which might among Englishmen require a Preposition" (195). Understanding "humanity" as a story we tell ourselves, Pynchon seems to recognize the novel's complicity in the creation of the modern subject because his own novel takes place on the cusp of modernity when even the fully developed agents of science and method—Mason and Dixon—still believe in ghosts and hauntings.

In earlier books, such concepts as subjectivity, epistemology, and the creation of history are hitched to plot and plotting so that the reader's interest in ideas is motivated by and coincident with the desire to make sense of plot. Developed character in Forster's definition was correspondingly weak. In *Mason & Dixon*, reader involvement with plot is largely absent because readers know the task contracted by Mason and Dixon, and they know the line was cut and drawn. There are mild, low-profile suspicions, like those that the two surveyors hold of the Royal Society, and there are departures and digressions from the novel's "line," but they do not structure the novel or motivate the major characters, who are (it might be said) largely unwitting and loveable agents of the Enlightenment and the Age of Reason.

On the other hand, if the act of surveying the Line is seen to participate in the Enlightenment project of bringing mystery into light, and magic under the reign of reason, one can argue that Mason and Dixon, like their ancestors in Pynchon's oeuvre, are also on a search, and in this general, abstract sense, there is a plot, but it is a plot of social and political formation. From an Althusserian point of view, Mason and Dixon might be said to advance the plot of history at the same time they participate, ideologically, in its creation. This redefinition of plot naturally has consequences for our understanding of character in Pynchon's novel.[14]

As many of the novel's reviewers have argued, *Mason & Dixon* is a novel rooted in characters rather than in plots and plotting, who even as they help construct the modern rationalized world encounter along the Line different cosmologies, the mysteries of the wilderness, and other characters whose understanding of the natural world, politics, and belief differs greatly from their own.[15] It might be argued, in fact, that Mason and Dixon are Pynchon's first sustained characters, capable of engaging reader interest and emotion, and as such constitute another dimension of Pynchon's fidelity to history, this time to the history of the novel and its roots in such characters as Clarissa, Tom, and Tristram. But to put it this way is to remain within the novelistic ideology of Forster, for we may now understand more accurately that Mason and Dixon are the interpellated subjects of plot, that it is they who practice the formation they reproduce. In ideological critique, then, the distinction between plot and character may be viewed as an aspect of false consciousness.

To take this argument yet further, we must approach the author himself and imagine Pynchon confronted by the quandary of his own recognition as a subject within ideology, for "this recognition," Althusser writes,

> only gives us the "consciousness" of our incessant (and eternal) practice of ideological recognition—its consciousness, i.e. its recognition—but in no sense does it gives us the (scientific) knowledge of the mechanism of this recognition.

The problem Althusser outlines at this point is at once the problem of any speaker or author:

> Now it is this knowledge that we have to reach, if you will, while speaking in ideology, and from within ideology we have to outline a discourse which tries to break with ideology, in order to dare to be the beginning of a scientific (i.e., subjectless) discourse on ideology.[16]

Clearly, this formulation is the Marxist version of Wittgenstein's early thoughts on language in which the "limits of my language are the limits of my world" or of William Burroughs's aphorism, "to speak is to lie."

In this context, one can argue that the novel's use of characterization and its corresponding affective claim on the reader's emotions is an effect of the cul-de-sac in which Pynchon finds himself, since he clearly lacks Althusser's confidence (or delusion) that one may speak outside of ideology. This affective characterization works to sentimentalize the Enlightenment and its projects, evoking sympathy in subtle counterpoint to the book's critique of reason, a counterpoint noiselessly collapsed into the double entendre of Mason's last words (quoted earlier):

> "'Tis a Construction," Mason weakly, "a great single Engine, the size of a Continent. I have all the proofs you may require. Not all the Connexions are made yet, that's why some of it is still invisible. Day by day the Pioneers and Surveyors go on, more points are being tied in, and soon becoming visible, as above, new Stars are recorded and named and plac'd in Almanacks." (772)

Punning on Mason's word "construction," Pynchon seamlessly embeds two opposed views: in one, which has the emotional force of Mason's "weakly," the New World is a "great single Engine" that pioneers and surveyors discover or make visible; in the other view (the framing narration mediated through Cherrycoke) the word "construction" denotes the emplacement of rationalized system upon natural and social heterogeneity; or, in the language of *The Crying of Lot 49,* a kind of right-angled tapestry that spills out the slit windows of reason and ownership, not into a void but into— and through—Otherness: in one, history seen by the individual; in the other, history understood through ideological recognition.

This yoking of sentiment and critique is a key structural principle of *Mason & Dixon,* one which gives new emphasis to the element of compassion present in Pynchon's fiction from at least *The Crying of Lot 49.* Readers of *Vineland* are still puzzling over the end of that novel, in which the dog Desmond licks Prairie's face, and still wondering over the status of McClintic Sphere's aphorism in *V.,* "keep cool, but care," but with *Mason & Dixon* we are now in a position to suggest that sympathy and compassion have always occupied a somewhat dissonant place within Pynchon's satiric analytic. Near the end of *The Crying of Lot 49,* the narrator's access to Oedipa's thoughts reveals a little-discussed rumination: "Though she could never again call back any image of the dead man to dress up, pose, talk to and make answer, neither could she lose a new compassion for the cul-de-sac he'd tried to find a way out of, for the enigma his efforts had created."[17] In

The Crying of Lot 49, this "cul-de-sac," it must be recalled, is an image of monopoly, patriarchy, narcissism, cultural incest, and entropy, yet Pynchon endows his character with "a new compassion" for Pierce and the "enigma his efforts had created."

Perhaps this is a key to what has happened: his own awareness of ideological complicity, his position on a "spectrum of impotence," has induced in Pynchon a forgiving pastoralism, always present but now emerged to occupy a more dominant place in his work.[18] In *The Crying of Lot 49,* Oedipa's melancholy compassion is quickly overshadowed by Oedipa's marvellous meditation on the republic and its "excluded middle," but in *Vineland* the novel ends on an affective note worthy of Frank Capra when Prairie—a name evoking the republic's pre-Columbian past—awakes from her fantasies of Brock Vond to the "warm and persistent tongue" of her dog Desmond, his "face full of blue-jay feathers, smiling out of his eyes, wagging his tail, thinking he must be home."[19]

To accomplish this about-face in his most recent novel, Pynchon has had to rewind time to the point where Mason's two sons by his first wife Rebekah are remembering their eagerness to travel to America:

> "Since I was ten," said Doc, "I wanted you to take me and Willy to America. I kept hoping, ev'ry Birthday, this would be the year. I knew next time you'd take us."
> "We can get jobs," said William, "save enough to go out where you were,—". . . .
> "The Stars are so close you won't need a Telescope," said Doc. "The Fish jump into your Arms. The Indians know Magick."
> "We'll go there. We'll live there."
> "We'll fish there. And you too." (773)

These last words are spoken by William and Dr. Isaac after their father's death, but because of Pynchon's subtle weave of mood and tense, they appear to issue from a time prior to their emigration, giving to the novel's close all the utopian expectancy of youth, a prospect already considerably compromised by their father's experience and the reader's ex post facto knowledge of what such dreams have become. A paragraph that begins with dependent consequences ("would" and "will prove") modulates backward in time to Doc's memory ("Since I was ten"), to present-tense declaration ("We can get jobs") and finally to future hopes: "We'll fish there. And you too." In these last three words, no doubt, readers are meant to hear the pastoral accents of Frost's farmer going out to clean the spring in "The Pasture" ("You come too"), and Whitman's invitation in "Song of Myself": "I stop some where waiting for you."

Pynchon's novels have always had their moments of pathos and compassion: the sailor in Oedipa's arms and Pökler putting his ring on the finger of a Camp Dora survivor are two examples, yet these emotions were invoked in the midst of satiric critique and apocalyptic outrage. These novels appeared in the midst of and seemed aligned with such initiatives as Earth Day, antiwar demonstrations, and coalitions for a nuclear freeze. The endings of *Vineland* and *Mason & Dixon* are qualitatively different. Both seem to be aesthetic strategies for getting over the hump of apocalypse, in which even the quality of anger has diminished. One has only to compare Dixon's whipping of the slave driver—itself possibly an apocryphal story handed down through the family generations—to "Mondaugen's Story" in *V.,* which vividly presents the colonial ruthlessness of von Trotha's 1904 genocide of the Hereros, to note the transition from the appalled imagination to one more forgiving. The result may be termed the genre of nostalgic (or bourgeois) tragedy: tragic because there is always some prior crime that makes our present moment "too late," and nostalgic because the novels end "at home," in moments of willed reconciliation with what has gone before. Readers might ask of Mason's sons, What stream shall we go a-fishing in? The polluted stream of our present moment, or the time of the novel, which is to say in the remembered futurity of a nation about to be born, the past already imperfect?

NOTES

1. Thomas Pynchon, *Slow Learner: Early Stories* (Boston: Little, Brown, 1984), 19.

2. Peter Brooks, *Reading for the Plot: Design and Intention in Narrative* (New York: Knopf, 1984; rpt., New York: Vintage, 1985), 37.

3. At the International Pynchon Week Conference, David Cowart asked, "does *Mason & Dixon* have a plot?" ("The Luddite Vision: *Mason & Dixon,*" International Pynchon Week Conference, London and Antwerp, June 1998).

4. Thomas Pynchon, *Mason & Dixon* (New York: Henry Holt, 1997), 511. Further references will be included parenthetically within the text.

5. Thomas Pynchon, *Gravity's Rainbow* (New York: Viking, 1973), 733.

6. Henry David Thoreau, *"Walden" and "Civil Disobedience,"* ed. with notes and introduction by Sherman Paul (Boston: Houghton Mifflin, 1960), 221.

7. Thomas Pynchon, *The Crying of Lot 49* (Philadelphia: Lippincott, 1966), 54.

8. Pynchon, *Gravity's Rainbow,* 136.

9. Richard Rorty, *Contingency, Irony, and Solidarity* (New York: Cambridge University Press, 1989), xiii.

10. *Gravity's Rainbow,* 722.

11. Louis Althusser, "Ideology and Ideological State Apparatuses," in *Contemporary Critical Theory,* ed. Dan Latimer (San Diego: Harcourt, Brace, Jovanovich, 1989), 61.

12. Althusser, "Ideology," 76, 95.

13. Ibid., 87, 90.

14. Brian McHale, for example, speaks of *Mason & Dixon* as a novel of "subjunctive space," which is the space of "wish, desire, possibilities" ("*Mason & Dixon* in the Zone, or, A Brief Poetics of Pynchon Space," International Pynchon Week Conference, London and Antwerp, June 1998); and Hanjo Berressem argues that "the line is the reason there is an 'if' in front of all the other possible worlds [in *Mason & Dixon*] ... the Line occupies fact" ("'Hit the Spot, Draw the Line': Cultural Inscriptions, Traumatic Wounds and the Multiplexity of Matter in *Mason & Dixon,*" International Pynchon Week Conference).

15. See, among others, Anthony Lane, "Then, Voyager," *New Yorker,* 12 May 1997, 97–98, 100; Rick Moody, "Surveyors of the Enlightenment," *Atlantic Monthly,* July 1997, 106–10; T. Coraghessan Boyle, "The Great Divide," *New York Times Book Review,* 18 May 1997, 9; Michael Dirda, "Measure for Measure," *Washington Post Book World,* 27 April 1997, 1–2; and Michiko Kakutani, "Pynchon Hits the Road with Mason and Dixon," *New York Times,* 29 April 1997, B1, B4.

16. Althusser, "Ideology," 95.

17. *The Crying of Lot 49,* 178.

18. Anthony Lane sees this as a more recent development: "Since the rocket-powered riffs of *Gravity's Rainbow,* Pynchon has learned how to stop worrying about the Bomb. He has even started loving a little, extending an amused tenderness in all sorts of directions" (100).

19. Thomas Pynchon, *Vineland* (Boston: Little, Brown, 1990), 384–85.

Mason & Dixon Bibliography

CLIFFORD S. MEAD

Listed below are all materials relating to *Mason & Dixon* known to me, beginning with prepublication notices in 1996 of the forthcoming novel, all book reviews (marked with an asterisk), subsequent features and news items, and scholarly essays that have been published through the spring of 1999. I gratefully acknowledge the assistance of Sherrill Leverich-Fries, Marie D. Wise, and John Krafft.

*Abbott, Lee K. "From Cherrycoke to Everybeet, Pynchon's Multitude of Voices." *Miami Herald,* 27 April 1997, 4L.

*Akst, Daniel. "Drawing the Line of North and South: Thomas Pynchon's Runaway Imagination Runs Away with Itself." *San Jose Mercury News,* 4 May 1997, 3. Reprinted as: "Gravity's Proof: Pynchon Goes Long." *Los Angeles Weekly,* 30 May–5 June 1997, 45.

*Alford, Steven E. "Pynchon's Line." *Houston Chronicle,* 11 May 1997, 18, 23.

Allen, Bruce. "Pynchon Redux." *Kirkus,* 1 May 1997, 657.

"Authentisch." *Focus,* 14 July 1997, 16.

*Battersby, Eileen. "A Great Opportunity Missed." *Irish Times,* 10 May 1997, 9.

*Battestin, M. C. "Pynchon, North and South." *Sewanee Review* 105, no. 3 (Summer 1997): R76–78.

*Baudino, Mario. "Pynchon, Don Chisciotte in America." *La Stampa,* 29 April 1997, 23.

*Begley, Adam. "Pynchon Still Has the Stuff, but You Can't Get to It." *New York Observer,* 28 April 1997, 32. Reprinted as: "Flattened History." *St. Petersburg Times,* 4 May 1997, 4D.

*Bencivenga, Jim. "The *Monitor*'s Guide to Bestsellers: Hardcover Fiction." *Christian Science Monitor,* 15 May 1997, 13.

Bergh, Magnus. "Gutenberggalaxens ytterligheter." *Bonniers Litterära Magasin,* September 1997, 50–51.

*Bigsby, Christopher. "The Subdividers of Eternity." *Daily Telegraph,* 3 May 1997, 4.

*Birkerts, Sven. "Pynchon's Metaphysical Landscape." *Washington Times,* 11 May 1997, B6.

*Blinkhorn, Lois. "Pynchon Back in Print." *Milwaukee Journal Sentinel,* 29 December 1996, 11.

*Bloom, Harold. "The Perplexity of the World after Eden." *Bostonia,* Fall 1997, 71.

*Bonca, Cornel. "Re-Dreaming the American Dream: And Re-Reading Pynchon's Latest." *Orange County Weekly* [CA], 29 August 1997, 23.

Bone, James. "Mystery Writer." *Times Magazine* [London], 14 June 1997, 26–29.

*Boomsma, Graa. "De geschiedenis als opera." *De Groene Amsterdammer,* 14 May 1997, 26–27.

*Bottum, J. "The End of His Rainbow: Thomas Pynchon Fails to Deliver." *Weekly Standard,* 19 May 1997, 36–37.

*Boyd, Greg. "All Lined Up: Pynchon Goes Long and Connects Again." *Eye,* 15 May 1997, 50.

*Boyle, T. Coraghessan. "The Great Divide: Thomas Pynchon's Novel Features Two Historical Figures Who Were Sent to America to Settle a Dispute." *The New York Times Book Review,* 18 May 1997, 9.

Brauner, David. "Book Bytes." *Jerusalem Post,* 21 August 1997, 7.

*Brazell, Bill. "Pynchon's Line Dance." *Metro,* 26 June–2 July 1997, 34.

*Bril, Martin. "De veel te gewone rug van Thomas Pynchon." *Het Parool,* 16 May 1997, 15.

*Brubaker, Jack. "Thomas Pynchon Examines Murder of the Conestogas in *Mason & Dixon.*" *Lancaster New Era* [PA], 7 October 1997, A12.

*Bukiet, Melvin Jules. "Boundaries: Thomas Pynchon's Line on Modernity." *Chicago Tribune,* 11 May 1997, 1, 5.

*Burgess, John. "A New Novel From a Great Writer." *American Reporter,* 16–17 August, 1997.

*Burkman, Greg. "Brilliant and Bawdy, Pynchon at Full Force." *Seattle Times,* 4 May 1997, M2.

*Carpenter, Humphrey. "The American Goon Show." *The Sunday Times Books* [London], 4 May 1997, 8.

*Carter, Ron. "Pynchon Creates a Work that 'Dances with Language.'" *Richmond Times Dispatch,* 18 May 1997, F-4.

*Cartwright, Justin. "All Language with No Heart." *Financial Times,* 3 May 1997, 5.

Cecchi, Sandra. "Dr. Pynchon e Mr. Salinger." *L'Espresso,* 30 April 1997, 114–15.

*Chesney, Alan. "Reclusive Author Pens Brilliant Novel." *Chattanooga Free Press,* 6 July 1997, M4.

*Cheuse, Alan. "*Mason & Dixon* Surveys Signature Pynchon Domain." *Dallas Morning News,* 27 April 1997, 8J.

*Cohea, David. "Pynchon Charts America's Divided Soul." *Orlando Sentinel,* 4 May 1997, F6.

*Cumyn, Richard. "Drawing the Line: At 60, Thomas Pynchon Is Still the *Enfant Terrible* of American Letters." *Ottawa Citizen,* 18 May 1997, M15.

De Pastino, Blake. "Cryptic Messages." *Weekly Alibi* [Albuquerque, NM], 16–22 July 1997, 16.

"Diary." *Sunday Times* [London], 30 March 1997, 8.

"Diary." *Sunday Times* [London], 27 April 1997, 6.

Di Filippo, Paul. "On the Line." *Asimov's Science Fiction,* February 1998, 149–51.

*Dirda, Michael. "Pynchon's Marvel-Filled Historical Novel." *Rocky Mountain News,* 4 May 1997, 2E.

*———. "Measure for Measure." *The Washington Post Book World,* 27 April 1997, 1, 10.

"Doubtin' Thomas?" *Entertainment Weekly,* 23 May 1997, 61.

Douglas, Ann. "High Is Low: Finally, the Wall Dividing the Art World Collapses." *The New York Times Magazine,* 29 September 1996, 175–78.

*Drexler, Mike. "Beautiful Colors and Strangely Put Together Shapes." *Mainichi Daily News,* 13 September 1997, 9.

Dugdale, John. "Good at Games." *Independent,* 7 May 1997, 2.

*———. "Pynchon's Back." *Guardian,* 24 April 1997, T9.

*Duyfhuizen, Bernard. "Worth the Wait." *News and Observer* [Raleigh, NC], 4 May 1997, G4.

*Eder, Richard. "Wrestling with History: Thomas Pynchon's New Novel Features the Famed Surveyors Charles Mason and Jeremiah Dixon, but There Is Hardly a Straight Line in Sight." *Newsday,* 27 April 1997, G9, 11.

*Ekbom, Torsten. "Till bristningsgränsen." *Dagens Nyheter,* 7 July 1997, B2.

*"Etáts-unis: le retour de Thomas Pynchon." *Le Monde,* 23 May 1997, 4.

*Factor, T. R. "Over the Line." *Willamette Weekly* [Portland, OR], 30 April 1997, 56.

*Feeley, Gregory. "Pynchon Reemerges: The Reclusive Author's First Novel in Seven Years Tells the Story of the Two Men Who Created the Mason-Dixon Line." *Philadelphia Inquirer,* 27 April 1997, Q1.

*Feeney, Mark. "Gravity's Boundary." *Boston Globe,* 4 May 1997, D17–20. Reprinted as: "Pynchon's Merry *Mason & Dixon* a Disappointingly Muddled Effort." *Seattle Post-Intelligencer,* 8 May 1997, C2.

*Fernandez-Armesto, Felipe. "Measuring up America." *Evening Standard,* 12 May 1997, 26.

"Fiction from America: Putting Readers' Stamina to the Test." *Economist,* 15 November 1997, 14–15.

*Fischer, David Marc. "Pynchon's Progress: David Marc Fischer Heralds the Coming of *Mason & Dixon.*" *NewCity* [Chicago, IL], 1 May 1997, 14.

*Fitzgerald, Judith. "An Unimaginably Gorgeous Tapestry." *Toronto Star,* 3 May 1997, K17.

*Foran, Charles. "Adventures in Pynchonland." *Montreal Gazette,* 17 May 1997, I1.

Fowles, John. "Christmas Books II: Books of the Year." *Spectator,* 22 November 1997, 40.

*Froehlich, Leopold. "Tom Crosses the Line." *Playboy,* September 1997, 28.

Frost, Betty L. "New at the Library." *Stuart News/Port St. Lucie News* [Stuart, FL], 11 May 1997, D9.

*Gardner, James. "The Bigger the . . . Better?" *National Review,* 30 June 1997, 44–46.

Geier, Thom. "Lone Writers: Do Not Disturb: Recluse at Work." *U.S. News & World Report,* 5 May 1997, 79.

Glassie, John. "Big Tom." *New York Times Magazine,* 27 April 1997, 15.

Goetz, Thomas. "Pynchon's Web of Influence." *Village Voice,* 6 May 1997, 45.

Goldstein, Sergei. "Adventures in Etymology: The Spinach Scones at Crudely's Pub & Breakfast by B. M. W. Schrapnel, Ph.D." *Oasis* 5, no. 4 (1997): 21–32.

*Gottlieb, Janus. "Excellence, by the Pound." *Spy,* July/August 1997, 16.

*Gray, Edward. Review of *Mason & Dixon. William and Mary Quarterly* 54, no. 4 (October 1997), 877–79.

*Gray, Paul. "Drawing the Line: Thomas Pynchon's Long-Awaited *Mason & Dixon* Is a Tale of Scientific Triumph and an Epic of Loss." *Time,* 5 May 1997, 98.

Groer, Annie, and Ann Gerhart. "The Reliable Source: Now You Know ... " *Washington Post,* 13 October 1997, C3.

*Hagen, W. M. Review of *Mason & Dixon. World Literature Today* 71 (Autumn 1997): 788–89.

*Hale, Julie. "The Adventures of Mason & Dixon in the Land of Pynchon." *Virginia-Pilot and Ledger-Star* [Norfolk], 1 June 1997, J2.

*Hamilton, Ian. "Pynchon and On and On." *Sunday Telegraph* [London], 4 May 1997, 14.

*Hanrahan, Phil. "Pynchon Delivers a Marvelous Buddy Tale." *Milwaukee Journal Sentinel,* 15 June 1997, 11.

*Hartnett, Michael. Review of *Mason & Dixon. Confrontation,* nos. 62–63 (Fall 1997): 361–63.

*Harvey, Miles. "The Woods Divided." *Outside,* June 1997, 144.

*Hayes, Ned. "Pynchon's Live Objects: Characters as ActiveX ." *Hot Ink,* 12 August 1997, 4.

*Hedgecock, Andrew. *The Edge,* August-September 1997, 38.

*Henderson, David W. Review of *Mason & Dixon. Library Journal,* 1 June 1997, 150.

*Hensher, Philip. "The Best Novel of the Decade." *The Spectator,* 3 May 1997, 35–36.

*Herman, Luc. "Het failliet van de rechte lijn." *De Morgen,* 29 May 1997, 23.

*Hintermeier, Hannes. "Unlösbares Gezerre." *Die Woche,* 30 May 1997, 33.

"Historical Line is Drawn Out to Great Lengths." *Lancaster Sunday News,* 8 June 1997, H8.

Hodgman, John. "Mason & Me: Taking a Page From Pynchon." *New York Observer,* 21 July 1997, 5.

Hoffert, Barbara. "Saving the Owl: Michael Naumann Inspires Henry Holt." *Library Journal,* 15 February 1997, 106–8.

Hoover, Bob. "Counting the *Mason & Dixon* Days." *Pittsburgh Post-Gazette,* 25 May 1997, F9.

———. "Fear and Loathing in Chicago: '*Mason & Dixon:* The Early Years,' cont." *Pittsburgh Post-Gazette,* 15 June 1997, G8.

———. "'M&D' Diary: The Governor Lends a Hand." *Pittsburgh Post-Gazette,* 29 June 1997, G8.

*Horvath, Brooke. "History, Imagination Cross Paths." *Plain Dealer* [Cleveland, OH], 27 April 1997, I13.

Hunt, Kevin. "Pixels: Rocket Science." *Hartford Courant* [CT], 17 July 1997, E1.

*Ingram, Lynette E. "Pynchon Maps History of a Country Divided." *Nashville Banner,* 30 July 1997, D4.

Ivry, Bob. "Pondering the Enigma of Pynchon." *The Record* [Bergen, NJ], 7 May 1997, YT1, 12.

Jacobs, Alexandra. "Exposing Hidden Talents." *Entertainment Weekly,* 9 May 1997, 71.

*Johnson, Malcolm L. "Delineating the New World in *Mason & Dixon.*" *Hartford Courant* [CT], 11 May 1997, G3.

*Jones, Malcolm, Jr. "The Master Surveyor." *Newsweek,* 28 April 1997, 77.

*Kakutani, Michiko. "Pynchon Hits the Road with *Mason & Dixon.*" *New York Times,* 29 April 1997, B1, B4. Reprinted as "Author Blurs Lines of Mason-Dixon History." *The Fresno Bee,* 4 May 1997, G2; reprinted as "Dark Comedy Energizes Saga." *Sun-Sentinel* [Ft. Lauderdale], 4 May 1997, D8; reprinted as "Pynchon and On and On . . . " *Dayton Daily News,* 4 May 1997, C8.

Kane, Pat. "Paging 1997." *Herald* [Glasgow], 11 December 1997, 19.

Keesey, Douglas. "*Mason & Dixon* on the Line: A Reception Study." *Pynchon Notes* 36–39 (1995–1996): 165–78.

*Keough, Peter. "Roman à Cleft: Thomas Pynchon's *Mason & Dixon* Surveys the Making of America." *Boston Phoenix,* May 1997, 4.

*Kipen, David. "Pynchon Draws the Defining Pair." *Los Angeles Daily News,* 27 April 1997, L20. Reprinted as "Pynchon's 773-page Punch Line is a Masterpeice." *Austin-American Statesman,* 4 May 1997, D8; reprinted as "Pynchon's *Mason & Dixon* a Challenge." *Star-Tribune* [Minneapolis-St. Paul], 15 May 1997, E5.

*Kirn, Walter. "Z. Pynchon's Tiresome Mind Games." *Slate,* 6 May 1997 [http:// www.slate. com/BookReview/97-05-06/BookReview.asp].

*Kisor, Henry. "Antic Author Retells Mason and Dixon Saga." *Chicago Sun-Times,* 27 April 1997, NC13.

———. "A Novelist Who Gives 'Recluse' New Meaning." *Chicago Sun-Times,* 27 April 1997, NC 13.

*Klepp, L. S. "Liner Notes." *Entertainment Weekly,* 9 May 1997, 71, 75.

Kloer, Phil. "Reclusive Novelist Breaks His Silence." *Atlanta Journal and Constitution,* 5 June 1997, 2C.

*Knipfel, Jim. "Crossing the Crooked Line." *New York Press,* 30 April 1997, 21–23.

*Koenig, Rhoda. "History and Tomfoolery." *Wall Street Journal,* 2 May 1997, A12.

*Kravitz, Peter. "The Marx Brothers of Dixieland." *The Scotsman,* 3 May 1997, 14.

*Krewson, John. "An Epic Literary Journey." *Onion,* 14–20 May 1997, 30.

Lago, Eduardo. "Carta de Nuevo York: Cibernesis y literatura." *Cuadernos Hispanoamericanos,* no. 571 (January 1998): 139–42.

*Lane, Anthony. "Then, Voyager: Thomas Pynchon's Time-Travelling." *The New Yorker,* 12 May 1997, 97–100.

*Larson, Susan. "Drawing the Line Somewhere." *Times-Picayune* [New Orleans], 6 May 1997, F1.

*Leader, Zachary. "The Final Frontier." *Independent,* 3 May 1997, 9.

*LeClair, B. *Quinzaine Litteraire,* no. 719 (1 July 1997): 2.

*LeClair, Tom. "The Map Is Not the Territory." *American Book Review,* July-August 1997, 5.

*Leonard, John. "Crazy Age of Reason." *The Nation,* 12 May 1997, 65–68.

*Lewis, Trevor. *Sunday Times* [London], 12 April 1998.

*Livingstone, David B. "Mystery Train." *Spike* September 1997 [http://www.hedweb.com/spike/0997pync.htm].

"The Loafer." *Guardian,* 3 April 1997, T10.

Logan, William. "Pynchon in the Poetic." *Southwest Review* 83, no. 4 (1998): 424-37.

*Logue, Bret. "What's the Topic? A Review of Thomas Pynchon's *Mason & Dixon.*" *The Stanford Daily,* 7 August 1997, 8.

*Lombreglia, Ralph. "Invisible Forces." *Boston Book Review,* July-August 1997, 46–47.

*Lowenkopf, Shelly. "Crossing the Line into a New, Wild World." *Fort Worth Star-Telegram,* 25 May 1997, 7.

*Lundgren, Caj. "Seklets märkligaste amerikanske författare." *Svenska Dag-bladet,* 1 October 1997, 14–45.

Lyman, Rick. "Finalists for Book Award Named." *New York Times,* 16 October 1997, B3.

*MacDougall, Carl. "The Myth of Mystery." *The Herald* [Glasgow], 24 May 1997, 15.

*Madsen, Deborah L. "Colonialism on the Couch." *Times Higher Education Sup-plement,* 23 May 1997, 22.

*Mars-Jones, Adam. "How a Quaker Gets his Oats." *Observer* [London], 15 June 1997, O17.

Mason & Dixon Home Page. Henry Holt & Co. October 1996 [http://www.hholt.com/pynchon/masonmain.htm].

Massie, Allan. "The Fashionable Reader's Choice." *Daily Telegraph,* 2 June 1997, 15. Reprinted as "Pynchon Novel: Newest Unread Stylish Stout?" *Chicago Sun-Times,* 15 June 1997, 13.

*Mattessich, Stefan. "Telluric Texts, Implicate Spaces." *PostModern Culture* 8, no. 1 (September 1997): 137–48.

McCarron, Bill. "Separation & Linkage in Pynchon's *Mason & Dixon.*" *Notes on Contemporary Literature* 28, no. 1 (1998): 12–14.

*McConnell, Frank. "Good & Plenty." *Commonweal,* 15 August 1997, 20–21.

*McLaughlin, Robert. *Review of Contemporary Fiction* 16, no. 3 (Fall 1997): 216–17.

*McLemee, Scott. "Weird Morning in America: Thomas Pynchon's *Mason & Dixon* Travels Back to Pre-Revolutionary Times to Map the 'Cryptic & Per-ilous' Contours of a Nation." *Salon,* 25 April 1997, 4.

*Melander, Christel. Review of *Mason & Dixon. Ord & Bild* 1–2 (1998): 182–84.

*Menand, Louis. "Entropology." *New York Review of Books,* 12 June 1997, 22, 24–25.

*Mesler, Corey. "Great American Novel? Pynchon's Latest Is a Feast." *Commercial Appeal* [Memphis], 1 June 1997, G1.

*Miller, Laura. "Pynchon's Line: The Great American Recluse's Postparanoid Epic." *Village Voice,* 6 May 1997, 43, 46.

Minzesheimer, Bob. "Big-Name Writers Still Pack a Punch." *USA Today,* 19 June 1997, 7D.

*Mitchell, Jim. "Over the Hill with Pynchon." *Courier-Journal* [Louisville, KY], 24 August 1997, 6I.

*Moody, Rick. "Surveyors of the Enlightenment: Thomas Pynchon's Powerfully Symbolic Language Gets Us Beneath the Rhetoric of Our Pretensions." *The Atlantic Monthly,* July 1997, 106–10.

*Mooney, Ted. "All Down the Line." *Los Angeles Times Book Review,* 11 May 1997, 3.

*Moore, John. "No Use Pynchon Yourself–It's Real." *Vancouver Sun* [Seattle, WA], 16 August 1997, B5.

*Moroney, Mic. "Far Out Again with Pynchon." *Irish Times,* 3 June 1997, 12.

Morris, Charles R. "Critics' Choices for Christmas." *Commonweal,* 5 December 1997, 15–16.

*Morton, Brian. "Defining Lines in Nation's History." *Scotland on Sunday,* 27 April 1997, 14.

*Nelson, Tod. "A Weighty Arrival." *Amazon.com,* 29 April 1997.

*O' Connell, Alex. *Times* [London], 28 March 1998, 4.

*Ottenhoff, John. "A Line in the Wilderness." *Christian Century,* 17 December 1997, 1199.

"Our 25 Favorite Books of 1997." *Voice Literary Supplement,* Winter 1997, 9–11, 14–15.

*Overbye, Dennis. "Pynchon Toes the Line." *Wired,* August 1997, 130.

"Panel's Prognosis Mixed for Publishing Industry." *BookWeb,* 6 October 1997.

*Passaro, Vince. "They Walk the Line: Age of Reason as Comedy?" *Daily News* [New York], 27 April 1997, 7.

"Passé Notes: No. 1028: Beach Novels." *Guardian,* 2 June 1997, T3.

Payne, Doug. "Dividing Lines." *The San Diego Union-Tribune,* 11 May 1997, 1–2.

*Pekar, Harvey. "Hitting below the Mason-Dixon Line." *Austin Chronicle,* 13–19 June 1997, 4.

*Pelovitz, David. "Linear Pynchon." *Enterzone* 11 (1997) [http://ezone.org:1080/ez/e11/articles/pelovitz/masondixon.html].

*———. *Book Report,* 12 September 1997 [http://www.bookwire.com/TBR/Lead-Reviews/read.review$4301].

*Pinsker, Sanford. "Pynchon Draws Line between Order and Chaos: Taken in Small Doses, *Mason & Dixon* Can Be an Enlightening Experience." *Providence Journal-Bulletin* [RI], 25 May 1997, E8.

*Pizzichini, Lilian. "Books: Paperbacks." *Independent* [London], 19 April 1998, 35.

*Porlock, Harvey. "Thomas Pynchon and Will Self: Privates on Parade." *The Sunday Times Books* [London], 11 May 1997, 2.

*Powe, B. W. "A Thomas Pynchon Lexicon." *Toronto Globe & Mail,* 17 May 1997, D11, D16.

*Pritchard, William H. "Actual Fiction." *Hudson Review* 50 (Winter 1998): 662.

"Private, but Not a Recluse." *Hartford Courant* [CT],11 June 1997, E1.

*Quamme, Margaret. "Pynchon Engages in Some Ornate Rambling." *Columbus Dispatch,* 27 April 1997, 7J.

*Quan, Adán. "Mason & Dixon." *Antioch Review* 56 (Summer 1998): 375–76.

Quinn, Judy. "Long Wait Over: New Pynchon Novel for Spring." *Publishers Weekly,* 28 October 1996, 24.

*Reid, James. "Author Pynchon Returns." *The Digital Collegian,* 13 June 1997 [http://www.collegian.psu.edu/archive/1997/06/06-13-97tdc/06-13-97d05-001.htm].

Riedel, Michael. "Author a Poor Excuse for a Recluse." *Daily News* [New York], 19 May 1997, 27.

*Rifkind, Donna. *"Mason & Dixon*—Pynchon at Last." *The Sun* [Baltimore], 27 April 1997, 5F. Reprinted as "A History with No Boundaries." *The Record* [Bergen County, NJ], 18 May 1997, 9; reprinted as "Pynchon's *Mason & Dixon* Is a Fine, Sloppy Monster." *The Salt Lake Tribune,* 18 May 1997, D5; reprinted as: "Pynchon's 'Mason' Breaks New Ground." *Cincinnati Enquirer,* 8 June 1997, E9

Rising, Gerry. "Account of Calendar Changeover Illustrates Generation Gap in Communicating about Science." *Buffalo News,* 9 June 1997, 4C.

*Rosenbaum, Jonathan. "Pynchon's Tangle." *In These Times,* 27 July 1997, 26.

Rosenbaum, Ron. *"Mason & Dixon." The New York Observer,* 18 November 1996, 43.

———. "The Edgy Enthusiast." *The New York Observer,* 28 April 1997, 43.

*St. John, Warren. "The Secret Selling of Thomas Pynchon." *New York Observer,* 2 June 1997, 1, 29.

Sandgren, Håkan. "Vem vill avslöja Thomas Pynchon?" *Smälandsposten,* 17 July 1997, 4.

*Sante, Luc. "Long and Winding Line." *New York,* 19 May 1997, 65–66.

*Schader, Angela. "Amerika als Traum und Theme Park." *Neue Zuercher Zeitung,* 17 May 1997, Buecher, 45.

*Scheck, Denis. "Halali am Hudson." *Focus,* 23 June 1997, 98–100.

*Schmidt, Peter. "Line, Vortex, and Mound: On First Reading Thomas Pynchon's *Mason & Dixon.*" [http://www.swarthmore.edu/Humanities/pschmid1/essays/pynchon/mason.html].

*Schmitz, Neil. "Thomas Pynchon and His Witty, Weary Land Surveyors." *Buffalo News,* 11 May 1997, 7F.

Schwartz, Nils. "Ankan flyger västerut." *Expressen,* 11 June 1997, 4–5.

*Seaman, Donna. *Booklist,* 15 April 1997, 1365.

*Shindler, Dorman T. *"Mason & Dixon* Maps Pynchon's Line on History." *The Denver Post,* 4 May 1997, 6E. Reprinted as "Our Best-Known Recluse Comes Out with Top Tale." *San Antonio Express-News,* 11 May 1997, J4.

*Shippey, Tom. "The Pynchon Line." *Times Literary Supplement,* 6 June 1997, 25.

*Siegel, Mark. *Journal of Popular Culture* 31, no. 4 (Spring 1998): 176–77.

*Singleton, Ruth. *New York Law Journal,* 8 July 1997, 2.

*Skenazy, Paul. "Pynchon Draws the Line: Cult Novelist Is All over the Map with His Huge, Antic *Mason & Dixon.*" *San Francisco Chronicle Book Review,* 27 April–3 May, 1997, 1, 8.

*Smith, Kyle. Review of *Mason & Dixon. People,* 19 May 1997, 50.

Startle, William. "Review of Books of the Year." *Sunday Telegraph* [London], 14 December 1997, 14.

*Stein, Joel. "Longer Than the Civil War." *Time Out,* 24 April–1 May 1997, 52.

*Steinberg, Sybil S. *Publishers' Weekly,* 14 April 1997, 56.

Streitfeld, David. "The Latest Line on Thomas Pynchon." *The Washington Post,* 21 October 1996, D1–D2. Reprinted as "Thomas Pynchon's *Mason & Dixon* Is a Tome on Lives of the British Surveyors." *Palm Beach Post,* 24 November 1996, J2.

Sullivan, Lorana. "The Makings of a Mystery Writer." *Daily Telegraph,* 3 May 1997, 7.

*Suter, Martin. "Der beste Roman des 18. Jahrhunderts." *Sonntags Zeitung,* 11 May 1997, 63.

*Syken, Bill. "Pynchon: *Mason & Dixon* Tells Some Strange Tales." *Augusta Chronicle,* 25 May 1997, E9.

*Taylor, D. J. "A Line Too Far." *Mail on Sunday* [London], 27 April 1997, 30–31.

*Tepper, Nanne. "Pynchon verdwaald in nieuwe roman: Krullen rapen in de prullenbak." *NRC Handelsblad,* 6 June 1997, Boeken, 3.

"This Summer's Epic Bestseller" [full-page ad for *Mason & Dixon*]. *Library Journal,* 15 June 1997, 95.

*Trachtenberg, Stanley. "Pynchon Draws Burlesque Mason-Dixon Line Burlesque." *St. Louis Post-Dispatch,* 27 April 1997, 5C.

*Tremblay, Mark. "Another Feast in Store for Pynchon Fans." *Calgary Herald,* 14 June 1997, J9.

*Trumm, James F. *Insouciance* 5 (1997).

*———. "*Mason & Dixon* Illuminates History." *The Blade* [Toledo, OH], 1 June 1997, E4.

*Turner, Jenny. "When the Sandwich Was Still a New Invention." *London Review of Books,* 17 July 1997, 23–25.

Ulin, David L. "Writers on the Storm." *Los Angeles Times,* 12 May 1997, E1.

*van Dixhoorn, Frank. "Verwikkelingen rond een Amerikaanse grenslijn." *Volkskrant,* 27 June 1997, 30.

"Vanity Publishing." *The Times* [London], 30 May 1997, 4.

Varadarajan, Tunku. "Trendy New Yorkers Lap Up Cult Writer's Indigestible Novel." *The Times* [London], 30 May 1997, 4.

Veale, Scott. "New and Noteworthy Paperbacks." *New York Times Book Review,* 26 April 1998, 36.

*Verble, Bill. "Let It Be Written." *Sack,* 16 June 1997 [http://sac.uky.edu/~wwgees0/sack/mason.htm].

*Vilmure, Daniel. *The Tampa Tribune,* 24 May 1997, 8.

"The Vulture." *The Times* [London], 21 June 1997, 4.

Wahlin, Claes. "Pynchonland." *Aftonbladet,* 29 June 1997, 4.

Warmbold, Carolyn Nizzi. "A Bunch o' Books for the Buck." *Atlanta Journal and Constitution,* 18 June 1997, D1.

*Webb, Don. *Nove Express* 4, no. 4 (1998): 41.

"Web Citations." *Atlantic Unbound,* 25 June 1997 [http://www.theatlantic.com/unbound/citation/wc970625.htm].

*Weeks, Jerome. "Meanderings Seem Almost a Maze without Center or Exit." *Dallas Morning News,* 27 April 1997, J8.

*Weisenburger, Steven. "Pynchon Surveys Troubled Land." *Post and Courier* [Charleston, SC], 22 June 1997, E5.

Werneburg, Brigitte. "Surfbrett: Die Briefe des Buchhändlers." *Tageszeitung,* 5 June 1997, 12.

White, Carolyn. "ShortList." *Mirabella,* March/April 1997, 44.

*Wiggins, Marianne. "Trouble in Toeing the Line." *The Times* [London], 1 May 1997, 4.

*Wiley, David. "Back to the Future: Thomas Pynchon Revisits Yesterday's America and Writes Tomorrow's Literature." *Minnesota Daily,* 22 May 1997, 1, 9.

Wilson, Jeff. "Searching for Pynchon." *CityBeat* [Cincinnati, OH], 12–18 December 1996, 35.

*Wood, James. "Levity's Rainbow." *The New Republic,* 4 August 1997, 32–38.

———. "Books: Crowd Pleasers." *Guardian,* 11 December 1997, 9.

*Wood, Michael. "Pynchon's *Mason & Dixon.*" *Raritan* 17 (May 1998): 120-30.

"A Writer as Elusive as His Plots." *Straits Times* [Singapore], 2 August 1997, 16.

Zane, J. Peder. "The New American Dream." *News and Observer* [Raleigh, NC], 8 June 1997, G6.

———. "The Stark Raving Genius of Thomas Pynchon." *News and Observer* [Raleigh, NC], May 1997, G4.

*Zinn, Christopher. "Pynchon: Fabulist of the Frontier." *The Oregonian,* 11 May 1997, G5–6.

Works Cited

Althusser, Louis. "Ideology and Ideological State Apparatuses." In *Contemporary Critical Theory,* edited by Dan Latimer, 61–102. San Diego: Harcourt, Brace, Jovanovich, 1989.

Ashbery, John. "They Dream Only of America." In *The Tennis Court Oath.* Middletown, CT: Wesleyan University Press, 1962.

Baker, Jeff. "Amerikkka Uber Alles: German Nationalism, American Imperialism, and the 60s Anti-War Movement in *Gravity's Rainbow,*" *Critique* 40.4 (1999): 323–41.

———. "A Democratic Pynchon: Counterculture, Counterforce and Participatory Democracy." *Pynchon Notes* 32–33 (1993): 99–131.

Bakhtin, Mikhail. "Forms of Time and of the Chronotope in the Novel." In *The Dialogic Imagination: Four Essays,* edited by Michael Holquist, translated by Caryl Emerson and Michael Holquist, 84–258. Austin: University of Texas Press, 1981.

Barruel, Abbé. *Memoirs, Illustrating the History of Jacobinism.* London, 1797–98.

Bartram, William. *Travels through North and South Carolina, Georgia, East and West Florida.* New York: Penguin, 1988.

Baumbach, Jonathan. *The Landscape of Nightmare: Studies in the Contemporary American Novel.* New York: New York University Press, 1965.

Beckett, Samuel. *Waiting for Godot.* New York: Grove, 1954.

Beitzinger, A. J. *A History of American Political Thought.* New York: Dodd, Mead, 1972.

Berressem, Hanjo. "'Hit the Spot, Draw the Line': Cultural Inscriptions, Traumatic Wounds and the Multiplexity of Matter in *Mason & Dixon.*" Paper presented at the International Pynchon Week Conference, London and Antwerp, June 1998.

"Bibliography (–1997)." *Pynchon Notes* 36–39 (1995–1996): 195–221.

Booth, Wayne C. *The Rhetoric of Fiction.* Chicago: University of Chicago Press, 1961.

Boyle, T. Coraghessan. "The Great Divide." Review of *Mason & Dixon. New York Times Book Review,* 18 May 1997, 9.

Bridenbaugh, Carl. *Silas Downer, Forgotten Patriot: His Life and Writings.* Providence: Rhode Island Bicentennial Foundation, 1974.

Brooks, Peter. *Reading for the Plot: Design and Intention in Narrative.* New York: Knopf, 1984; rpt., New York: Vintage, 1985.

Brown, Robert, ed. "Focus on Thomas Pynchon and the Law." Special issue of the *Oklahoma City University Law Review* 24, no. 3 (1999).

213

Bullock, Steven C. *Revolutionary Brotherhood: Freemasonry and the Transformation of the American Social Order, 1730–1849.* Chapel Hill: University of North Carolina Press, 1996.

Burchard, Edward L., and Edward B. Mathews. "Manuscripts and Publications Relating to the Mason and Dixon Line and Other Lines in Pennsylvania, Maryland, and the Virginias." In *Report on the Resurvey of the Maryland-Pennsylvania Boundary,* 205-403. (Harrisburg, PA: Harrisburg Publishing, 1909).

Byrd, William. *Prose Works of William Byrd of Westover: Narratives of a Colonial Virginian.* Edited by Louis B. Wright. Cambridge: Harvard University Press, 1966.

Calvino, Italo. "Why Read the Classics?" Translated by Patrick Creagh. *New York Review of Books,* 9 October 1986, 19–20.

Capra, Fritjof. *The Tao of Physics: An Exploration of the Parallels between Modern Physics and Eastern Mysticism.* Boulder, CO: Shambhala, 1975; rpt., New York: Bantam, 1977.

Chakrabarty, Dipesh. "Postcoloniality and the Artifice of History." In *The Post-Colonial Studies Reader,* edited by Bill Ashcroft, Gareth Griffiths, and Helen Tiffin, 383–93. New York: Routledge, 1995.

Cleary, Thomas, ed. and trans. *The Essential Tao: An Initiation into the Heart of Taoism.* San Francisco: HarperSanFrancisco, 1991.

Clemens, Samuel Langhorne. *Pudd'nhead Wilson and Those Extraordinary Twins.* 1894. Edited by Sidney E. Berger. New York: Norton, 1980.

Cohea, David. "Pynchon Charts America's Divided Soul." Review of *Mason & Dixon. Orlando Sentinel,* 4 May 1997, F6.

Cooper, James Fenimore. *The Prairie: A Tale.* 1827. Edited by James P. Elliot. Albany: State University of New York Press, 1985.

Cope, Thomas D. "The Astronomical Manuscripts which Charles Mason Gave to Provost The Reverend John Ewing during October 1786." *Proceedings of the American Philosophical Society* 96 (1952): 417–23.

———. "A Frame of Reference for Mason and Dixon." *Proceedings of the Pennsylvania Academy of Science* 19 (1945): 79–82.

———. "When the Stars Interrupted the Running of a Meridian Line Northward up the Delaware Peninsula." *Proceedings of the American Philosophical Society* 100 (1956): 557–66.

Corner, George W. Preface to *The Journal of Charles Mason and Jeremiah Dixon.* Philadelphia: American Philosophical Society, 1969.

Cowart, David. "The Luddite Vision: *Mason & Dixon.*" Paper presented at the International Pynchon Week Conference, London and Antwerp, June 1998.

Cox, Harvey. *Turning East: The Promise and Peril of the New Orientalism.* New York: Simon & Schuster, 1977.

Cummings, Hubertis M. *The Mason and Dixon Line: Story for a Bicentenary 1763–1963.* Harrisburg: Commonwealth of Pennsylvania, 1963.

Dawson, Henry B. *The Sons of Liberty in New York* [paper read before the New York Historical Society on 3 May 1859], Mass Violence in America series. New York: Arno Press and the *New York Times,* 1969.

Dinn, Andrew. "Pynchon Server List Archive." 26 September 1999 [http://waste.org/pynchon-l].

Dirda, Michael. "Measure for Measure." Review of *Mason & Dixon. Washington Post Book World,* 27 April 1997, 1–2.

Duyfhuizen, Bernard. *Narratives of Transmission.* Rutherford, NJ: Fairleigh Dickinson University Press, 1992.

———. "Worth the Wait." Review of *Mason & Dixon. News and Observer* [Raleigh, NC], 4 May 1997, G4.

Dwight, H. G. "The Mason and Dixon Line." *Yale Review* 15 (1926): 687–702.

Eco, Umberto. *"Lector in Fabula:* Pragmatic Strategy in a Metanarrative Text." In *The Role of the Reader: Explorations in the Semiotics of Texts.* Bloomington: Indiana University Press, 1979.

Eddins, Dwight. *The Gnostic Pynchon.* Bloomington: Indiana University Press, 1990.

Faulkner, William. "Nobel Prize Address" (10 December 1950). In *The Harper American Literature,* 2 vols., edited by Donald McQuade, et al., 2:1368–69. New York: Harper & Row, 1987.

Fitzgerald, F. Scott. *The Great Gatsby.* 1925. Edited by Matthew Bruccoli. New York: Cambridge University Press, 1991.

Foucault, Michel. Introduction to *Anti-Oedipus: Capitalism and Schizophrenia,* by Gilles Deleuze and Felix Guattari. Translated by Robert Hurley, Mark Seem, and Helen R. Lane. Minneapolis: University of Minnesota Press, 1983.

———. "Of Other Spaces." Translated by Jay Miskowiec. *Diacritics* 16 (1986): 22–27.

———. *The Order of Things: An Archeology of the Human Sciences.* Translated by Alan Sheridan-Smith. New York: Pantheon, 1970.

Gardner, James. "The Bigger the . . . Better?" Review of *Mason & Dixon. National Review,* 30 June 1997, 44–46.

Genette, Gérard. *Narrative Discourse.* Translated Jane Lewin. Ithaca: Cornell University Press, 1980.

Gen-X Susan's Pynchon Links. 17 May 1998 [http://www.city-net.com/~argus/pynchon.html] (20 May 1999).

Gitlin, Todd. *The Sixties: Years of Hope, Days of Rage.* New York: Bantam, 1987.

Gray, Paul. "Drawing the Line." Review of *Mason & Dixon. Time,* 5 May 1997, 98.

Hacker, Louis M. "An Economic Interpretation." In *The American Revolution: How Revolutionary Was It?,* edited by George Athan Billias, 30–41. 2d ed. New York: Holt, Rinehart, and Winston, 1974.

Harley, J. B. "Maps, Knowledge, and Power." In *The Iconography of Landscape,* edited by Denis Cosgrove and Stephen Daniels. Cambridge: Cambridge University Press, 1988.

Himmelfarb, Gertrude. Review of *Isaiah Berlin,* by John Gray. *Wilson Quarterly* 20, No. 2 (1996): 72–74.

Hipkiss, Robert A. *The American Absurd: Pynchon, Vonnegut and Barth.* Port Washington, NY: Associated Faculty Press, 1984.

Hite, Molly. *Ideas of Order in the Novels of Thomas Pynchon.* Columbus: Ohio State University Press, 1983.

Hollis, H. P. "Jeremiah Dixon and His Brother." *Journal of the British Astronomical Association* 44 (1934): 294–99.

Huggan, Graham. "Decolonizing the Map: Post-Colonialism, Post-Structuralism and the Cartographic Connection." *Ariel* 20, no. 4 (1989): 115–31.

Hutcheon, Linda. *A Poetics of Postmodernism: History, Theory, Fiction.* New York: Routledge, 1988.

Huxley, Aldous. *Brave New World.* London: Chatto & Windus, 1932; rpt., London: HarperCollins, 1994.

Irwin, John T. *American Hieroglyphics: The Symbol of the Egyptian Hieroglyphics in the American Renaissance.* New Haven: Yale University Press, 1980.

Jacob, Margaret C. *Living the Enlightenment: Freemasonry and Politics in Eighteenth-Century Europe.* New York: Oxford University Press, 1991.

———. *The Radical Enlightenment: Pantheists, Freemasons, and Republicans.* London: George Allen and Unwin, 1981.

Jameson, Fredric. *Postmodernism, or, The Cultural Logic of Late Capitalism.* Durham, NC: Duke University Press, 1991.

Jarvis, Brian. *Postmodern Cartographies: The Geographical Imagination in Contemporary American Culture.* London: Pluto Press, 1998.

Jones, Malcolm, Jr. "The Master Surveyor." Review of *Mason & Dixon. Newsweek,* 28 April 1997, 77.

Joyce, James. *Ulysses.* New York: Modern Library, 1946.

Kakutani, Michiko. "Pynchon Hits the Road with Mason and Dixon." Review of *Mason & Dixon. New York Times,* 29 April 1997, B1, B4.

Keesey, Douglas. "*Mason & Dixon* on the Line: A Reception Study." *Pynchon Notes* 36–39 (1995–1996): 165–78.

King, Geoff. *Mapping Reality: An Exploration of Cultural Cartographies.* London: Macmillan, 1996.

Kirn, Walter. "Z. Pynchon's Timesome Mind Games." Review of *Mason & Dixon. Slate,* 6 May 1997 [http://www.slate.com/BookReview/97-05-06/BookReview. asp].

Lane, Anthony. "Then, Voyager." Review of *Mason & Dixon. New Yorker,* 12 May 1997, 97–98, 100.

Latrobe, John H. B. *The History of Mason and Dixon's Line.* Philadelphia: Historical Society of Pennsylvania, 1855.

LeClair, Tom. *The Art of Excess: Mastery in Contemporary American Fiction.* Urbana: University of Illinois Press, 1988.

Lefever, Barbara Susan. *The Stargazers.* York, PA: Printing Express, 1986.

Lemisch, Jesse. "The Revolution as a Mass Movement." In *The American Revolution: How Revolutionary Was It?,* edited by George Athan Billias, 101–13. 2d ed. New York: Holt, Rinehart, and Winston, 1974.

Leonard, John. "Crazy Age of Reason." Review of *Mason & Dixon. The Nation,* 12 May 1997, 65–68.

Letters of Wanda Tinasky, n.d. [http://members.aol.com/tinasky/links.html] (20 May 1999).

Lewis, R. W.B. *The American Adam: Innocence, Tragedy, and Tradition in the Nineteenth Century.* 1955. Chicago: University of Chicago Press, 1958.

MacLeod, Duncan J. *Slavery, Race and the American Revolution.* Cambridge: Cambridge University Press, 1974.

Madsen, Deborah. *The Postmodernist Allegories of Thomas Pynchon.* New York: St. Martin's Press, 1991.

Maskelyne, Nevil. "The Length of a Degree of Latitude in the Province of Maryland and Pennsylvania Deduced from the Foregoing of Operations." *Philosophical Transactions of the Royal Society* 58 (1768): 323–25.

Mason, A. Hughlett. Introduction to *The Journal of Charles Mason and Jeremiah Dixon.* Philadelphia: American Philosophical Society, 1969.

Mason, Charles. "Observations for Determining the Length of a Degree of Latitude in the Provinces of Maryland and Pennsylvania in North America." *Transactions of the Royal Society* 58 (1768): 274–328.

Mason, Charles, and Jeremiah Dixon. "Astronomical Observations, Made in the Forks of the River Brandywine." In *Philosophical Transactions of the Royal Society* 58 (1768): 329–30.

———. *The Journal of Charles Mason and Jeremiah Dixon.* Edited and transcribed from the original by A. Hughlett Mason. Philadelphia: American Philosophical Society, 1969.

Mason & Dixon Home Page. Henry Holt & Co. 1997–1998 [http://www.hholt.com/pynchon/masonmain.html] (20 May 1999).

Mathews, Edward Bennett. "History of the Boundary Dispute between the Baltimores and the Penns Resulting in the Original Mason and Dixon Line." In *Report on the Resurvey of the Maryland-Pennsylvania Boundary Line,* 103–203. Harrisburg, PA: Harrisburg Publishing, 1909.

McClure, John A. "Postmodern/Post-Secular: Contemporary Fiction and Spirituality." *Modern Fiction Studies* 41 (1995): 141–63.

McHale, Brian. Class discussion, West Virginia University, Morgantown WV, 9 October 1997.

———. *Constructing Postmodernism.* New York: Routledge, 1992.

———. "*Mason & Dixon* in the Zone, or, A Brief Poetics of Pynchon Space." Paper presented at the International Pynchon Week Conference, London and Antwerp, June 1998.

———. *Postmodernist Fiction.* London: Metheun, 1987.

McHoul, Alec, and David Wills. *Writing Pynchon: Strategies in Fictional Analysis.* Urbana: University of Illinois Press, 1990.

McLaughlin, Robert. Review of *Mason & Dixon. Review of Contemporary Fiction* 16, no. 3 (1997): 216–17.

Menard, Louis. "Entropology." Review of *Mason & Dixon. New York Review of Books,* 12 June 1997, 22, 24–25.

Miers, Earl Schenk. *Border Romance: The Story of the Exploits of Charles Mason and Jeremiah Dixon.* Newark, DE: Spiral Press, 1965.

Miller, Laura. "Pynchon's Line." Review of *Mason & Dixon. Village Voice,* 6 May 1997, 43, 46.

Moody, Rick. "Surveyors of the Enlightenment: Thomas Pynchon's Powerfully Symbolic Language Gets Us beneath the Rhetoric of Our Pretensions." Review of *Mason & Dixon,* by Thomas Pynchon. *Atlantic Monthly* July 1997, 106–10.

Moore, Steven. Review of *The Tunnel,* by William Gass. *Review of Contemporary Fiction* 15, no. 1 (1995): 159–60.

Moore, Thomas. *The Style of Connectedness: "Gravity's Rainbow" and Thomas Pynchon.* Columbia: University of Missouri Press, 1987.

Nicholson, C. E., and R. W. Stevenson. "'Words You Never Wanted to Hear': Fiction, History and Narratology in *The Crying of Lot 49.*" In *Tropic Crucible: Self and Theory in Language and Literature,* edited by Ranjit Chatterjee and Colin Nicholson, 297–315. Singapore: Singapore University Press, 1984.

Olster, Stacey. "'A Patch of England, at a three-thousand-Mile Off-set': Representing America in *Mason & Dixon.*" Paper presented at the International Pynchon Week Conference, London and Antwerp, June 1998.

Pavel, Thomas. "Narrative Domains." *Poetics Today* 1 (1980): 105–14.

Plater, William M. *The Grim Phoenix: Reconstructing Thomas Pynchon.* Bloomington: Indiana University Press, 1978.

Pope, Alexander. *Alexander Pope: Selected Works.* Edited by Louis Kronenberger. New York: Modern Library, 1948.

Porush, David. "'Purring into Transcendence': Pynchon's Puncutron Machine." In *The Vineland Papers,* edited by Geoffrey Green, Donald J. Greiner, and Larry McCaffery, 31–45. Normal, IL: Dalkey Archive Press, 1994.

Price, Victoria. *Christian Allusions in the Novels of Thomas Pynchon.* New York: Lang, 1989.

Prince, Gerald. "The Disnarrated." *Style* 22 (1988): 1–8.

Pynchon Files. 1998–1999 [http://www.pynchonfiles.com/] (20 May 1999).

Pynchon Notes Homepage. 2 July 1998]http://www.ham.muohio.edu/~krafftjm/pynchon.html] (20 May 1999).

Pynchon, Thomas. *The Crying of Lot 49.* Philadelphia: Lippincott, 1966.

———. *Gravity's Rainbow.* New York: Viking, 1973.

———. "Is It O.K. to Be a Luddite?" *New York Times Book Review,* 28 October 1984, 1, 40–41.

———. *Mason & Dixon.* New York: Henry Holt, 1997.

———. "Nearer, My Couch, to Thee." *New York Times Book Review,* 6 June 1993, 3, 57.

———. *Slow Learner: Early Stories.* Boston: Little, Brown, 1984.

———. "Under the Rose." *Slow Learner.* Boston: Little, Brown, 1984.

———. *V.* Philadelphia: Lippincott, 1963.

———. *Vineland.* Boston: Little, Brown, 1990.

"Reading Group Guide." *Mason & Dixon Home Page.* Henry Holt, 1997–1998 [http://www.hholt.com/pynchon/md_readinggde.html] (20 May 1999).

Rifkin, Donna. "*Mason & Dixon*—Pynchon at Last." Review of *Mason & Dixon. The Sun* [Baltimore], 27 April 1997, 5F.

Robinson, H.W. "Jeremiah Dixon (1733–1779)—A Biographical Note." *Proceedings of the American Philosophical Society* 91 (1950): 272–74.

Robison, John. *Proofs of a Conspiracy against All the Religions and Governments of Europe.* London: 1798.

Ronen, Ruth. *Possible Worlds in Literary Theory.* New York: Cambridge University Press, 1994.

Roosevelt, Theodore. *History as Literature and Other Essays.* New York: Scribner's, 1913.

Rorty, Richard. *Contingency, Irony, and Solidarity.* New York: Cambridge University Press, 1989.

Rosenbaum, Ron. "The Edgy Enthusiast." *The New York Observer,* 28 April 1997, 43.

Rossbach, Sarah. *Feng-Shui: The Chinese Art of Placement.* New York: Dutton, 1983.

Ryan, Marie-Laure. *Possible Worlds, Artificial Intelligence and Narrative Theory.* Bloomington: Indiana University Press, 1991.

Safer, Elaine B. *The Contemporary American Comic Epic: The Novels of Barth, Pynchon, Gaddis, and Kesey.* Detroit: Wayne State University Press, 1988.

Said, Edward W. *Culture and Imperialism.* London: Chatto & Windus, 1993.

Sales, Nancy Jo. "Meet Your Neighbor, Thomas Pynchon." *New York,* 11 November 1996, 60–64.

San Narciso Community College Thomas Pynchon Home Page. San Narciso Community College, 1995–1997 [http://department2.pomona.edu/pynchon/ or http://www.pomona.edu/pynchon/] (20 May 1999).

Sasuly, Richard. *IG Farben.* New York: Boni and Gaer, 1947.

Schaub, Thomas H. *Pynchon: The Voice of Ambiguity.* Urbana: University of Illinois Press, 1981.

Seed, David. *The Fictional Labyrinths of Thomas Pynchon.* Iowa City: University of Iowa Press, 1988.

Skertich, Mark. "'This Palpable Disregard of the Plain Provisions of Nature': The Role of the Royal Society in the Mason-Dixon Survey." Master's thesis, West Virginia University, 1993.

Smith, Kyle. Review of *Mason & Dixon. People,* 19 May 1997, 50.

Sobel, Dava. *Longitude: The True Story of a Lone Genius Who Solved the Greatest Scientific Problem of His Time.* New York: Walker, 1995.

Spermatikos Logos. N.d. [http://www.rpg.net/quail/libyrinth/pynchon] (20 May 1999).

Stark, John O. *Pynchon's Fictions: Thomas Pynchon and the Literature of Information.* Athens: Ohio University Press, 1980.

Stein, Joel. "Longer than the Civil War." Review of *Mason & Dixon. Time Out New York,* 24 April–1 May 1997, 52.

Sterne, Laurence. *Tristram Shandy.* Ed. Howard Anderson. Norton Critical Editions. New York: W. W. Norton, 1980.

The Subculture Pages. 1996–1999 [http://fringeware.com/subcult/Thomas_Pynchon.html] (20 May 1999).

Suzuki, D. T. "The Meaning of Zen Budhism." In *Selected Writings on Zen Buddhism,* edited by William Barrett, 3–27. Garden City, NY: Doubleday-Anchor, 1956.

Swenson, May. "The Cross Spider." *In Other Words.* New York: Knopf, 1992.

Thoreau, Henry David. *Journal.* Edited by Bradford Torrey. Boston: Houghton Mifflin, 1906. Reprint edition edited by Francis H. Allen. 10 vols. New York: Dover, 1962.

————. *"Walden" and "Civil Disobedience."* Edited with notes and introduction by Sherman Paul. Boston: Houghton Mifflin, 1960.

Ware, Tim. *Hyperarts Pynchon Pages,* n.d. [http://www.hyperarts.com/pynchon/] (20 May 1999).

————. "Thomas Pynchon's *Mason & Dixon.*" *Hyperarts Pynchon Pages,* n.d. [http://www.hyperarts.com/pynchon/ mason-dixon/masondixon-nf] (20 May 1999).

Watts, Alan W. *The Way of Zen.* New York: Vintage, 1957. Reprint New York: New American Library, 1959.

The Way of Lao Tzu. Translated by Wing-tsit Chan. Indianapolis, IN: Bobbs-Merrill, 1963.

Weisenburger, Steven. *A "Gravity's Rainbow" Companion.* Athens: University of Georgia Press, 1988.

————. "Hyper-Embedded Narration in *Gravity's Rainbow.*" *Pynchon Notes* 34–35 (1994): 70–87.

White, Curtis. "Fiction's Future." *ANQ: A Quarterly Journal of Short Articles, Notes and Reviews* 5 (1992): 250–52.

————. *The Idea of Home.* Los Angeles: Sun & Moon, 1992.

————. "Italo Calvino and What's Next: The Literature of Monstrous Possibility." *Iowa Review* 14, no. 3 (1984): 128–39.

Whitman, Walt. "When I Heard the Learn'd Astronomer." In *Poems, Poets, Poetry,* ed. Helen Vendler, 300. Boston: St. Martin's-Bedford Books, 1997.

Wilgus, Neal. *The Illuminoids: Secret Societies and Political Paranoia.* London: New English Library, 1980.

Wilmshurst, W. L. *The Meaning of Masonry.* London: Rider, 1927. Reprint of 5th edition, New York: Bell, 1980.

Zoran, Gabriel. "Towards a Theory of Space in Narrative." *Poetics Today* 5 (1984): 309–35.

Contributors

Jeff Baker teaches at Moorpark College. He received his Ph.D. from Purdue University, where he wrote a dissertation on *Gravity's Rainbow*.

Joseph Dewey, associate professor of American literature at the University of Pittsburgh, Johnstown, is the author of *In a Dark Time: The Apocalyptic Temper in the American Novel of the Nuclear Age* and *Novels from Reagan's America: A New Realism*. He is currently completing a study of the novels of Richard Powers.

Bernard Duyfhuizen is professor of English and associate dean of Arts and Sciences at the University of Wisconsin, Eau Claire. He is the author of *Narratives of Transmission* and numerous articles on Thomas Pynchon and other topics in narrative theory. With John Kraft and Khachig Tölölyan he edits the journal *Pynchon Notes*.

David Foreman is a student in the master's program at West Virginia University and an editor with Envision Development Group.

Donald J. Greiner holds the chair of Carolina Distinguished Professor of English at the University of South Carolina, where he also serves as associate provost and dean of undergraduate affairs. The author of many books and articles on John Updike, John Hawkes, Frederick Busch, Robert Frost, and others, he is also executive editor of *Critique: Studies in Contemporary Fiction*.

Brooke Horvath is the author of numerous essays on American fiction as well as of two collections of poetry, including most recently *Consolation at Ground Zero*. A professor of English at Kent State University and an editor with the *Review of Contemporary Fiction,* he has recently coedited books on William Goyen and George Garrett.

Irving Malin is the author of many books devoted to modern American literature and coeditor of recent collections on William Gass's *The Tunnel,* Vladimir Nabokov's short fiction, George Garrett's Elizabethan trilogy, and the fiction and criticism of Leslie Fiedler. His reviews have appeared widely in journals, newspapers, and magazines.

Brian McHale is Eberly Family Distinguished Professor of American Literature at West Virginia University. Coeditor of *Poetics Today,* he is the author of two books, *Postmodernist Fiction* and *Constructing Postmodernism,* and of a number of articles on modernist and postmodernist fiction, literary theory, and poetry.

Clifford S. Mead is associate professor at the Valley Library of Oregon State University, where he is head of Special Collections. He is the author of *Thomas Pynchon: A Bibliography of Primary and Secondary Materials.*

Arthur Saltzman, professor of English at Missouri Southern University, is the author of six books, most recently *This Mad "Instead": Governing Metaphors in Contemporary American Fiction.* A contributor to *Modern Fiction Studies, Gettysburg Review, Twentieth Century Literature* and many other journals, he was in 1998 the inaugural winner of the Roy T. Ames Memorial Essay Contest sponsored by *Literal Latte.*

Thomas H. Schaub is the author of *Pynchon: The Voice of Ambiguity* and of *American Fiction in the Cold War.* Editor of *Contemporary Literature,* he is the current chair of the Department of English at the University of Wisconsin, Madison.

David Seed is reader in the English Department at Liverpool University. He has published books on Thomas Pynchon, Joseph Heller, Rudolph Wurlitzer, and James Joyce. Series editor for Liverpool University Science Fiction Texts and Studies, his most recent book is *American Science Fiction and the Cold War.*

Victor Strandberg, an English professor at Duke University since 1966, has published numerous essays on twentieth-century American literature as well as books on William Faulkner, William James, Cynthia Ozick, and Robert Penn Warren.

Index

223